Crisis Without End?

Praise for *Crisis Without End?*:

'Theoretically informed and empirically grounded, and taking its subject as seriously as it deserves, this is the most penetrating account yet of the ongoing crisis of neoliberal capitalism.' – **Wolfgang Streeck, Max Planck Institute, Munich, Germany, and The New School for Social Research, New York, USA**

'A sobering analysis of the structural crisis of the neo-liberal order. Andrew Gamble grapples with remarkable dexterity and erudition with the big issue it confronts: no hegemon any longer able to manage the system and no credible political alternatives as yet able effectively to challenge it.' – **Loukas Tsoukalis, Athens University, Greece**

'Thoughtful and thought-provoking, Andrew Gamble explains lucidly how the disagreements about the current economic crisis between realistic pragmatists and their radical critics are grounded in murky data and contestable conjectures. In the twilight only Hegel's sharp-eyed owl discerns dawn from dusk.' – **Peter J. Katzenstein, Cornell University, USA**

'Undoubtedly the best book I have read on the crisis – seamlessly drawing together analytical insights from a wonderfully rich career. This is essential reading for all those who have lived through the crisis and especially for those who would claim to be leading us out of it. Its central message and clear warnings are simply too important to be ignored.' – **Colin Hay, Sciences Po, Paris, France**

'Andrew Gamble asks exactly the right question: have we bested the tempest of 2008 or busted the neoliberal growth model? He gives us four possible answers to this question, none of them comforting, all of them plausible. *Crisis without End?* is the new benchmark for sober and scholarly assessment of the (supposedly) post-crisis world.' – **Mark Blyth, Brown University, USA, and author of *Austerity***

'A brilliant book, remarkable for its insights into the origins and trajectory of the crisis of neo-liberal capitalism, and the key challenges it faces. A must read for anyone who wants to know not just why the crisis happened but also why and how it may – or may not – be resolved.' – **Vivien A. Schmidt, Boston University, USA**

'Andrew Gamble's contribution to the study of political economy is second to none. *Crisis Without End?* is a crowning achievement: wise, pellucid and challenging. Gamble is no Doctor Pangloss, but he shows that, given courage and skill, we can master events instead of allowing them to master us.' – **David Marquand, Oxford University, UK**

Also by Andrew Gamble

The Conservative Nation
Britain in Decline
The Free Economy and the Strong State
Hayek: The Iron Cage of Liberty
Politics and Fate
Between Europe and America
The Spectre at the Feast

Crisis Without End?

The Unravelling of Western Prosperity

Andrew Gamble

First published 2014 by
PALGRAVE MACMILLAN

Palgrave Macmillan in the UK is an imprint of Macmillan Publishers Limited, registered in England, company number 785998, of Houndmills, Basingstoke, Hampshire RG21 6XS.

Palgrave Macmillan in the US is a division of St Martin's Press LLC, 175 Fifth Avenue, New York, NY 10010.

Palgrave Macmillan is the global academic imprint of the above companies and has companies and representatives throughout the world.

Palgrave® and Macmillan® are registered trademarks in the United States, the United Kingdom, Europe and other countries

ISBN 978–0–230–36707–4 hardback
ISBN 978–0–230–36708–1 paperback

This book is printed on paper suitable for recycling and made from fully managed and sustained forest sources. Logging, pulping and manufacturing processes are expected to conform to the environmental regulations of the country of origin.

A catalogue record for this book is available from the British Library.

A catalog record for this book is available from the Library of Congress.

Typeset by Cambrian Typesetters, Camberley, Surrey, England, UK

Printed and bound in the UK by The Lavenham Press Ltd, Suffolk

For Joni, Nye and Louis

Contents

Preface and Acknowledgements

My earlier book *The Spectre at the Feast*, published in 2009, attempted to make sense of the financial crash in its immediate aftermath. The aim of this new one is to provide a more comprehensive and considered account of the nature of the cataclysm through which we have passed and the predicament we still face, five years on – focusing on the aftermath of the crash as well as its causes. It was harder to write than I expected, and took longer.

Many of the ideas in this book have been developed and stimulated through invitations to participate in other projects and networks, and I would particularly like to thank the editors and organizers of various research projects and edited volumes over the last few years in which I have been involved, including: Vivien Schmidt and Mark Thatcher (*Resilient Liberalism in Europe's Political Economy*); Wyn Grant and Graham Wilson (*The Consequences of the Global Financial Crisis*); Tony Payne and Nicola Phillips (*The Handbook of the International Political Economy of Governance*); Michael Freeden (*The Oxford Handbook of Political Ideologies*); Olaf Cramme, Patrick Diamond and Michael McTernan (*Social Justice in the Global Age*, *After the Third Way* and *Progressive Politics after the Crash*); Peter Taylor-Gooby and the New Paradigms in Public Policy project at the British Academy; John Eatwell, Terry McInley, Pascal Petit and the Augur project of the EU Seventh Framework programme; Amrita Narlikar (*Deadlocks in Multilateral Negotiations*); and Mario Telo and the Garnett and Green projects and conferences at L'Université Libre de Bruxelles (ULB). I am also fortunate to have been closely involved in recent years with the Sheffield Political Economy Research Institute's *The Political Quarterly*, of which I was a co-editor with Tony Wright for 13 years until 2012, and *Policy Network*.

Karim Amijee provided some invaluable research assistance at an early stage, and was tireless in searching out material and contributing ideas. William Brett worked with me on the AUGUR project and researched and wrote an excellent paper on the rise of nationalist and populist parties in Europe which was incorporated into the final AUGUR report as part of Chapter 9. I am also very grateful for the opportunities I have had to present my arguments at seminars, conferences and events in many parts of the world and to many different audiences.

The Department of Politics and International Studies and Queens' College at Cambridge have provided a very supportive and intellectually challenging environment these last few years, and I have learned a great deal from my colleagues, particularly Helen Thompson, with whom I have worked closely on the innovative course she has devised on the politics of the international economy. I have also benefited enormously from being able to engage with students on many different courses at Cambridge, both undergraduate and postgraduate. I have always found teaching more rewarding than research, as well as more fun, and it is hard to imagine doing research without teaching, not least because discussing ideas with students has always been such a stimulus to thinking through my arguments and clarifying them, and to seeing things in new ways. I would particularly like to thank the five doctoral students I have supervised since I returned to Cambridge: Michael Salvagno, Luke Fletcher, Hassan Akram, Tom Barker and Christian Bluth. They have been a constant source of new ideas and fresh ways of thinking.

My publisher, Steven Kennedy, has been very patient as always in waiting for me to finish this book, and has been very supportive and encouraging along the way. He must sometimes have wondered if I was in danger of taking the title too literally and writing a book without end. It is the kind of book that strictly is never finished. Steven's critical engagement with the arguments has improved the text enormously. I am also grateful to three anonymous reviewers whose criticisms helped me to focus the argument.

Three grandchildren have arrived since I started writing this book. I dedicate it to them.

Queens' College, Cambridge   ANDREW GAMBLE

Introduction: Living in a Neo-Liberal World

On 15 September 2008, the fourth largest investment bank in the United States filed for bankruptcy protection. A small event in itself, it triggered a cataclysm. We are still living with the consequences. The US authorities who had been quick, earlier in the year, to ease the sale of another ailing investment bank, Bear Stearns, and had intervened swiftly as well over the summer to prop up the public sector mortgage lenders, Freddie Mac and Fanny Mae, decided to treat Lehman Brothers differently. They wanted to send a signal to the markets that banks, however large and prestigious, would no longer be bailed out. If they got themselves into an unsustainable position they would be allowed to go bankrupt.

Fiscal conservatives applauded the decision, as their counterparts had applauded similar decisions almost 80 years earlier. After the 1929 crash Andrew Mellon, the long-serving and highly regarded US Treasury Secretary, a former industrialist and banker who had cut taxes during the great boom in the US economy in the 1920s to boost enterprise and consumption, argued strongly for an orthodox policy response to the crash. In a memo to the President, Herbert Hoover, he wrote that the guiding principle of the government's response should be 'liquidate labour, liquidate stocks, liquidate the farmers, liquidate real estate ... purge the rottenness out of the system. People will work harder, live a more moral life' (Hoover 1952, p. 30). In following that advice President Hoover presided over the greatest slump in the history of capitalism.

In September 2008 the failure of Lehman threatened to unleash a similar storm, but this time the authorities blinked. The consequences of 'purging the rottenness from the system' were judged too high; so Hank Paulson, the US Treasury Secretary, put together emergency measures to stop the contagion spreading. Like Mellon, Paulson was both a strong Republican and a former banker; he had been head of Goldman Sachs before moving to the Treasury. It fell to him to invoke the power of government to save the financial markets and the financial traders, the 'masters of the universe', who were plainly in no condition

1

to save themselves. A coordinated rescue package was put together and rushed through by governments in the US and Europe which stabilized the financial system and resolved the immediate crisis. Every policy lever that could be pulled was pulled. Interest rates were pushed down close to zero in the US and also in the UK, a level without precedent in the 300-year history of central banking in Anglo-America. Some banks were nationalized, others bailed out. A large fiscal stimulus was announced, and central banks increased the money supply through the new form of alchemy known as quantitative easing to prevent economies falling into deflation. QE as it was affectionately known in the markets meant that the monetary authorities purchased financial assets from the banks, which raised asset prices and improved bank balance sheets. Huge transfers were made in this way from the public to the private sector.

These policies were dictated by the urgent need to hold the line. Governments were determined to do enough to stabilize the financial system and prevent collapse. But they had no time to think of what the long-term implications of their actions would be. They took the actions they did without intending to change the system in a radical way. They wanted to return it to how it had been before the crash as quickly as possible. They did not intend their rescue to be a prelude to a new policy direction, still less to change the assumptions which had governed policy for so long, or to recast the neo-liberal order. The rescue package was conceived primarily as fire-fighting, the kind of measures that had to be adopted in an emergency, but would no longer be needed once the moment of danger had passed.

The financial crash was followed by an economic recession in 2009 in all the major western economies, the most severe recession since the Second World War. Output plunged by up to 9 per cent in some of the leading western economies. Confidence was badly shaken and remained fragile, with markets subject to wide swings on thin trading volumes. A politics of austerity and retrenchment took hold as governments struggled to deal with the fall-out. It took five years for many western economies to regain their pre-crash levels of output; the most severely affected economies in the eurozone, like Greece, did not achieve even that. This is outside the recent experience of western countries. The recessions experienced in the last 60 years, even in the 1970s, were relatively short-lived. The normal pattern was a rapid dip in output and employment, followed by a short period of adjustment and then the beginning of recovery, with the economy quite quickly returning to its trend rate of growth. Such recessions, formally defined as two consecutive quarters of declining output, were uncomfortable but easily survivable. Most recessions in the recent past have been like this – shallow and short – with a V-shaped recovery.

This time was different. Many of the emergency policies introduced to deal with the financial crash were still in force five years later. Interest rates were still at historic lows, many banks were still in intensive care, while several central banks were on their third or fourth round of quantitative easing. Fears grew of secular stagnation – the emergence of a new form of stagflation, only with deflation rather than inflation now the greater danger.

We are still coping with the aftermath of the financial crash of 2008 and the credit crunch which preceded it. The events themselves of that autumn may already be receding in political memory as new events and problems clamour for attention, but their impact is nonetheless enduring and their consequences still unfolding. For western economies the immediate crisis of 2008 is over and there were many signs in 2013 that a more sustained recovery had at last begun in some countries. But there was not much confidence that the foundations of this recovery were secure. There is as yet no end in sight to the deeper crisis of the neo-liberal order for which the 2008 crash was such a portent. We are only in its early stages.

We live in a neo-liberal world, which emerged after the last great economic and political cataclysm in the 1970s. It brought an end to the era of fixed exchange rates, capital controls, universalist welfare, strong trade unions, full employment and large autonomous public sectors which had become established in many countries after 1945. This neo-liberal order was established through a new international monetary regime to control inflation, based on floating exchange rates and the removal of capital controls, the abandonment of full employment as a policy objective and the implementation of new rules for containing inflation and public spending, and for creating flexible labour markets. This was accompanied by a rhetoric of cutting back the state and freeing the market. But the neo-liberal order has always been paradoxical. There has been no straightforward roll-back or retreat of the state. Instead the state and the economy have become more interpenetrated than ever before. Privatization, marketization, deregulation and low business and income taxes, all trade-mark neo-liberal policies, have been pursued by an increasingly active and interventionist state, which gives selective support to the private sector, from sub-prime mortgages to defence spending and investment in human capital, creating in the process a large number of companies dependent on government contracts and public subsidies. The 'smart states' of the neo-liberal era emerged in response to the increasing pace of globalization, especially after the fall of Soviet Communism in eastern Europe and the new rising economies of the East. They helped unleash a new boom in Anglo-America which spread outwards to all the western economies.

There was no uniformity in this neo-liberal order, any more than there had been in its predecessor, the international market order set up at Bretton Woods. Different countries adjusted to the new international order in different ways, and considerable variety in institutions and policies remained. The full force of the neo-liberal revolution was felt in Anglo-America, and especially in its two core states, the United States and the United Kingdom. Both saw a huge expansion of financial services and the growth of consumer debt, as well as a radical reorganization and marketization of their public sectors and public services, a large increase in welfare dependency and unemployment, and a dramatic widening in inequality.

A cautionary tale of our neo-liberal times is told by Ferdinand Mount in *The New Few*. It concerns the owner of a US mortgage business called Household, which was bought by one of the UK's big five banks, HSBC, in 2003. The remuneration package for the chief executive was £35 million over three years, together with fringe benefits which included a private jet and free dental treatment for life for himself and his wife. Sir John Bond, the CEO of HSBC, was asked at the shareholders' meeting that year how he justified the size of this remuneration package, compared with that of Abdul, who cleaned his office for £5 an hour. Sir John, who was earning 400 times what Abdul was, explained that the bank paid the going rate for the job in both cases. In the financial crash Household collapsed leaving HSBC with losses of $50 billion (Mount 2013).

Levels of inequality which narrowed for a time in the 1950s and 1960s are now back to where they were 80 years ago and on present trends will return to where they were 150 years ago. The neo-liberal order has not only created much more unequal national societies, but also a much more unstable international economy with vast uncontrolled financial flows, huge international imbalances and rising private as well as public debt (Hutton 2011).

The neo-liberal order appeared fatally wounded in 2008, and looked as if it might follow the banks, one of its major pillars, and collapse – so intense was the public anger. But it survived, and five years later seemed remarkably unscathed, preparing for another spin of the wheel as though nothing had happened. Bankers' bonuses are still being paid, inequality is as marked as ever, the same constellations of business and political power rule unchallenged, the same ideological mantras are endlessly rehearsed. Why has the neo-liberal order proved so resilient? And will this resilience last? Does it have the capacity to renew itself in the face of the challenges to its effectiveness, its sustainability and its legitimacy which the crisis has revealed? These are the questions with which this book is concerned.

Summary of the argument

I argue in Chapter 1 that the depth of the 2009 recession and the slowness of the recovery can be interpreted in three ways. The first is that it was just a *blip*, quite a long blip, but still a blip, a one-off episode brought about by a unique financial crash, but signifying nothing of great long-term importance. It was cyclical rather than structural. Normal service will shortly be resumed, with growth and living standards back to their former trajectory in an international order in which the US is still the leading power. Nothing fundamental has changed or needs to change. A little bit of tidying around the edges will suffice. The second possibility is that some kind of *watershed* has been crossed, and that we are now in the early stages of a gradual political and economic transformation which will re-order the international economy and international politics in the course of the next two decades. The neo-liberal order has been shattered and cannot be put back together in its old form. Signs of this transformation are the new stagflation, the increasing assertiveness of the rising powers, the new importance of the G20, the coordinated financial regulation introduced under its auspices, and the changed public mood in many countries. The expectation is that these changes will lead to further changes and gradually a new order will emerge. The third possibility, which I argue is the most plausible, is that it is an *impasse*. There has indeed been a fundamental change, but because the immediate crisis has been successfully contained, many of the economic, political and ideological challenges posed by the crash have been defused. This has made it possible to stave off calls for more radical change and to plan a return to business as usual. I explore the reasons for this resilience of the neo-liberal order and its roots in key characteristics of our political economy. The current calm is deceptive, however. The crisis is not over, because it is structural rather than cyclical. It has been postponed, but will erupt again, if nothing is done. The neo-liberal order has become highly unstable, and attempts to return to business as usual will either lead to further breakdowns, or will perpetuate existing deadlocks and impasses. If change does not come western prosperity may start to unravel. The crisis will rumble on, with occasional shocks and upheavals, but with no decisive turning point. Structural crises of this kind can persist for decades without being resolved. If this happens the malaise of the western economy will not heal, and more turbulence can be expected. It will be a crisis without end.

In Chapter 2, I explore the relationships between crisis, order and change, and how the resilience of the neo-liberal order is to be explained. I distinguish between two kinds of crisis. The 2008 crash was an *existential* crisis, created by a sudden emergency, a moment of danger, which required quick decisions and firm action. But it was also a symptom of a much deeper, *structural* crisis. Such crises are characterized by enduring strains or contradictions between the basic institutions and organizing assumptions which constitute an order. These strains are often expressed through transient short-term crises, but resolution of the underlying problems generally requires a radical reshaping of power relationships, both within and between states – and this only occurs rarely. I will argue that the 2008 crash and its aftermath, the recession and the recovery, are the first phase of a new structural crisis, which makes it the third such structural crisis of the international market order, following the crises in the 1930s and the 1970s. Such structural crises create the possibility but not the certainty of fundamental change in our political economy. The 1930s crisis led ultimately to a fundamental reconstruction of the international market order, and major changes in policies, institutions and organizing assumptions. The 1970s crisis was on a smaller scale, but still led to significant change in policies, institutions and organizing assumptions. The present crisis, although at least as profound as its predecessors, has not so far produced any major change. Yet the neo-liberal order, like its predecessors, has become increasingly ungovernable and is an amalgam of unstable and unpredictable forces. Its internal contradictions are specific expressions of three great interlinked conundrums – governance, growth and fiscal – which confront those who seek to govern international market orders.

In Chapter 3, I examine in more detail the events leading up to the crash of 2008, and how the aftermath, both the recession of 2009 and the slow and halting recovery, has been managed. I chart the resilience of the neo-liberal order. Despite the scale of the crisis in 2008 and its troubled aftermath there has so far been little radical challenge to the ruling policy regime of the last 30 years at either the elite or popular level. There has been relatively little dissent, radicalism or resistance. The absence of alternatives has been marked. Orthodox narratives around debt, retrenchment and austerity have for the most part defined the crisis and determined how it has been perceived, and protest has been muted. No insurgent populist anti-system party of right or left has yet succeeded in breaking the hold of mainstream parties over government in any western state, despite the economic pain inflicted on their citizens.

In Chapter 4, I focus on the resilience of the international market order and the uneven impact of the 2008 crisis. I argue that the effects of the 2008 financial crash were primarily located in the OECD economies of the West, and that its direct impact on other parts of the international economy was at first limited. Many of the rising economies continued to grow rapidly, highlighting the great historical shift in the balance between western and rising powers that has been taking place since the 1990s. Within the OECD states the impact of the crisis and the response to it has also varied. The crisis was at its most severe in some parts of Anglo-America, notably the US, the UK and Ireland. Its initial impact in the eurozone was more limited, but this quickly changed once the dependence of European banks on the Anglo-American financial markets became clear. But as events since the crash have unfolded, the instabilities in the western economies have begun to affect all regions of the world. In the deeper structural crisis of the neo-liberal order the rising economies are leading players, and have a major stake in the outcome.

In Chapter 5, I explore the first of the three conundrums at the heart of the structural crisis of the neo-liberal order, which threatens the unravelling of western prosperity: how order can be achieved in an increasingly interconnected world in the face of the global shift in the balance of the international market order towards multipolarity – creating many centres of power rather than a single centre. The perennial tension between a unified market order and a fragmented state system has been sharpened by the emergence of new rising powers and by the growth in the power of networks outside the control of governments, ranging from transnational corporations, off-shore finance centres, the internet, the illegal trafficking in drugs, arms and people, to social movements and international terror networks. The implications for the present neo-liberal order are profound. The US played the key role in establishing the neo-liberal order, just as it did for its predecessor. It is now called on again to take the lead in refashioning the international market order in the new circumstances following the crash. But this will require sharing power with countries which up to now have been largely excluded from international governance, and reforming international institutions to recognize new realities. The US may have to learn to play a different and less dominant role, if an international market order which is also liberal is to be sustained.

In Chapter 6, I ask how sustainability can be achieved, given the pressures on reproducing the social and ecological conditions for growth in the face of the new stagflation and environmental change. Capitalism works by privatizing gains and socializing losses, but there is a perpetual tension between the two, which has become increasingly pronounced in the neo-liberal era. Private accumulation constantly undermines the social, political and environmental conditions which are required for its success. The most visible signs are the return of stagflation in western economies, marked by the stagnation of living standards and a new bias towards deflation, threatening to bring falling prices and declining confidence. The prospects for a return to sustained long-term growth are clouded both by this risk of secular stagnation in the western economies and by the much larger emerging ecological risk to the conditions under which life can be sustained on this planet. Many of the social and environmental foundations of growth in the past on which market orders have relied, such as technological innovations, rising population, immigration and an inexhaustible natural environment, are becoming less secure. Western economies appear for the moment to have reached a technological frontier, and having picked all the low-hanging fruit are struggling to find ways to increase productivity which can sustain rising living standards and provide the resources to adjust to climate change.

In Chapter 7, I ask how legitimation of the market order can be achieved in the face of threats to social cohesion, which include rising inequality, falling living standards, cuts in public services and a flat economy. The fiscal conundrum reflects the persistent tension between global markets and national democracies in the neo-liberal order, which shows itself through the growing polarizations in western societies of rich and poor, and of the increasing inequality of income and wealth, and through the erosion of the fiscal basis for universal welfare states. Partly as a result of the intensification of global competition and the reduced prospects for growth, the entitlement culture built up in western economies since 1945 is threatening to precipitate a deep long-term fiscal crisis, depressing living standards and putting legitimacy and social cohesion at risk. The current austerity drive has been targeted in particular at welfare recipients, and the political lines are hardening. Maintaining consent for redistributive welfare states, and affording universal pensions, universal health care and universal education, is becoming ever more difficult given the resistance to higher taxes as well as current taxes. Yet an extended state is indispensable for the health of private accumulation on which market orders are founded. The long-term fiscal crisis is also exacerbated by the current decline in the legitimacy of public institutions and trust in politicians which has become widespread in western democracies. It makes resolving the first conundrum, the task of building support for greater regional and international cooperation, that much more difficult.

In Chapter 8, I outline four scenarios. The first scenario reflects the view discussed in Chapter 1 that nothing much changes or needs to change. This is the default scenario, the crisis without end. Despite further shocks the neo-liberal order stays resilient, and liberalization and globalization both proceed further. The world remains unipolar as far as the state system is concerned, with the US retaining its dominance, but with its global reach shrinking. The rising powers fail to progress, beset with crises of their own, and their challenge fades; although non-state networks continue to expand and to undermine the power of states, an order of sorts is maintained. The western powers avoid a further major crisis, but have to devote considerable effort to managing the tensions within the neo-liberal order. The price of resilience is a deadlock over reform. The other three scenarios all assume a fundamental change in one or more aspects of the neo-liberal order, which to a greater or lesser extent resolves the crisis by making possible a transition to a different, although not necessarily a better, order. In the second scenario the world is bipolar because a new geopolitical rivalry develops between the US and China, increasing competition for resources and markets, and providing a major stimulus to the US economy through a new arms race. Fiscal problems, however, worsen as a result, and another major financial crisis eventually erupts, this time involving the dollar. In the third scenario the world is multipolar. There is an enhanced role for the G20 and multilateral negotiations which make possible wide-ranging international agreements covering currency, trade, finance and aid, creating a much more diversified and representative international market order, which establishes the basis for higher levels of cooperation and a new era of prosperity across the world, and eases western fiscal problems. In the fourth scenario the world is also multipolar, both because of the balance of power between states and the growth of non-state networks, but this time cooperation breaks down and a new era of rivalry, conflict and fragmentation develops. The West falls into secular stagnation and decline, exacerbated by persistent and unresolved fiscal crisis. The chapter concludes with a summary of the argument of the book and a discussion of the prospects for a benign outcome to the crisis of the neo-liberal order.

Chapter 1

The New Stagflation

The crash of 2008 presents a paradox. If it was such a cataclysm, why five years later has so little apparently changed? The basic structures of the political economy are still in place. There have been some reforms, most notably in financial regulation, but banks are still paying bonuses, corporate power is unruffled, key international institutions are still unreformed, international negotiations on climate change and on trade are still deadlocked on the big issues, and the dominant ideologies of the last 30 years – the various strands of neo-liberalism – remain dominant and for the most part unchallenged. Despite the extraordinary state rescue of the financial system, states are still in retreat, shrinking their spending and their employment in accordance with the dictates of the new austerity. The G20 has emerged as an important international forum, eclipsing the G8, but most countries are still excluded from it. Parties belonging to the political mainstream and accepting the political orthodoxies of the last 30 years still rule in all the centres of western power. The neo-liberal order seems resilient and secure. In which case, should we speak of a crisis at all? Were the events of 2008 nothing more than a blip, similar to the stock exchange crash of 1987, a brief interruption in the otherwise smooth upward path of the neo-liberal era?

The evidence is contradictory, but in this chapter I will make the case that the crisis of 2008 was not a blip, and that what it signalled was the beginning of a prolonged period of contestation over the basic issues of political economy at both the national and international level. The contest is driven by conflicts of interest between different states, groups, classes and organizations, framed through different ideologies and sometimes different cultures. Conflicts of this kind are nothing new, and are inseparable from politics. During crises, however, they become much more intense and can trigger major changes, sometimes deliberately, sometimes inadvertently. The conflicts are open, there is no certainty about the outcome, but the participants in the conflicts come with specific resources, capabilities, knowledge and beliefs so that the odds are weighted in favour of particular outcomes.

Times of crisis often encourage radicalism, a proliferation of new ideas and the polarization of political opinion around strongly contrasting alternatives. Political imagination comes alive. Radicals of all shades of opinion start to believe that the dreams they have entertained for so long might be realized, either in whole or in part. To be radical means to take things by the root and to imagine something different from the established order and the present way of doing things. Radicals flourish during times of crisis precisely because things do not seem to be working in the old way, and many more people than in normal times can be persuaded that something fundamentally different should be tried.

But radicals never have it all their own way. They are opposed in every epoch by pragmatists and realists, who dislike thinking about politics in terms of fundamentals, whether this means going back to old certainties or creating new ones. They seek rather to keep afloat what already exists, to use existing institutions and approaches, to repair and patch where necessary, to experiment and improvise – but not to alter radically either institutions or policies. It is the realists and pragmatists who are most often in power, and who often come to power after revolutions. As that supreme realist, Prince Tancredi, observed in *The Leopard*: 'everything must change so that everything can remain the same'.

It is an open question whether radicals or realists will prevail after a crisis. There is always a contest to define the crisis, what caused it, who is to blame for it, whether it was a crisis at all and what the response should be. In the fluid state of politics after the 2008 crash it seemed possible for a while that radicals might seize the initiative and start to reshape and reorder international politics and the international economy, as they had done in a number of countries after the 1929 crash, most notably in Germany and the US. The events of 2008 were dramatic and at first it seemed they might also be cathartic, purging and purifying the system of the financial toxins which had so damaged it, and heralding major shifts in the international political economy. The dominant doctrines of the political economy of the previous 20 years appeared for a time discredited, and there was talk of the need for new frameworks and the recasting of the assumptions on which the economy had been based. But once the immediate crisis had passed the feeling that nothing would ever be the same again soon gave way to an old conservative refrain: why not leave it alone? The old doctrines and the old ways began to reassert themselves as if nothing had happened. In 2010 and then again in 2013 confidence rose that the worst was over and that the world would soon return to business as usual. Normal service could be resumed, with only minimal changes necessary in the way that economies were organized. The storm had been weathered. Only minimal adjustments had proved necessary. A few new precautions against a financial collapse had been put in place but nothing too burdensome that might cramp the style of the financial sectors which were so central now to their national economies and to prospects for recovery and growth.

The case that nothing fundamental has changed

The argument that the 2008 crash did not change anything fundamental does not dispute how serious the crisis was but points to specific features which allowed its effects to be contained. First among them is that the emergency measures did stabilize the economy. The crisis was successfully managed; disaster was averted. As a result confidence has slowly revived that the Anglo-American financial growth model is still viable, and that the crash was a one-off event which will not be repeated. The recovery from the recession was slow and painful, but after five years there were signs that it was on track. The contrast with the 1930s is most stark here; there is greater similarity with the 1970s, when again the crisis was successfully managed, although out of that crisis a new order did ultimately arise, the neo-liberal order (Helleiner 1996; Frieden 2006; Glyn 2006).

A second reason is that there has been no change in the hierarchy of states. The US remained the dominant power within the international market order. The contrast here is both with the 1930s, when the crisis exposed Britain's incapacity to remain the leading power, and with the 1970s, when the US used the opportunity of the crisis – which it partly precipitated when it unilaterally withdrew from the fixed exchange rate system agreed at Bretton Woods – to reshape its own role in the system and the rules which were to be imposed on everyone else. Since 2008, the US has so far proposed only minor changes to the way the international system is governed (Germain 2009; Payne 2010; Wade 2011).

A third reason is that there is no significant bloc of business interests pushing for an alternative policy and that countervailing forces to business, such as trade unions, have been seriously weakened over the last 30 years. Although there are divisions within business, it no longer faces significant opposition outside itself. This was not the case in the 1930s and 1970s. The space for policy alternatives has shrunk. The privileged position of business which Charles Lindblom analysed in the

1970s, which resulted both from its ability to shape the political agenda through the deployment of its superior resources and from its structural power as the source of employment and growth, has become significantly more privileged in the neo-liberal order (Lindblom 1977). There are major civil society pressure groups which harass business, but it no longer has to contend with a major organized opposing interest (Crouch 2011).

A fourth reason is that there is little appetite in the political class or in the state agencies for radical experiments. Mainstream political parties in the western democracies have become increasingly interchangeable in the eyes of their electorates as a single political class. Voters find it hard to discern major differences in the policies they pursue in government. State agencies, particularly regulators, are sometimes more interventionist, but many of them are successfully captured or neutralized by business lobbies. An example of this was the light-touch regulation enjoyed by the financial services industry in the run-up to the crash. The symbiotic relationship between business and government makes the power structure increasingly monolithic. It has become a single enterprise. In the neo-liberal era the international system has achieved a new level of interconnectedness through globalization and liberalization, and awareness of this complex interdependence has made mainstream political actors aware of their limited scope for departing from the mainstream consensus. This consensus is technocratic, cosmopolitan and liberal. The opposition to it tends to be populist, nationalist and authoritarian – but so far, as I show in Chapter 3, these forces have not become majority ones (Eatwell et al. 2014, ch. 9, part I).

A fifth reason is that neo-liberal ideas have become hegemonic to a much greater extent than liberal ideas achieved in earlier times (Schmidt & Thatcher 2013). Neo-liberal ideals have become embedded both at the level of common sense, helped by the modern media, and as operational codes through the influence of modern economics. There are no longer many political economy alternatives to the neo-liberal model (the Nordic model of the Scandinavian states is one), and there is no alternative international order or alternative socio-economic system, a role that was filled by the USSR in the two earlier structural crises of the international market order. Since 1989, the western international market order has had no challengers (Fukuyama 1989). The contrast with the 1930s and the 1970s is marked.

These five reasons help to explain why the neo-liberal order has been so resilient. Big as the crash was, it has not yet led to the emergence of new interests or new alternatives. Muddling through in any case is always the default policy stance. On this reading the fallout from the crisis was just not big enough to galvanize radical action. If it ain't broke, don't fix it has always been a powerful slogan, and by 2013 the bulk of business and political opinion was coming round to the view that the economy was not broke after all. The western economy did not experience a 1930s slump. The crisis response was enough to prevent that. The crisis was certainly a moment of danger, but the patient survived, and no great shift in direction has so far taken place. The politics of the first five years after the crash were taken up with deciding how much damage there had been to the relationships which existed before the crash, and how quickly confidence could be restored to allow a return to business as usual. Realists point out that the show is still on the road, and that the worst has so far not happened. The US survived its fiscal cliff in 2013, and the eurozone survived a succession of near-death experiences in 2011 and 2012. David Runciman (2013) has argued in *The Confidence Trap* that democracies when pushed generally do just about enough to stay afloat. The structural aspects of the crisis may not have been fixed, but realists argue that in time they will become less relevant and so can be ignored.

The strongest evidence that nothing has changed is the resilience of the dominant framework of institutions, policies and ideas which existed before the crash and, though briefly shaken, was still largely intact five years afterwards (Engelen et al. 2011; Schmidt & Thatcher 2013; Grant & Wilson 2014). There have been a number of reports about banking reform, and some legislation, notably the Dodd–Frank Bill in the US passed in 2010, which introduced new rules for the operation of banks, as well as the international agreement in the G20 to establish a Financial Stability Board and to introduce a new set of rules for financial regulation which became the Basel III rules. But although these measures have tightened financial regulation, the changes look rather modest compared to the uncompromising reforms of the 1930s, such as the US Banking Act of 1933 (the Glass–Steagall Act) which split retail and investment banking. It lasted until 1999 when it was repealed by the passing of the Gramm–Leach–Bliley Act, just in time for the final irrational exuberance of the great financial boom.

The same is true of international financial regulation. The G20 summit held after the crash, in London in 2009, held out the hope of a radical agreement on international financial regulation to curb the excesses of the international financial system and re-establish some control over financial flows. But despite the personal commitment of some leaders, particularly Gordon Brown, and despite important changes, including the establishment of the Financial Stability Board run by the central bankers (Mackintosh 2013), agreement on a comprehensive set of rules has proved elusive (Baker 2010, 2013; Engelen et al. 2011) and has disappointed some of the original protagonists (Brown 2013). The Basel III rules in particular have attracted many critics. The financial sector remains almost as large, almost as unregulated, as ever. The talk of a new Bretton Woods quickly faded (Helleiner 2010), and little attempt has been made to reassert political control over financial flows, apart from the addition of a few extra safeguards which are unlikely to prevent the next bubble and the next crash (Stiglitz 2010). The banks have recovered their confidence and have been lobbying hard against new measures of financial regulation. As the recovery takes hold there will be pressure to relax the rules of Basel III, or allow the banks to circumvent them. It will be said that they were appropriate for the period immediately after the crash but not now that the economy is back on its feet. Politicians on both sides of the Atlantic have been voicing concern that the banks should not be hobbled and that a flourishing financial sector is essential to the recovery. Unpopular though banks and bankers have become, the Anglo-American financial model of growth which flourished so strongly in the two decades before the crash has not been abandoned, partly because no clear alternative to it has yet emerged. If all countries followed the export-led growth model of Germany and China it would be self-defeating and lead to competitive devaluations and trade wars. The willingness of some countries to run debt-fuelled import-led growth models was essential in the last period to underpin growth. All politicians have talked of rebalancing their economies to promote more exports and more manufacturing, but the actual rebalancing that has occurred is small.

Colin Crouch (2011) has written the most persuasive account of why this is so in his book *The Strange Non-Death of Neo-Liberalism*. The previous boom depended on what he calls 'privatized Keynesianism'. The neo-liberal turn in public policy in the 1970s and 1980s had discredited 'public' Keynesianism, which had advocated using public spending to boost demand in the economy and return it to full employment. The solution adopted by neo-liberalism using the financial sector was to rely on a huge increase in private debt. The US as the leading economy and in control of the dollar could afford to run both public and private deficits, but in other countries public deficits were kept under tight control through EU and IMF rules, and it was private debt, for both households and companies, which increased dramatically and fuelled the boom and the asset bubbles associated with it. There was always a risk it might get out of hand, but the prevailing wisdom was that the markets themselves would be able to sort it out by pricing in all risks and steering the economy away from the cliff, helped by some discreet central bank intervention if necessary.

Privatized Keynesianism, the encouragement of a steady increase in the indebtedness of private households through the encouragement to borrow through mortgages, credit cards and bank loans, became addictive. As Crouch shows it served everyone, but most of all it served the interests of the corporate sector. The flow of easy money was essential to enable them to sell their goods and services and make profits. In this process most large companies have become major financial players themselves, dependent upon the banks but also taking full advantage of the financial opportunities which the banks were creating for them. Crouch's point is that in modern political economies business interests have become hard to disentangle. There is no manufacturing sector yearning to be free of finance. In the Anglo-American heartland of the modern capitalist economy finance is the driver of everything (Gowan 2009; Baker 2010; Green 2013). The complex of interests which has been formed in the modern corporate sector and its symbiotic relationship with the state means that there is no appetite in the business community for a drastic restructuring of the economy or the direction of policy. The 2008 crash was a huge shock, but it has not fundamentally shaken the belief in the indispensability of the financial growth model. The addiction to rising asset values, from property to shares, as the driver of the economy remains as strong as it ever was, and recovery is still measured in the old terms (Hay 2013).

The burden of adjustment during the recession has fallen mainly on the public sector. House prices have declined, particularly in the US, but much less so in some other western economies, including the UK, and by 2014 a new housing bubble was under way. Tentative steps were being taken to start a new consumption-led boom in Anglo-America, sustained by another big increase in credit in the absence of a surge in business investment. In contrast, the main drive of austerity in Europe has been to cut public spending and shrink the size of the public sector. The economic contraction of 2009 meant that public sectors overnight represented a much larger proportion of economic output, and the primary effort was put into scaling them back. They were also swollen by the cost of the bank rescues and the bailouts. But although public sector deficit reduction became the test of a sound fiscal policy, regarded as essential for laying the basis of recovery, it became clear that there could be no recovery unless a way could be found for consumers to start taking on new debt again. Only then might companies have the confidence to invest. The economy in most western states has proved resilient in the sense that it has at last recovered. But it remains very fragile (Wolf 2013).

The case that something fundamental has changed

In the last six decades there have been a great number of financial crises affecting various national economies and regions. The Asian crisis in 1997/98 for example was a severe check to the rapid growth of many emerging economies there, but its effects proved temporary (Haggard 2000). It is possible to see the 2008 financial crash in the same way, as a crisis mainly of the OECD or North Atlantic economy (although not all its members were equally affected). This is discussed in Chapter 4. What makes the 2008 crisis different is firstly that the financial centres involved were the leading financial centres of the international economy in New York and London (Gowan 2009); secondly that large parts of the liberalized international financial system were caught up in the backwash of the crisis and this ultimately affected all parts of the international economy; and thirdly there was no quick bounce back as there was after the Asian crisis. The overhang of debt and the uneven and subdued prospects for recovery persisted in many western economies.

There are many forms which crises can take. One of the most important distinctions, explored further in the next chapter, is between an existential crisis and a deep or structural crisis. The first is a critical situation, an emergency, a moment of danger, a climax, in which the intentions, the choices, the decisions and the responses of agents are crucial. The second is the product of slow-moving forces and trends, which although constituted by human actions and choices, appear often to constrain human agents rather than to be under their control. There is not much doubt that the 2008 crash was an existential crisis, a real moment of danger. The financial authorities were blindsided, caught unawares, and although they reacted in time, it was a close call. There seems little doubt that if the crisis had been handled differently there would have been a financial meltdown in 2008 on the scale of 1929, with far-reaching political and economic consequences, including a slump of 1930s proportions. This was averted, but only narrowly (Paulson 2010; Darling 2011). The events which led up to 2008 represented a major failure of regulation and oversight, a loss of control which almost precipitated the kind of classical capitalist crisis which it was thought had been banished since the experience of the 1930s.

Was this simply a temporary existential crisis, a short sharp shock ending in a return to normal, to business as usual, or did it signal instead the presence of a much deeper crisis, whose resolution requires a lengthy period of adjustment and reconstruction? If it is the latter then the 2008 crash may come to be viewed as inaugurating another great upheaval in the history of capitalism. An upheaval can mean both a sudden convulsion and a fundamental reordering. The 2008 crash was certainly a sudden convulsion. The dispute is over whether it will lead to a reordering – and, if so, what kind.

The first reason for thinking that something fundamental changed with the financial crash was the scale of the events themselves. Many commentators argued in the immediate aftermath that the assumptions which had guided policy for three decades had been overturned. The long retreat of the state was over. In the emergency it had had to ride to the rescue of the markets. All the nonsense that had been spouted about efficient markets was revealed to be just that – nonsense. Many were quick to claim that the forceful use of state intervention to save the banks vindicated Keynes (Clarke 2009; Skidelsky 2009), and that, after 30 years during which Keynesianism had been derided as a failed and outdated method of managing the economy, the boot was suddenly on the other foot, and there was a lot of kicking to be done (Eatwell & Milgate 2011; Mirowski 2013). Many argued that the old policy regime was holed beyond repair and that a radical reconstruction would be necessary at both the national and international level (Stiglitz 2010; Reich 2011).

That radical reconstruction has not yet taken place, nor has any comprehensive new policy framework yet emerged. But neither has the old policy regime been entirely restored, and certain changes are taking place which may in time lead to lasting change. The state is active again in certain fields, particularly in financial regulation. But the most convincing evidence that something fundamental has changed is the length of time it took for the recovery to become established. Exceptional measures such as interest rates close to zero and quantitative easing proved not to be temporary crisis measures. They were still considered essential in 2013, five years after the crash. The length of the recession and the scale and duration of the intervention which national governments and central banks deemed necessary to support the economy underlined the severity of the crash and how hard it was to restore pre-crash conditions. Policy-makers were forced to grapple with a new reality; instead of the main problem of economic management being inflation, as it had been in the 1970s, the fear now was deflation (Summers 2014; Cassidy 2014) and of a deflationary spiral taking hold in the manner of the 1930s. Efforts to arrest that threat through fiscal stimulus and monetary easing had created a new stagflation, although this time the stagnation was combined with a persistent tendency to deflation rather than inflation.

The experience of Japan over the previous two decades, which had been thought unique to the circumstances of that country, now seemed to have a much more general application. After 1990, Japan had suffered a major financial crash followed by a long period of slow growth, considerably less than the rates it had achieved in the previous four decades. The country experienced an L-shaped recovery, during which output stopped falling but grew very little. The episode came to be called 'Japan's lost decade', which extended into the twenty-first century. Japan for 40 years had been a rising power. It had grown so rapidly and continuously that it had become not only the second largest economy in the world but was talked about as a potential rival to the US. Books with titles like 'Japan in the passing lane' filled airport book-stalls. By 2000 they were mostly out of print. At the time of the financial crash Japan was still the third largest economy in the world, but its growth rate had slowed, its population was ageing, and it was increasingly seen not as a rising but as a declining power. In 2013, a new government under Shinzo Abe set out to change all this with a radical programme to tackle the causes of the decline. Many of them were deep-seated, reflecting geopolitical, demographic and resource constraints; but there was a widespread perception in Japan and outside that the abruptness of the end of Japan's challenge to be the world's leading economy was accelerated by the way it had handled its own financial crash at the end of the 1980s. Japan had become caught in a deflationary trap, in which the need to eliminate its deficits and pay down its debt came to predominate over everything else, blighting the prospects for growth by creating a pervasive pessimism about the future and a reluctance to invest (Koo 2009; Hutton 2013).

In the aftermath of the 2008 crash, the struggle to stop deflation taking hold has preoccupied policy-makers, who suddenly became aware that the Japanese experience might not be exceptional, but the harbinger of a new set of circumstances. The confounding of expectations that recessions are followed fairly quickly by recoveries, which push economies to higher levels of output than existed before the downturn, induced a new caution about the state of the economy. An

L-shaped recovery was averted; but the recovery turned out to be W-shaped rather than V-shaped. In several countries the economy has moved forward and gathered pace, only to fall back again. In 2010, confidence began rising that perhaps after all this recession was not so different from those in the past. Output fell sharply during 2009 in most western economies, reaching 9 per cent in some, but during 2010 there were marked signs of recovery, allowing hopes that the worst was over. These hopes then in turn evaporated during 2011, amidst signs that economic growth was slowing again and that predictions that some economies, particularly in Europe, would suffer a further recession in 2012. Most western economies escaped that, but the overall verdict on the first five years following the crash was that after the initial slump they had at best flat-lined, experiencing weak rallies which then subsided again. Some countries in the eurozone did much worse than this, but elsewhere economic activity was buoyant enough to prevent steep rises in unemployment. The avoidance of a collapse in employment was one of the major policy successes of the period since the crash, although in several eurozone countries, including Spain and Greece, unemployment had reached very high levels by 2012, with more than 25 per cent of the total work force, and more than 50 per cent of young people, out of work.

The durability of the recovery evident in 2013 and 2014 in many western economies has still to be tested, and many obstacles in the path of a robust and sustained recovery remain. The real test will come when interest rates are at last allowed to rise and quantitative easing is phased out. All governments have been pursuing varying degrees of austerity (Blyth 2013) to reduce the level of public and private sector debt, but their dilemma is that if they are too successful, wages will be too low, demand will contract and confidence will fade again. The Abe government during 2013 made great strides in relaunching the Japanese economy, pushing up internal prices through quantitative easing and pushing down the value of the yen. The government pledged itself to raise the rate of inflation. This would have been unheard of in the 1970s, but it has become necessary in the new deflationary age. Even so, doubts remained as to whether the momentum could be sustained, since the government knew that once confidence revived the yen might start appreciating again, making exports less competitive and driving confidence back down. Japan also has one of the highest national debts of any advanced economy (over 200 per cent of GDP), so balancing the need to contain the rise of its debt with providing additional public finance to support the recovery will be difficult.

If Japan succeeds and returns to a more normal rate of growth it will give some comfort to other western economies struggling to cope with the deflationary bias of this new stagflation. But it still points to something fundamental having changed in the western economy. Why were rising prices (inflation) the prime symptom of disorder in the 1970s, while today it is falling prices (deflation)? Despite the record low interest rates and the amount of quantitative easing, none of the western economies has a problem with inflation. Several, however, have a problem with deflation. Once the question is posed like this it focuses attention on a number of other recent trends in the political economy, several of which predate the 2008 crash. One of these is the stagnation of living standards for the great majority of wage earners, which started in the early 2000s (Parker 2013). This was one of the drivers behind the increase in household indebtedness in the last years of the boom, as individuals borrowed to maintain their standard of living and to afford the rising cost of housing. A lasting recovery will need to see wages and productivity rising again. The 20 years before the crash saw widening inequality in income and wealth, particularly in the economies of Anglo-America, and this trend has continued since the crash, because quantitative easing is very regressive in its effect on the distribution of income and wealth, by boosting asset prices at a time when other incomes are frozen or reduced. A second trend has been the growing imbalances in the international economy between deficit and surplus economies, with certain economies being very free spending and allowing public and particularly private debt to rise to pay for it, while other economies have given priority to investment and exports, building up huge surpluses as a result (Thompson 2010). Imbalances can always be managed so long as there is an agreed framework in which to manage them, such as the world had for a time in the 1950s and 1960s, and again in the 1990s and 2000s. The framework was already under strain before 2008, and the crash has increased that strain. The events since then are further evidence that something fundamental has happened and that we are in a new economic time.

This view has been championed by policy insiders as well as outsiders. In its *World Economic Outlook* published in October 2012, just before rather better economic news began arriving, the IMF downgraded the growth forecasts for most major economies, and warned of the dangers of another major global recession. It pointed to the approaching 'fiscal cliff' in the US, the polarization between Democrats and Republicans over how to deal with the country's debt problem. It pointed also to the severe strains within the eurozone and urged those countries to persevere in moving towards full fiscal and banking union in order to stabilize the euro. The IMF team had also started worrying that the sluggish recovery in the western economies was now affecting the rising powers, with China, India and Brazil all noticeably slowing too, reflecting the declining global demand as well as specific internal problems. In the past, the IMF had championed the cause of fiscal consolidation, arguing that the surest path to recovery was for national governments to adopt credible deficit reduction plans, to seek to eliminate their deficits and to start paying down the accumulating debt. By 2012, the IMF had recognized that this strategy was not working for many states and that the degree of financial repression and fiscal austerity which many countries were experiencing meant that debt was actually rising rather than falling, because the policy had weakened growth and reduced output. The IMF admitted that some of its previous calculations on growth had been wrong. It had assumed the effect of cutting spending and raising taxes to reduce deficits would have been much less than turned out to be the case. The fiscal multipliers had not healed the economy but made the problem of stagnation more severe – the IMF, while still supporting fiscal consolidation, now urged governments to impose their cuts more gradually so as not to damage growth.

The IMF belatedly recognized that this was not an ordinary recession or an ordinary recovery and that orthodox austerity politics, which it had up to then supported, now risked becoming self-defeating. In doing so it echoed arguments made by Paul Krugman, Mark Blyth and other critics of the ruling orthodoxy (Krugman 2008; Skidelsky 2009; Blyth 2013). The problem that had to be tackled was growth, not public debt, if prosperity was to be rebuilt. Too much emphasis on debt risked a deflationary trap. But these warnings had been largely brushed aside. Priority had been given to austerity and deficit reduction, ahead of other goals. From the other side, fiscal conservatives argued that much of the austerity on display was a mirage. Far from there being too much austerity there had been too little. The fiscal adjustment had not been tough enough and it had been drawn out much too long. The actions of governments had not matched their rhetoric. If greater pain had been embraced from the start, in terms of bankruptcies and reductions in expenditure and incomes, these fiscal conservatives argued, the economy might have bounced back more quickly (Ryan 2012).

At the end of 2012, both sets of critics could (and did) claim they were right. It was plain that the global economy was still in poor shape, that the recovery on which so many political hopes were pinned was still sluggish and fragile, and that austerity and fiscal pain stretched endlessly into the future. Finance ministers and financial journalists kept comforting themselves with the thought that all recessions end sometime. The economy always had recovered in the past and moved on to higher levels of output and prosperity. There were also some positives about the economic outlook. Unemployment was generally lower than expected and inflation was subdued. But, as the IMF report indicated, the uncertainties about the economic future were still high and confidence remained low. It seemed a crisis without end. The crash of 2008 had revealed not just a serious malfunctioning of the financial system but deeper underlying problems which needed fixing before a sustained recovery could be put in place and stability and growth restored.

The case that something fundamental needs to change

By 2013, the signs were contradictory. There was evidence that nothing had changed – the neo-liberal order seemed remarkably resilient – but there was also evidence that something fundamental had changed – the shift in the balance in the international economy between East and West, and the worrying symptoms of a new (deflationary) stagflation. Those in the first camp pointed out with growing optimism that the worst was now over and that healthy growth would soon return to western economies. If this turned out to be true, and if it could be sustained, then the 2008 crash might come to be regarded as more limited in its long-term impact than many had supposed.

Those in the second camp rightly argued that it was still much too soon to tell. They discounted the short-term focus of much of the media which exaggerates good news and bad news alike and disregards longer-run perspectives. In the previous two periods of major upheaval in the 1930s and 1970s there were many occasions of relative optimism and relative pessimism, periods of recovery and then further shocks. Most policy-makers therefore remained cautious, fearing that a long period of adjustment, austerity, deleveraging and slow growth still lay ahead. Living standards had still not recovered for most western citizens. Although most governments had pledged to pay down debt and eliminate deficits, the slow progress that had been made five years after the financial crash, in part because of fears of falling into a deflation trap, forced governments to adjust their assumptions and their expectations and to try and persuade electorates to do the same. A very different politics from the more optimistic time of the boom years had begun to take shape across the western world, a new politics of austerity, a politics of less, stretching ahead as far as anyone could see.

Major breaks in political continuity are extremely rare, but they do happen, most often as a result of wars or revolutions, when authoritarian regimes break down. The disintegration of the Soviet Union or more recently the events of the Arab Spring provide examples, even if sometimes the breaks turn out to be less radical than they first appear. Less dramatic breaks in political continuity can also happen in democracies, most often in the form of major shifts in the framework of assumptions governing policy, such as the new direction associated with the Thatcher government in the UK in the 1980s (Gamble 1994; Heffernan 1999). The ability of democracies to generate political projects that can renew their social institutions is one of their most important features and, once that ability atrophies, a country becomes vulnerable to decline, and ultimately to breakdown. One of the questions in the present crisis is whether western democracies still possess the capacity to renew themselves and respond adequately to the challenges they face (Posner 2010; Schäfer & Streeck 2013; Coggan 2013).

It seems doubtful that the changes which have so far occurred have laid the basis for a more fundamental change, but there is a strong case to be made that such a change is needed if western prosperity is not to unravel in a long debilitating crisis without end. Change particularly needs to happen not just in one country or a few countries, but in transnational forms of governance. Although the crisis has forced a recognition of certain new realities, such as the growing importance of the rising powers, and the G20 has been given new importance as the main forum for discussing the issues facing the international economy, the changes need to go much further. The bulk of political effort is still being devoted to patching and mending the existing frameworks and institutions and hoping that the forces which had so often regenerated the economy in the past will do so again. But if the deeper structural crisis of the neo-liberal order is not addressed, these efforts will fail.

The Clinton campaign in 1992 used the slogan 'It's the economy, stupid' to emphasize that how voters view their personal economic prospects and those of the country is strongly related to how they view the competence of politicians and therefore how they decide to vote. But the deeper dilemmas of public policy are better captured in the slogan 'It's the politics, stupid'. The constant capacity of politics to disappoint and to disillusion, the seeming ubiquity of deadlocks and impasses, the frustration of hopes and ideals for progress, makes understanding the politics around any problem in public policy essential for explaining why rational and technocratic solutions to social and economic problems so often fail, why governments so often decline to take long-term decisions, and why achieving cooperation is often so hard. In the aftermath of a major event like the 2008 financial crash the temptation is often to start with economic, psychological or cultural explanations for what has happened, and the obstacles preventing recovery. But many of the problems reside in the politics. Starting with the politics helps to explain why the problems appear so intractable, why agreement is so hard to reach, why recovery is so long delayed, and why we seem to lurch from one crisis to the next (Dunn 1979; Caplan 2009; Runciman 2013).

The unending nature of this present crisis and the difficulty of resolving it encourages fatalism, a sense that the world is in gridlock and that there is nothing politicians or governments can do to sort it out. Yet while there are indeed many problems about which politics can do nothing, the organization of national economies and of the international economy is not one of them, since so much of our political economy is either a deliberate or an accidental political construction from the past. Understanding why there are problems which are in principle capable of resolution, and yet cannot be resolved, is baffling to many people and leads to widespread disillusion with politics and disengagement from it. That then becomes part of the problem and increases its intractability. The paradox is that the way politics works is responsible for the problem, but politics is indispensable if ways are to be found to address it (Stoker 2006; Hay 2007; Flinders 2012).

Deadlocks and impasses are familiar from the history of conflict between states and within states, but they arise in all forms of politics and are common in political economy (Narlikar 2010; Hale et al. 2013). At their simplest they imply that changes are stalled and reforms blocked. A great deal of politics is about attempting to block or to unblock particular paths, to make viable particular policies, and to facilitate particular forms of cooperation. A typical example of a deadlock is when negotiations between two or more parties to a dispute become blocked, while an example of an impasse is when institutions and sometimes entire regimes become blocked, either because of their internal culture and forms of decision-making or by the veto power of entrenched interests, or by both. A great deal of political activity is about the managing of the inescapable blockages and rigidities which must necessarily arise in any society. It is their existence which makes politics as an activity indispensable, seeking to resolve and manage conflicts which are often intractable. At times the way politics works often seems to make the problems more rather than less intractable.

However, politics can also produce breakthroughs and lead to substantial reordering of institutions and policies.

As the crisis has unfolded, it has also begun to cause an upheaval in previously settled views of the world: in our assumptions and expectations. It has begun to raise deeper questions about the economic and political viability of the international market order, which has dominated world politics and world economics for so long, and whether in particular the neo-liberal order, its latest variant, has the capacity to renew itself. The harder it proves to remove the obstacles to progress and recovery, the more the threats grow to the complex fabric of western prosperity, and the more fears rise that it might be unravelling. This prosperity has rested on the interweaving of many different institutions, ideas and interests. Key among them has been the sustaining of a particular kind of liberal capitalism. There have been other models of capitalism, some of them highly successful (Coates 2000; Clift 2014), but the most successful and resilient of them all has been the model first pioneered in Britain and then developed to a new level in the US. This Anglo-American model has had many internal variants and conflicts, but its most consistent thrust has been to promote a liberal international market order, comprising a liberal form of democracy, a liberal form of economy, and a set of international rules (Gamble 2003, ch. 5). It is the successful weaving together of these three strands that have made the West so prosperous and its leading states so stable and resilient. The prospects for all three are currently clouded, and the means by which this model can make the adjustments it needs to regain its vitality have not yet been clearly identified. It has come through worse crises in the past, and may well do so again, but it faces a stern test and an unfamiliar set of circumstances and dilemmas. Reknitting the fabric of western prosperity depends crucially on resolving three conundrums which currently threaten it and which are at the heart of the structural crisis within the neo-liberal order. What these conundrums are, and how they express perennial dilemmas at the heart of international market orders, is explored in the next chapter.

Chapter 2

Understanding 'Crisis'

'Crisis' has become such a ubiquitous term in modern politics that it often seems to have lost any precise meaning. The media turn every event into a crisis, so much so that crises are now weekly or daily, even hourly, occurrences. In this usage, 'crisis' means little more than a critical situation, a sudden emergency, something which requires concentrated effort and quick decision, but which normally passes as quickly as it has arisen. Such a crisis is situational, precipitated when something happens which was not anticipated, but is judged to require an immediate response, which is consequently often hasty and improvised, sometimes in an atmosphere of panic, a resort to desperate measures to stop the boat capsizing. But in many situational crises of this kind the boat is not really in danger of capsizing, although it may feel like that to those caught up in the rush to deal with the emergency. Such crises are moments of difficulty rather than danger and arise from pressures and circumstances at a particular time and place and which are generally ephemeral and soon forgotten when the next 'crisis' strikes. They are not *existential* crises which threaten the survival of the individual, the organization or the regime.

Existential crises come about in different ways. One common form is the result of natural disasters. Such crises may be triggered by freak events, like sudden floods following storms, or they may be the result of natural processes long in gestation which culminate in earthquakes, volcanic eruptions, typhoons or tsunamis. Such natural events create genuine existential crises for human communities, by suddenly putting their survival at risk. The crisis is not the natural event itself but the emergency it creates for human communities. The dilemma at the heart of such crises is how to respond most effectively to the disaster; but often what such crises do is expose the powerlessness of human communities. When a hurricane approaches the Atlantic seaboard of the US, states of emergency are declared and the media go on full crisis alert. The course of the hurricane is tracked, the eye of the storm identified, the moment of greatest danger pinpointed, the extent of the devastation mapped, until it begins to subside. What human societies cannot do is change the course of the hurricane.

Another form of existential crisis comes from medical understandings of certain illnesses. The crisis is the culmination of a process, summing up all that has gone before, and providing a climax, a moment of resolution and therefore a turning point which shapes subsequent events. The moment of crisis is that moment in the course of an illness which is decisive for recovery or death of the individual human being. The illness may be long-standing, and its symptoms the expression of a complex medical history. The climax comes when the patient either fights off the illness or finally succumbs to it. Although elements of human agency, such as whether the individual has the will to live and triumph over the disease, can also be involved, the process described is essentially a natural one in which human agency is limited. The individual is powerless to do more than endure the natural process.

'Crisis' as the Greeks understood it was not a natural but a social process. The original Greek word *krino*, from which 'crisis' is derived, means the moment of decision and judgement, typically in battle, but later extended to a wide range of political and social situations. In a crisis, radically different outcomes are at stake, which is what makes the decision about how to act so crucial and agonizing. Once the decision is taken there can be no going back. In this usage a crisis has come to be associated with an ordeal, involving uncertainty and suffering, a situation in which the future is uncertain, and individuals are forced to make quick judgements and to act decisively under pressure from some urgent necessity (Habermas 1976; Kosellek 2002). From this perspective, political crises, economic crises and social crises present human agents with choices and dilemmas. How they resolve them may determine their own survival as well as the survival of their communities. The rise or fall of states and civilizations is punctuated by crises; some are resolved in ways that bring new life and development, others lead to ruin and extinction.

These crises have their origins in human wills and purposes, and although powerful analogies from nature and from medicine have been borrowed and applied, analogies from drama have also been influential. In a drama, a crisis arises through human agency, the result of the actions of protagonists who often do not understand the implications of what they are doing. The crisis is often the climax of the action, that moment in a play where all the issues and characters introduced earlier are brought together and make possible a resolution. The crisis makes sense of everything that has gone before and provides a climax. In classical Greek tragedy the resolution is the working out of an ineluctable fate, which the human agents are incapable of changing. Individuals are prisoners of their past decisions and actions whose consequences unfold inexorably. In many modern dramas the crisis is the resolution of a dilemma. The protagonists are forced to choose between alternatives which up until then they have avoided. Crises created by human actions and beliefs are resolved by human actions and decisions.

Crises in drama are almost by definition existential. They allow the possibility of closure and a definitive resolution of the action. Most of the events to which the term 'crisis' is commonly applied in everyday politics are not existential because relatively little is at stake, and little changes as a result of them. But some crises are different, and the medical and dramatic analogies are often useful in helping to illuminate what makes them existential crises. The medical analogy is particularly used in the understanding of those crises which are moments of danger but also of opportunity, leading to decisions and outcomes that make the crisis a turning point. The dramatic analogy is particularly used in the understanding of crises as the resolution of key dilemmas, where the outcome is not predetermined but depends on the choices which individual protagonists make. The way in which they understand the crisis determines the range of options for resolving it. By choosing differently, the outcome would be different. Crises in this sense are about contingency rather than fate. In a crisis, things come to be seen as they really are, individuals see the world as if with new eyes, and discover their capacity to judge and respond. Notable examples of such existential crises in politics include the Cuban Missiles Crisis in 1962 (Allison 1971) and the Falklands Crisis in 1982 (Freedman 1990), both security crises in which new leaders were tested, and in surviving the test, consolidated their authority. What makes these crises existential is that they can as easily break leaders as strengthen them.

Existential crises in politics focus on agency, either in the way human agency directly brings about the crisis, or in the way it responds to a threat to the existence of an individual or a group. A very different form of understanding 'crisis' conceives it as structural, although still arising from social rather than natural processes. Instead of the drama of highly charged events, and the focus on individual leaders and the decisions they take, crises are understood as deep, structural phenomena in human societies and polities. The analogy in the physical world is with the slow grinding of tectonic plates creating unbearable tensions which eventually are released as an earthquake, even if their timing is extremely hard to predict. The faults and the movement of the plates can be described, and the reasons why earthquakes happen can be understood, but not where and when the quake will occur. Structural crises in the political and social world are often seen in the same way. The deep-seated tensions and conflicts associated with such crises can be described and their causes analysed, leading to a diagnosis that the crisis has deep historical roots and multiple causes. Historians speak of the crisis of the *ancien régime* in eighteenth-century France, or the crisis of the USSR, or the crisis of the Roman Empire, as they may in future speak of the crisis of the eurozone. A structural crisis may persist for a very long time, for all practical purposes indefinitely, but ultimately some external or internal shock may lead to an earthquake resulting in one final existential crisis for the regime, which proves terminal. In such a crisis a regime which may have survived for a very long time can finally succumb; or it can find the means to transform itself into something new.

Such a structural crisis therefore is a 'deep crisis', a crisis which can persist over a long period of time. It is a condition rather than an event. In talking of the crisis of the seventeenth century or the crisis of the Ottoman Empire what is meant are long-term and persistent deadlocks and impasses from which there appears to be no exit, and which lead to repeated short-term crises. They are resolved after some fashion, but this does not overcome the deeper problems. If the idea of a deep crisis is to have substance and not be simply a metaphysical conceit, then it has to be anchored in political processes which can be described and investigated empirically, specifically in the deadlocks and impasses which prevent the problem from being resolved. 'Crisis' in this sense should be used rather sparingly if it is to be useful, but it does capture something important about certain political eras and regimes. In politics, crises are rarely resolved neatly and finally as they can be in a drama or in an illness. They are often messy and there is unfinished business. The same problem can recur, because the underlying tension is still there.

What are the political implications of structural or deep crises? The complexity of these crises means that they cannot be resolved by acts of will alone. The problems are too intractable for one new leader, however energetic or charismatic, to overcome. This encourages the view that those caught up in them are not able to alter the trajectory of the crisis and must endure the outcome. They may try to resist, but their efforts will be fruitless. This view is too fatalistic, because it treats the crisis as though it arose from a natural condition beyond the human power to shape or change. But a structural crisis in the social and political world is not natural but social, which means that it does not exist separately from the speech that identifies and describes it, and the larger discourse which gives the speech its meaning. A structural crisis finds expression through short-term crises, which resolve some of the immediate pressures and conflict, but leave the underlying structural problems unchanged, so that similar crises then recur. Very occasionally one of these crises or a succession of them can swell into a much bigger event, a major turning point, a crisis when a fundamental choice can no longer be evaded. Such a moment becomes recognized, usually retrospectively, as *transformative* because it changes the direction of events decisively. The collapse of the USSR in 1990–91 is a recent example.

One of the major differences for crises defined by natural events and processes and those defined by social events and processes is that the latter, whether they are situational, existential, structural or transformative, are products of the human mind and human interaction, and many aspects of them will always be contested. There is never agreement on either the causes of a crisis or the remedies for it, whether it is really a moment of danger which requires decisive leadership to resolve, or whether it is of little significance. The ability to define a situation as a crisis and to prescribe the appropriate response to it is one of the most important expressions of political power (Hay 2011). It matters a great deal how a crisis is interpreted and framed, because that determines non-agendas as well as agendas, the options for action, and the appropriate response. The way a crisis is defined makes certain actions possible while ruling out others. Many of the basic facts about a natural disaster are difficult to dispute, but there are few hard facts when it comes to a political or an economic crisis. History is usually written by the victors, and crises come to be defined by those who take advantage of the opportunities which they create.

Crisis as creative destruction

Economic crises are endemic to capitalism, but the understanding of 'economic crisis' has changed radically in the last hundred years as capitalism has changed. In the classical view, crises were treated as quasi-natural events, the result of the impersonal workings of markets, over which human beings could have little sway. In part, this view was maintained in order to deter intervention by governments into the workings of markets, but it was always heavily contested, not least by the losers. The impact of financial crises in the nineteenth century were severe. Large numbers of firms and banks failed, and large numbers of workers lost their jobs with no support from the state. In 1857, 62 out of 63 banks in New York had to suspend payments (Flamant & Singer-Kérel 1968). Wages fell often by 10 or 20 per cent as unemployment rose to 20–25 per cent of the labour force. Recoveries, however, tended to be swift, but most workers had little security and felt at the mercy of the sudden swings of economic activity.

The defenders of free markets maintained that crises were necessary, a means of purging the system both morally and economically, forcing all economic agents to be honest, responsible, accountable and frugal. Crises were associated with destruction – but a creative destruction, a necessary destruction, which took out inefficient firms and activities, as well as many efficient ones, and allowed new initiatives and enterprises to bloom. This was elaborated by Joseph Schumpeter into a theory of capitalist progress. Building on Marx he argued that the secret of the great advance of productivity under capitalism depended on competition being as uninhibited as possible within a rule of law, and that by denying security to everyone, capitalists and workers alike, individuals were forced to experiment and discover new and more successful ways of doing things. For the advocates of capitalism the more unbridled it was the better, because then the more rapid the advance, the more colossal the achievements. Capitalism could discover much more through constant experimentation and allowing firms and individuals to fail. By this means the most effective and efficient ways of doing things could be discovered and the old cleared out of the way. The commitment to change and constant revolution required regular crises to act as the catalyst for destroying the old and making way for the new (Schumpeter 1943).

A key problem, however, with this model of capitalism was that it risked generating far more losers than winners, raising serious problems for its legitimacy. It hurt many of those who already had established property interests, as well as those who lacked property altogether. Maintaining a classical liberal market order was not easy against the interests of the growing numbers of those who felt threatened and insecure. Many of the classical understandings of 'crisis', particularly the Marxist and Austrian schools, saw economic and financial crises performing the same kind of function which war did between nations. It destroyed the weak and inefficient and elevated the strong and successful. It cleared the ground and removed obstacles to new growth. The difference between the two schools was that the Marxists thought that every crisis successfully surmounted only pushed the system towards much larger crises in the future, which eventually would confront capitalism with a crisis it could not surmount, a final crisis, a last judgement. Until that moment every crisis contained the seeds of the next, by creating the condition for the next upswing, which in time would come to be exhausted and turn into fetters. The Austrians agreed with the Marxists that crises were an essential aspect of a capitalist economy, the means by which capitalism periodically renewed itself, but they did not think it was building to some insurmountable, final crisis. They saw no reason why the cycle of capitalist production should not continue indefinitely, provided states did not attempt to step in to prevent crises from happening.

This classical understanding of 'crisis' still has its advocates, but they no longer decide policy. During the financial crash of 2008 many lamented that the crisis was not being allowed to run its course and that too many large companies and banks were considered too big to fail and were being protected by the state. The last time a major crisis was allowed to erupt and run its course was the 1929 crash in the US. The effects were very dramatic, but partly because they were so dramatic they created political obstacles to that course of action ever being taken again. Governments since have always intervened to try and prevent the kind of downward spiral which followed the 1929 crash, which brought 6 million unemployed in Germany and 14 million unemployed in the US by 1932. After the Great Crash it was recognized that doing nothing was itself a kind of intervention, and that a truly non-interventionist stance was impossible. Governments had the capacity to intervene, the question was whether they had the political will. There has still been much dispute about what kind of intervention was appropriate, whether for example, as monetarists urged, it should be focused on preventing the money supply from contracting, or whether, as Keynesians urged, the priority should be to keep the level of demand in the economy high to realize its full productive potential. Very different lessons were drawn from the 1929 crash and its aftermath by the different schools of political economy, and many Austrian school economists continued to insist that the proper lesson from the crash was that the slump should be allowed to run its course. What weakened this argument was that there was little spontaneous market recovery in the 1930s. Those countries which achieved a recovery, like Britain and Germany, did so through protectionism and subsidies, and in Germany's case large-scale spending programmes which boosted demand and restored full employment. It was the first demonstration of the power of military Keynesianism. It was not to be the last.

Crisis as system management

After 1945, the main policy lesson which was drawn from the 1929 crash and the depression which engulfed the US and some other states was that the economy had become too complex and interdependent for government to sit back in a crisis and allow market forces to perform the work of restructuring. Theoretically it might seem attractive, but there were too many casualties and the violent conflicts which were unleashed threatened the legitimacy of the state. Governments had to intervene to try and mitigate the effects of the slump and hasten the recovery. That has been the default position ever since, and 2008 showed how much it remained so, even after 25 years in which neo-liberal doctrines had been in the ascendancy. Joseph Schumpeter saw the trend clearly, and greatly regretted it, but thought it inevitable. The dynamism of the capitalist economy would be restricted to moderate the effects of a crisis, and this meant that a crisis would no longer be the main mechanism by which capitalist economies achieved competitive efficiency. Schumpeter was sure capitalism was heading for relative stagnation and bureaucratic inertia. As will be argued in Chapter 6, although he was wrong about that in the short term, the problem he identified has not gone away, and he correctly predicted that future crises in capitalism would be carefully managed by the state.

During the long boom of the 1950s and 1960s, still the most success-ful period ever in the history of western capitalism, the normal capital-ist business cycle seemed to have been suspended and economic crises of the old kind abolished. The recessions that did take place were mild by previous standards, with unemployment rising only a little and growth quickly resuming. How far this was due to intelligent economic management by governments is disputed, but many observers claimed that a revolution had taken place in the understanding of how the capi-talist business cycle worked (Shonfield 1966). The old role of the economic crisis in clearing out unprofitable and inefficient industries and putting in place the conditions for the next boom was now being performed as effectively and with far less social cost and disruption by the new planning agencies of the state. Reconstruction could take place through state intervention, and the state came to be seen not just as the arbiter between labour and capital but also as the strategic planner of the economy, charged with creating an environment in which enterprise would flourish, citizens would feel financially secure, and technological innovation and new organizational techniques were encouraged (Baran & Sweezy 1966; Galbraith 1971). The task of government was to

deliver growth; and the idea that growth should be regularly interrupted by an economic crisis, involving a sharp fall in the price level, the
bankruptcy of numerous firms and the unemployment of many workers, came to be regarded as unacceptable and belonging to an earlier
less developed age. As the *Economic Report of the President* put it in
1965, 'no law of nature compels a free market economy to suffer from
recessions or periodic inflations' (Council of Economic Advisors 1965,
p. 38). It became almost a mark of civilization to have moved beyond
the old rhythm of the capitalist business cycle and to have created an
economy which was immune from the economic catastrophe which
overtook the world in the 1930s.

Despite the sharp conflicts between Keynesians and monetarists
over macro-economic policy they were united by their attitude to crisis
management. Both believed they had the tools to manage a crisis and
control it. Alan Greenspan, as chair of the Federal Reserve through the
1990s, argued that the monetary authorities could allow local financial
bubbles to develop and then puncture them, without threatening the
viability of the whole system (Greenspan 2007). The regulatory system
was considered robust enough that it could deal with any problems
which emerged in increasingly liberalized financial markets. Greater
volatility was not seen as a problem but as a sign of healthy innovation
and competition. The ability of the financial system to survive the Asian
crisis in 1997–98 and the dot.com bubble collapse in 2000 were taken
as proof of the Greenspan doctrine and of the ability of the governing
institutions of the international economy to manage the more liberalized environment which followed the stagflation of the 1970s. Many
aspects of the post-war settlement were changed as a result of the crisis
of the 1970s, but the involvement of the state in crisis management was
not one of them. President Truman had declared after the war: 'in 1932
the private enterprise system was close to collapse. There was real
danger that the American people might turn to some other system. If we
are to win the struggle between freedom and communism, we must be
sure that we never let such a depression happen again' (Barraclough
1974, p. 16).

The change has been profound and marks one of the sharpest divides
between the classical liberal era and the liberal collectivist era which
followed it. The neo-liberal era repudiated many aspects of the liberal
collectivist era, but in important respects it still works within some of
its structures and constraints, notably the size of the extended state.
Despite the rhetoric of some of its more enthusiastic admirers the neo-
liberal era from the 1980s onwards has not succeeded in restoring some

of the key tenets of the earlier liberal era. What has changed is the very idea of an economic crisis, the belief that it has purely economic causes, and that the regular pattern of booms and slumps in the capitalist business cycle are a necessary part of keeping capitalism healthy and ensuring its progress. Techniques for managing the problems of a social system, evening out fluctuations and keeping the progress of the economy as smooth as possible, have been adopted (Habermas 1976). There has been a trend to make this management more and more technocratic and depoliticized. Elected politicians increasingly cede powers to unelected expert bodies such as central banks and regulators of all kinds. Economic crises are reduced to steering problems of complex systems which need not concern the citizen. But when crisis management fails and citizens suddenly find themselves unprotected then the legitimacy of the system itself can come into question. Crisis is displaced from the economic realm to the political. It is the failure of the regulators to protect the citizens that comes to the fore. This can lead on to much more basic questions about whether the economic and social order is organized in a just way.

In the classical liberal era letting the crisis take its course, and allowing the fallout from it to teach moral lessons about virtue and vice and about wisdom and folly in a market economy, were deeply ingrained. To read some of the nineteenth-century libertarians now, like Herbert Spencer, is to enter a different moral universe. As Spencer wrote: 'is it not manifest that there must exist in our midst an immense amount of misery which is a normal result of misconduct and ought not to be dissociated from it?' (Spencer 1994, p. 81). He assumed that capitalism would not be capitalism unless there were regularly large numbers of casualties and high levels of insecurity. He viewed with apprehension the first tentative steps towards the state providing insurance against the insecurities of unemployment, ill-health and old age, because this would take away the supreme value of the economic crisis as a way of sorting out the fit from the unfit and periodically ridding society of the latter.

This is an uncompromising view of personal responsibility as the bedrock of a free and progressive society, and although this kind of libertarianism revived at the end of the twentieth century it has remained a minority current. What instead has triumphed, at least in the established capitalist democracies, are welfare states, social minimums and safety nets, social justice, human rights and social democracy. The culture of entitlements, although frequently under attack in times of austerity, has continued to march on, as libertarians often complain. The fundamental roll back of the state so often promised has yet to materialize. This has become one of the key contradictions at the heart of the neo-liberal order.

Crisis as system management is a statist perspective and is often associated with production-centred rather than market-centred views of capitalism, in which technological innovation and the diffusion of technology throughout the international economy are considered the great drivers in the development of the modern economy. Crises are temporary breakdowns in that smooth diffusion. Growth for any economy on this view depends on the regular absorption of the technologies generated by the investment in science and technology in the leading states and sectors (Rostow 1978). From this kind of technocratic perspective, the magic of markets is strictly limited and their failures and frailties are all too apparent. Monetary systems and fiscal and monetary policy are considered to be of secondary importance compared to supply-side factors, such as the investment decisions of firms in leading industrial sectors and the movement of raw material, energy and food prices. It is the interaction between these different aspects of an economy which causes cycles and occasional hiccups. Crises are the result of problems of adjustment and alignment, frictions between the moving parts in the productive process, and although they cannot always be avoided, they can be mitigated by intelligent policy. The idea of allowing spontaneous adjustment and periodic uncontrolled crises to sort out the efficient from the inefficient is regarded as a most inefficient method of managing a modern economy. Crises will still occur, but their purpose in a technocratic perspective is to help with system adjustment, by pointing to problems and weaknesses which must be addressed. Understanding the drivers of change is crucial to informing public policies and enabling an active state to anticipate problems and undertake planning to minimize them.

From this perspective, the 2008 crash demonstrates the problems of a financial sector which was not properly regulated or controlled. It became a priority to fix the governance of that sector, if necessary by breaking up the banks, and finding ways to instil a new culture and new forms of banking which can assist the real economy. The financial sector is regarded as a perennial problem for modern capitalism. It is a necessary feature of a modern economy, but unless it is kept tightly controlled and subservient to the needs of industry and innovation, it becomes a disruptive and potentially very harmful factor in economic development. The freedom given to finance since the 1980s, in a number of major national jurisdictions, is a disease of an economy which uses money, and it has to be sorted out by putting the focus back on the real economy and on production (Mazzucato 2013).

There is a version of the technocratic perspective which is more sympathetic to the renewed emphasis on markets following the breakdown of the Keynesian order. There is still an emphasis on the importance of technological innovation as the main driver of economic growth, but less emphasis is placed on the role of the state in planning and directing production. Instead the role of the state becomes one of ensuring that markets, particularly labour markets, are as flexible as possible to encourage firms to invest (Crafts 2012). Obstacles to the smooth working of markets, such as restrictive practices or barriers to the free movement of goods and people, need to be removed. If there is a case for direct government investment, it is in forms of education that equip workers with skills which make them more employable and eliminate bottlenecks in the market. Flexible markets are the way to maximize economic growth and ensure that an economy grows as fast as it is able. From this perspective, the problem since 2008 has been that it is harder in a climate of economic insecurity to press the case for further liberalization of markets. Instead, pressure has grown to boost living standards by raising the minimum wage or freezing certain prices. The advocacy of flexible markets clings to the existing paradigm, arguing that the financial crash has not altered the case for neoliberal supply-side policy, and that what the economy needs is more privatization, marketization and deregulation, not less.

Crisis as risk management

Risk perspectives have become increasingly influential in managing crises. They rely on the fundamental distinction between risk and uncertainty (Knight 1964; Bernstein 1996). Risk management deals in probabilities, and in many practical activities, such as insurance, very accurate ways of calculating risk have been developed. An example is actuarial tables. Risk assessments have now become standard in a wide range of organizations, and risk management regimes vary widely in sophistication and complexity (Hood 2001). Risk management is an attempt to forecast the future and provide human beings with more certainty about what will happen. Not all kinds of uncertainty can, however, be reduced in this way. A risk is calculable, but true uncertainty is not. The models which many financial traders and regulators used during the financial boom were good at measuring certain risks, but missed altogether some of the larger uncertainties which surrounded the operation of finance (Haldane 2012). The systemic risk of the new financial practices was not understood; it was outside the models, and therefore was not truly a risk at all, but a form of uncertainty, which arose from the complexity of the system that had been allowed to develop, against which there could be no defence, because no one had anticipated it. Since the crash, major efforts by central bankers and regulators have been devoted to developing models which might account for systemic risk and give some early warning of dangers developing. But the lesson of every past financial crisis is that eventually people forget and the precautionary measures introduced after the previous crisis come to seem irksome and unnecessary and are removed (Kindleberger 1978; Reinhart & Rogoff 2009). So long as political economies are constituted as they are with deep structural tensions in their systems of governance, growth and distribution, there are always likely to be large uncertainties about how the system is operating which will never be known, and therefore the continuing possibility of a major crisis (Hay & Payne 2013). As Alan Greenspan explained to the Committee of Government Oversight and Reform on 23 October 2008:

> In recent decades, a vast risk management and pricing system has evolved, combining the best insights of mathematicians and finance experts supported by major advances in computer and communications technology. A Nobel Prize was awarded for the discovery of the pricing model that underpins much of the advance in derivatives markets. This modern risk management paradigm held sway for decades. The whole intellectual edifice, however, collapsed in the summer of last year. (Greenspan 2008)

Measuring risks is a key part of crisis management, but the complexity of the international market order was growing faster than the capacity of the models of the regulators or the traders to understand it.

Crisis as shifting policy paradigms

Public policy perspectives focus on the policy response which crises generate. In a stable regime, policy is pursued within a relatively fixed set of goals, assumptions, settings and instruments, which together make up a policy paradigm. If it is true that the response to a crisis can bring about a fundamental change, then one way to understand that change is by examining shifts in policy paradigms. The analyst has to separate claims made by political agents, who may exaggerate the changes which have taken place, from the evidence of what actually can be shown to have changed. One of the most influential accounts of how changes in policy paradigms happen has been proposed by Peter Hall, who distinguishes between first order, second order and third order change. First order change is where some of the settings of the instruments of policy change but the goals of the policy and the instruments themselves remain the same; in second order change, instruments as well as settings change; in third order change, the instruments, the settings and the goals of policy all change. Only where third order change is involved, Hall argues, is it right to speak of a paradigm shift (Hall 1993).

Hall has applied this approach to the transition from Keynesianism to monetarism. Changes in the instruments and settings of a policy regime are reasonably common, prompted by policy failure or by responding to a sudden emergency. Changes involving the assumptions and goals of policy tend to be much rarer and go beyond crisis management: there has to be a reordering, a rethinking of basic assumptions, leading to the emergence of a new policy regime in certain areas, even while many other elements remain constant (Kaletsky 2010). A true paradigm shift in political economy only occurs when there is a major change at all levels, including the international and national market order. There is always some continuity: not all elements will change; nor will they change all at once – and many of the changes will emerge gradually and become established as practical ways of doing things, long before they are recognized as a new direction.

The language of policy paradigms reminds us that crises have to be identified as such through discourse, and it is changes in the way we define situations which leads to changed responses and new understandings. Within a discourse perspective, crises are not like natural disasters which are beyond human capacity to control. Crises are instead socially constructed through language and discourse, and so do not exist in an objective measurable sense. They are always constructed out of particular interpretations and beliefs. One important consequence of this approach is that there is never one perspective on a crisis but many different ones arising from the participants who all have different interests, different knowledge and different beliefs. A crisis exists when enough people believe that it exists and act on that belief (Hay 2011).

Crises are therefore constructed out of many different discourses, each of which may highlight different aspects, ascribe different causes and advocate different responses to the same event. The discourse that becomes dominant in defining the crisis does so not just through its persuasive power, its ability to get everyone to see the crisis in the way its proponents already do. It also succeeds by legitimating and prompting particular courses of action. In the great majority of crises this implies that the meaning of the crisis is defined by a discourse which was dominant before the crisis, and remains dominant after the crisis. The way the crisis is defined and the response that is authorized has the effect of confirming existing structures of power (Blyth 2013).

Structural dilemmas in liberal political economies

The basic structures of liberal political economies have not altered much in 300 years, although the context of the everyday through which they are expressed has changed radically. These structures give rise to certain perennial dilemmas which policy-makers have to confront, and which I analyse in this book as the governance conundrum, the growth conundrum and the fiscal conundrum. These conundrums are inter-linked, which adds to the complexity of the political task, but the basic principles which give rise to them are simple enough.

The governance conundrum arises from the tension in international market orders between global markets – which create ever greater inter-connectedness and interdependence, and tend towards universality and inclusivity – and national sovereignties which claim jurisdiction over particular territories and populations and which tend towards particularity and exclusivity. The conundrum from a global perspective is how to provide governance for an increasingly interconnected world when political authority is fragmented in competing national jurisdictions and there are expanding networks of non-state actors outside the control of any single state. From a national perspective the conundrum is how to manage the competing external and domestic pressures which membership of the international market order involves (Thompson 2008). The conundrum creates political agendas around currency, trade, capital flows, people, knowledge, standards, resources and transnational cooperation over issues from fishing rights to climate change.

The growth conundrum arises from the tension between private accumulation and social reproduction. Private accumulation constantly undermines the social, political and environmental condi-tions which are required for its success (Harvey 2011). Capitalism works by privatizing gains and socializing losses. It relies on a system of property rights to ensure the first. For the second it relies on domestic households – whose unpaid labour nurtures and sustains past, present and future workers – and public households (states) which are able to raise sufficient taxes to provide public goods to reproduce the conditions under which private accumulation can continue to prosper (Fraser 2013). These public goods include currency, law, security, health, education, schools and dealing with the negative consequences of economic development, particularly on the natural environment. Private accumulation proceeds in cycles, and one of the public goods government provides is trying to moderate the violence and destructiveness of the cycle and to avoid depressions and periods of stagnation as well as too exuberant booms, which never end well. These attempts are only ever partially successful. The growth conundrum sets up political agendas around property rights, corporate governance, industrial relations, innovation, technology, the rule of law, security, human capital, domestic labour, childcare, the infrastructure and macro-economic policies.

The fiscal conundrum arises from the tension between markets and democracies. Achieving legitimation of the market order is hard because the way competitive markets work often undermines social cohesion and social solidarity. It leads to problems of securing consent for a fiscal base that is strong enough to meet the demands of the people for security and redistribution and to reproduce conditions necessary for successful private accumulation, yet at the same time maintaining external competitiveness and openness (O'Connor 1971). It creates political agendas around issues such as the gap between rich and poor, inequality, universal welfare, immigration, living standards and job protection.

Since the end of the First World War there have been three major structural crises of the international political economy, which are most easily denoted by their decades: the 1930s, the 1970s and now the 2010s. The starting event in each case was different. The 1930s crisis began with the stock market crash on Wall Street in 1929; the 1970s crisis began with the floating of the dollar in 1971; and the 2010s crisis began with the 2008 financial crash. Each of these crises can be analysed in terms of the three conundrums outlined above, which brings out their distinctive political contexts and sheds light in particular on the current crisis and the continued resilience of the neo-liberal order.

The 1930s crisis

The 1930s crisis began with the stock market crash in 1929, but in relation to international governance the key event was the collapse of the gold standard in 1931, brought about by the financial turmoil sweeping across North America and Europe. The crisis marked the end of the attempt to resurrect the basic elements of the international market order, which had existed before the First World War, and the leading financial and commercial role of Britain at the centre of this order. The failure to agree on anything that could go in its place at the London Economic Conference in 1933 led to a fragmenting of the international economy and the creation of currency and trading blocs, which also increasingly took the form of military blocs.

In the 1930s and following the dramatic events of the First World War and its aftermath, which sparked a series of revolutions and changes of regime, and saw the emergence of many new states, numerous Marxists linked together economic and political crises(*Krisen, Kriegen, Katastrophen*), seeing one flowing inexorably into the next. The final crisis of capitalism, the *Zusammenbruchsgesetz*, would be marked by external wars and internal revolutions. When the 1929 crash occurred many predicted this would lead to the sharpening of the conflict between the major capitalist powers and the descent once more into war. A war between Britain and the US was regarded as likely, given Britain's reluctance to give up its hegemony and empire and make way for the rising power. However, Anglo-American rivalry never came close to open conflict, in part because both states were challenged by the two anti-system powers, Germany and Japan, whose expansionist ambitions culminated in the Second World War, another all-out struggle between the world's great powers for survival and dominance (van der Pijl 2006). Anglo-America, the old hegemon and the new, prevailed – with the aid of the USSR.

This second major world security crisis of the twentieth century, coming so soon after the first, brought about a second and even more profound transformation of the international market order, although the outcome was not the destruction but the strengthening and ultimate triumph of western capitalism under the new leadership of the US. The conditions were laid for both economic and political recovery, although its extent could hardly be imagined in the midst of the conflict and devastation of the 1940s.

After 1945 the new international market order which emerged was based on a determined effort to manage the external and internal politics of states, so as to avoid war and revolution, and to link this with the economic policies which recognized the risks of leaving capitalism unmanaged and the business cycle unregulated. The result was concerted efforts to construct governance and legal frameworks to create an international market order that would be much more robust than the ones which had foundered in 1914 and 1939. The US emerged as the supreme western power, and through a network of military alliances and economic cooperation it secured unity within the West and helped secure the foundations for recovery and prosperity (Armstrong et al. 1984; Schwartz 1994).

The collapse of the gold standard and the liberal international framework had a direct impact on growth. It forced all countries, many willingly, into national protectionist policies, many of which were interventionist and collectivist. Cartels were encouraged through mergers, and state investment in infrastructure and science and technology was increased. Several countries, including Germany, began experimenting with what would become recognized as Keynesian policies, using the power of the state to boost demand and move economies back to full employment. Control of borders, control of trade, control of investment, control of currency – these were all ways in which national governments sought to protect their national economies and the economic security of their citizens. There was a general paradigm shift to statist solutions, even in the US, and away from economic liberalism.

In redistributive terms, states solved the fiscal conundrum through the policies which stimulated growth and helped to enlarge the fiscal base. The retrenchment policies pursued at times in the 1920s and again after 1929 were abandoned. State spending was on the rise in the 1930s, and there were no longer strong external constraints imposed by membership of an international market order to restrain it. Cohesive national communities were now the watchword. This also chimed with increasing militarization and preparations for war in many countries. After 1945, this turn was consolidated in many countries through social democratic settlements (Ruggie 1998) and the emergence of welfare Keynesianism.

The 1970s crisis

One key difference between the 1930s crisis and the 1970s crisis is that there was no breakdown of the international market order. US dominance remained, and the change that took place was guided by it, which sought a new role and a new set of rules for the governance of the international market order. The governance conundrum which had arisen under the Bretton Woods dispensation was identified by Robert Triffin. The 'Triffin dilemma' arose from the role of the dollar as the international reserve currency. The US experienced increasing conflict between its international obligation to supply the world with dollars to fund trade (and therefore to increase them) and its domestic interest in maintaining the value of dollars (and therefore to limit them) (Triffin 1964). Under the Bretton Woods system the US moved very quickly from being the main international creditor to being a major debtor. American debts were funded through the printing of dollars, and other countries were obliged to hold them; but foreign holders became increasingly concerned about the value of their holdings. The issue was resolved by the US floating the dollar and imposing new monetary rules on everyone else through the IMF. This meant it could continue its borrowing, but was no longer under direct pressure to control what it spent. The US decision was critical, domestically, to the paradigm shift away from Keynesianism to monetarism – yet the shift did not have domestic roots but international ones. This could not have been accomplished had the US not taken the lead. As already discussed in the previous chapter, since 2008 the US appears to have few plans to adjust its role in the international economy and this has slowed domestic adjustments. If the international rules are to remain much as they are, most governments will not see much urgency in changing their domestic policies.

The growth conundrum and to an extent the fiscal conundrum of the Keynesian order were analysed by Peter Jay when he suggested in the early 1970s that the Keynesian political economy of the post-war years had become 'inherently unstable, because it insists upon a level of employment which is unattainable without accelerating inflation under existing labour market arrangements' (Jay 1976, p. 33). The interaction of democracy, free collective bargaining and full employment in a market economy was proving explosive and leading to an inflation trap. Free collective bargaining led workers to demand higher wages. Democratically elected governments committed to full employment accommodated these wage demands by increasing the money supply and allowing prices to rise. The consequence was an accelerating inflation. Jay suggested that if inflation was to be halted one of the other pillars of the Keynesian political economy would have to be sacrificed. In the event both free collective bargaining and full employment were abandoned as the neo-liberal order emerged. But the neo-liberal turn in the 1980s created its own version of Jay's conundrum. It set out to resolve the tensions between the different logics of the political market place and the economic market place, which Jay had identified, by diminishing the first and strengthening the second. In its quest to control inflation it adopted strict monetary targets, as well as minimal government and policies to promote flexible markets, by removing all obstacles and opposition. Inflation was brought under control, but over time the mix of neo-liberal policies created a strong deflationary bias in the economy, highly inegalitarian distributive outcomes and a resulting threat of stagnation, both of output and living standards, which undermined the legitimacy of the neo-liberal order. This has driven governments operating within the constraints of the neo-liberal order to pursue privatized Keynesianism rather than welfare Keynesianism, encouraging consumer debt, asset bubbles, financial experimentation and often public deficits in order to boost spending and incomes and correct the deflationary bias. Trying to escape the deflationary trap leads to financial crashes and the prescription of austerity and retrenchment. However, if economies are not to be stuck in deflation and austerity for ever, sooner or later the policies that led to the crash will be tried again. Neo-liberal political economies turn out to be as unstable as Keynesian political economies.

A weakness of Jay's analysis was that it was focused on domestic politics and on the contradictions within a national political economy. His analysis needs to be combined with an analysis of the governance conundrum so we can understand the way domestic and international politics interact in our modern political economy. It was the collapse of Bretton Woods, and the new assertive US international policy on currencies and on the control of inflation, which brought the internal contradictions of the Keynesian political economy to a head and launched bitter redistributive struggles in many countries, polarized opinion and led to the canvassing of radical alternatives by both the Left and the Right. It created the conditions for the major paradigm shift which was eventually consolidated as the neo-liberal order.

The 2010s crisis

This brief outline of how the internal tensions of previous political economies played out in the 1930s and 1970s provides insights into the nature of the present crisis and its likely time span. Change took a long time to come after 1971 and still more after 1929. A decade and a half was required before new institutions and policies became embedded. Analysing the crisis in terms of the conundrums which are posed by governance, growth and fiscal politics allows us to identify more precisely the stage which the current crisis has reached and the ways in which it might develop.

What the handling of the 1970s and the 2010s crises show is that the international economy and the international state system are now so intensively managed that even the most serious crises can be controlled and defused. The 'retreat of the state' is misleading if by that phrase is meant a return to a separation between the state and the economy. In the neo-liberal era there is ever closer interpenetration of the two. One consequence is that the system gains in resilience but loses some of its former ability to transform itself and respond to new challenges. War and slumps are great catalysts for change; without them, effecting transformative change becomes that much harder. The bursting of the great financial bubble in 2008 and the long recession in the western economy which followed it threatens not just the neo-liberal order but the era of managed capitalism under US leadership since 1945. If the ability to continue to manage crises declined, we could return to a more uncertain and less predictable world. The international economy would become fragmented again between territorial jurisdictions, and the fear that war was coming back as a possibility between the great powers would revive. So far such fears have not materialized, and the international market order shows no sign of breaking up in the disorderly fashion which characterized the 1930s. Governments are still attempting to manage the fallout from the financial crash and to limit the amount of change that is necessary, both in the international economy and in the international state system. It is possible these efforts will fail and that a new cataclysm will erupt, which will become an existential crisis for the West. But so far there is not much sign of it. It is more likely that we are stuck – the old order has been saved from collapse but cannot be fully restored. The forces able to reform it in a progressive direction are not yet strong enough. We may have to get used to living with a permanent crisis, a crisis without end.

One reason it is hard to be sure in which direction the world is moving is that the crucial catalyst for unleashing the transformative potential of the 1930s crisis was a world war, ten years after the Great Crash. The transformative potential of the 2008 crisis may take even longer to emerge. The association of economic crisis and war belongs to the earlier period of the development of the modern international system. This link has been broken for 70 years, partly because economic crises are no longer allowed to run their course, and partly because direct war has become too costly an option in the nuclear age for resolving conflict between the great powers. This raises the question of what could be the catalyst for change this time. Without one, the international market order will become subject to increasing gridlock.

While the neo-liberal order is no stranger to crises and shocks in its short history, the 2008 crisis is on a different scale to any it has previously experienced. It is unlikely to be the last. The neo-liberal order has become increasingly unstable, and has revealed some deep flaws and tensions. The 2008 crisis was not supposed to happen. That type of crisis had been banished by improved risk management and regulation, and by the ever increasing sophistication of the markets. It turned out, however, that no one was in control, and this poses a big question. Is the price of regaining control the adoption of a different set of policy goals and policy instruments? Or are we so far into the neo-liberal model that we have already foreclosed that option? The neo-liberal order has many strengths and it has shown itself very resilient up to now, but whether it is truly capable of renewing itself remains to be seen.

Explanations of the 2008 crash divide into those that emphasize structural features of the neo-liberal order which made the crash possible, and those that focus more on specific triggers which caused it to take the form that it did. The structural features include the transformation of the international economy in the 1980s and 1990s by liberalization – firstly of western economies and then by the partial opening of key eastern economies to the world market – and the beginnings of a profound global shift in wealth and power from West to East. One of the consequences of this to which many accounts draw attention was the huge increase in global financial flows in this period (Thompson 2010), dwarfing most national economies, and the creation of a financial growth model, which depended on cheap exports from the new manufacturing plants of the East and high consumption in the West. The financial markets recycled the vast export surpluses in the East to support the private consumption and public deficits of the western economies. It created what Larry Summers (2004) called a financial balance of terror between China and the US. China was dependent on access to the US market to sell the products of its factories and maintain growth, employment and political stability. The US was dependent on China to lend it the money to finance its ballooning deficits. Neither side could afford to pull the plug on the other. The US debt was $1 trillion at the start of the neo-liberal era. By 1992 it had risen to $3 trillion, and by 2013 to $17 trillion and still rising. Other structural features include the nature of cycles under capitalism, the release of irrational exuberance, the herd behaviour of markets and the complacency among traders, regulators, commentators and politicians that 'this time is different' (Shiller 2008; Reinhart & Rogoff 2009).

The triggers for the crash most often identified are the reckless behaviour of the banks, the mistakes of the regulators, particularly the Fed's decision to raise interest rates in 2005, and political intervention in the US in the housing market which encouraged low-income households to take out sub-prime mortgages in a bid to spread home ownership. The housing bubble and the regulatory decisions of politicians and regulators which made it possible was the most important of these triggers (Thompson 2009, 2010). It was a typical expression of neo-liberal capitalism, the interpenetration of the public and private sectors. A major public programme, spreading home ownership, was delivered by a partnership between public sector corporations, Fannie Mae and Freddie Mac, and private banks. It is the weakening of countervailing forces, either in the state or in the market, that is most characteristic of neo-liberalism in practice, whatever neo-liberal theories may say.

This is why the crash can be seen as the result of both too much and too little regulation, too much and too little intervention. The neo-liberal order encourages both at the same time. Its central aim in practice has not been 'rolling back the state' but marketizing the state, using the private sector to deliver public services, and using public services to support the private sector. This makes it at times highly unstable, but also helps to make it resilient, because it encourages flexibility and pragmatism. The events leading up to the crash and how the neo-liberal order demonstrated its resilience are the subject of the next chapter.

Chapter 3

The Crash and the Recovery

In the five years since the crash, the international market order has proved resilient. This was the biggest convulsion since the 1930s but so far with less impact on economics, politics and ideology than the smaller convulsion in the 1970s. What looked like breaches in the walls have since been repaired, and now that the recovery is again under way, there is a new willingness to draw a line under the past and turn to the future. But the underlying reasons for the crisis have not gone away.

The resilience is particularly marked in the way the recession was handled and in the degree of political and ideological stability seen in the period since the crash. The recession did not turn into a slump, and although many governing parties lost office, there were no break-throughs by anti-system parties. The international economy has passed through four main phases since 2007. The first saw the onset of the crisis in 2007–08 leading inexorably to the dramatic events of September and October 2008. The second phase was dominated by the recession in the western economies in 2009 and the first tentative recovery in 2010. In the third phase, progress was interrupted by the euro-zone crisis and over-zealous austerity policies which derailed the recovery in 2011 and 2012. The fourth phase has seen strong signs of a second recovery in the western economies. This gathered pace in 2013, although it was accompanied by the faltering of growth in some of the rising economies and concern increased that they might in their turn become engulfed in the financial crisis.

Phase 1: from the credit crunch to the financial crash

An often noted aspect of the financial crash of 2008 and the deep recession which followed was that everyone expected it and yet no one did. The boom in the international economy which began in the 1990s had acquired such momentum that it seemed unstoppable, yet there were many market traders who expected that at some stage there would have to be a correction. Commentators of a melancholy disposition

51

predicted a final reckoning every year. But until 2007 it failed to materialize. Even when it did, few thought the outcome would be such a hard landing, with such widespread consequences for western economies. Since the boom began in the 1990s there had been episodes of financial turbulence, such as the Asian financial crisis in 1997 and the bursting of the dot.com boom in 2001. These had had serious local effects but had not derailed economic growth elsewhere, and the countries and sectors affected soon bounced back. Even when the first signs of financial strains began to appear in 2006 and 2007 they were not regarded as particularly threatening.

There were many reasons for this but one of the most important was that the economic fundamentals were judged to be sound. The international economy achieved an average growth rate of 5 per cent per annum from 2004 to 2007, up from an average 3.5 per cent in 1999–2003. The main force behind this performance was the exceptional economic growth of a number of countries, but in particular a few very large and populous ones – China, India and Brazil. Jim O'Neill, Chief Economist at Goldman Sachs, coined the term BRICs for this group, adding Russia (O'Neill 2001). In 2007, all the rising economies were still expanding at a very rapid pace and it was clear that there was still vast scope for them to continue to grow as they made the transition to being fully industrialized societies. The main concern of international policy-makers in 2007 and 2008 was not whether growth in the international economy could be sustained, but whether demand in the western economy for the output of the emerging economies could be financed in ways which did not lead to growing and ultimately insupportable imbalances between countries in surplus and countries in deficit. In its July 2007 *Update of the World Economic Outlook*, published just before the first major manifestation of the credit crunch on 9 August, the IMF observed that the international economy was continuing to grow strongly and revised its growth target for both 2007 and 2008 upwards to 5.2 per cent, 0.3 per cent higher than in April. Growth was above trend in both Japan and in the euro area, while it remained robust in China, India and Russia. Some downside risks were noted but these were not sufficient to outweigh the positives. There was no anticipation of the storm about to break.

In retrospect it is now easy to pick out the signs that not all was well with the international economy. Some of these were noticed at the time, but few imagined the economic and financial cataclysm that was about to erupt. The immediate trigger for what happened was the decision of the Federal Reserve to raise its interest rates in 2005 in order to cool the housing market in the US which it considered, with good reason, to be overheating. House prices were increasing at an unsustainable rate. The intention of the Federal Reserve was to raise the cost of borrowing and oblige financial institutions to reduce their lending. This should have been a normal market correction, but in hindsight it became a spark thrown into a gunpowder store. Households, companies and banks had become highly leveraged, having borrowed far in excess of the assets they owned on very optimistic forecasts of future income. As a result, when the rates increased many could not afford the increased interest payments, and their balance sheets plunged into the red (Peston 2012). For many households it meant they could no longer afford their mortgage repayments and had to give up their properties. In July 2007, Bear Stearns, one of the leading investment banks on Wall Street, and one of the most highly leveraged (its ratio of liabilities to capital had reached 35:1), announced major losses on two of its hedge funds. One of them was the quaintly named Bear Stearns High-Grade Structured Credit Enhanced Leveraged Fund. Many of its assets in mortgage related securities were now judged worthless. The realization that this was representative of a much wider problem sent shockwaves through the whole financial sector. On 9 August the wholesale money markets froze. Banks were suddenly unwilling to lend to one another, because no one was confident anymore that they could get their money back. From a situation where credit was easy and seemingly inexhaustible, the market switched and credit became tight and exceptionally hard to obtain as everyone scrambled to protect their bottom line and reduce their exposure by calling in the loans which they had made to others. This credit crunch as it was soon called received attention in the financial press but was at first largely ignored by the rest of the media. The Federal Reserve responded quickly by cutting its lending rate to 4.75 per cent, but the damage had been done.

The first sign that this was not just a problem for the US but a problem for the international financial system as a whole came with the run on Northern Rock in September. Northern Rock was one of the new breed of demutualized building societies in the UK which had become aggressive players in the mortgage market. At the height of the boom Northern Rock offered some mortgages at 125 per cent of the value of the property. Its business model depended on being able to borrow cheaply on the wholesale money markets and then loan the money at higher but still very attractive rates as mortgages. The seizing up of the money markets in August left Northern Rock stranded. If it could no longer borrow on the wholesale markets it could not continue to offer mortgages, and its outstanding liabilities were far in excess of its assets. It experienced a severe cash flow problem and quickly became insolvent. To stay afloat it needed a huge injection of funds to service its debt and continue to pay interest on its deposits. News of its precarious situation was revealed by Robert Peston on the BBC, which helped ignite widespread anxiety among investors about the safety of their money. An old fashioned bank run developed, with depositors queuing outside branches of Northern Rock to take their money out, the first time this indignity had happened to any British bank since the nineteenth century. But although this caught the headlines the real damage, as Peston has argued, was done not by small depositors clamouring for the return of their money but by the silent decision by major investors to withdraw their loans to Northern Rock (Peston 2008). The government was forced to step in to arrange emergency funding. There was a concerted attempt to treat the event as a one-off, a bank which had been poorly run and had adopted an unsustainable business model. But many in the financial markets were now seriously worried, because they knew that many other banks were in a similar perilous position. Many had over-extended themselves and could no longer borrow from the markets to repair their balance sheets and service their debts. A cascade of bankruptcies in the financial sector was threatened. Since the option of borrowing more from the financial sector itself was now foreclosed, the only alternative was to seek a bail out from the government, but that meant admitting failure and bankruptcy.

The regulators on both sides of the Atlantic were aware now of the risks facing the whole financial sector and took steps to offset them. The Federal Reserve made a further cut in its lending rate to 4.25 per cent to try and ease the position of the banks. Through the autumn of 2007, however, there was a stream of bad news as a series of major international banks announced big losses and, in an ominous development, the credit ratings of bond insurers were reduced. There was no longer any trust in the ability of financial institutions to make good their commitments. At the end of the year the Federal Reserve announced a major loan package to the banks to try and help them repair their balance sheets and avoid the need for defaults. That such steps were necessary further alarmed the markets and in January 2008 there were sharp falls in stock markets across the world as traders digested the implications of the precautionary actions of the regulators and the uncertainty surrounding the balance sheets of the banks. Another sign of the increasing seriousness of the situation was that house prices in the US now began to fall. But it was too late.

Through the autumn of 2007 there was a growing recognition that something was badly amiss in the financial system and that it was linked to the huge inflation of house prices in some western economies. This was the time when awareness of the existence of a special category of mortgages in the US – the sub-prime mortgages – first became general, although how these mortgages had been sold, and why extending credit to poor households to buy houses might trigger problems for the whole financial system, were not well understood beyond a circle of specialists (Shiller 2008; Schwartz 2009; Sinclair 2010; Davies 2010; Posner & Friedman 2011; Financial Crisis Inquiry Commission 2011). But everyone could appreciate that the banks no longer lending to one another was bad news for the economy, if it meant that the well springs of credit for banks and private households were beginning to dry up. The financial markets had become so central to the growth model of so many countries during the boom years that any question mark over their ability to continue to function normally threatened a major catastrophe. Yet in the early stages of the credit crunch most observers continued to think the problem was confined to the financial markets and could be ironed out once the financial authorities took appropriate action to sort out the bad banks and force them to get rid of their bad debts. But as the scale of the problem began to be appreciated, so the mood changed. By January 2008, the IMF was warning that financial turbulence was clouding the growth prospects in western economies, both in the US and Europe, where growth had markedly slowed in the final quarter of 2007. China and India appeared unaffected and were still expanding strongly, but the effects of the credit crunch on Europe and the US led the IMF to downgrade its global growth forecast for 2008 to 4 per cent, with sharp falls in the rate of growth expected in the US and in the euro area. Even growth in China was expected to slow – but only from 11 to 10 per cent.

During 2008, the problems in the financial markets grew steadily worse. The Federal Reserve cut its lending rate to 3 per cent in February. In March the British Government was forced to nationalize Northern Rock, conceding that the attempt to find a private buyer for the troubled bank had failed. No one was prepared to take on the risk. In April, Bear Stearns in the US narrowly avoided a similar fate. It was no longer able to keep trading, so the US Government and the Fed arranged for the bank to be taken over by JP Morgan Chase for a nominal sum. By July 2008, the IMF mood had become darker. The credit crunch had now lasted for almost a year, and there was no sign of it ending. Financial losses in the banking sector were now predicted to top $1 trillion. The more that banks evaluated their assets the more concerned they became about what they were worth. Many banks had become grossly over-leveraged, lending far more in relation to the assets they held than was prudent, so it was a natural reaction that each bank individually should seek to limit the damage by seeking to reduce its exposure by stopping new lending and calling in existing loans. The result of all these individual decisions for the whole system was a disaster. Confidence drained away as this process took hold, punctuated as it was by a succession of bank failures and mergers, as the most exposed firms in the market got into difficulty and had to be bailed out. These failures were not just individual failures but pointed to the failure of the entire banking system. The risk of individual failures had been allowed for in the regulators' models, but not this collective failure (Hindmoor & McConnell 2013; Bell & Hindmoor 2014).

Nevertheless, the financial authorities even at this point still thought it was manageable. They conceded that the financial turbulence would have a price. They expected there to be a global slowdown and rising inflation. The IMF forecast that global growth would decelerate significantly in the second half of 2008, but would then recover gradually through 2009. At this point (July 2008) the IMF did not expect a recession, defined as an actual fall in output over two consecutive quarters, for any of the world's main economies. The main danger it saw was inflation, so the top priority was to contain the rising inflationary pressure. This turned out to be fighting the last war. What triggered it was that commodity prices were rising steeply: oil alone had increased by 50 per cent in the previous six months, peaking at over $147 a barrel in July 2008 (it had been $60 a barrel in early 2007). The IMF was not complacent but saw no reason to panic:

> Forceful policy responses to the financial turbulence and encouraging progress toward bank recapitalisation seemed to have reduced concerns about a financial meltdown but ... markets remain fragile amid concerns about losses in the context of slowing economies. (IMF 2008)

This proved much too optimistic. What was not anticipated was the sudden acceleration of the financial crisis over the summer in the US. The major lenders there, which had been the prime movers in the issuing of sub-prime mortgages, were all in serious trouble. In September IndyMac collapsed, while Freddie Mac and Fannie Mae, both public sector institutions, received major federal bailouts. But the financial authorities were also aware that the way sub-prime mortgages had been securitized through the innovative financial products devised by the banks over the previous 20 years meant that much more than just the mortgage lenders were affected. A large number of banks across the world had toxic assets on their books and were now in difficulties and needed bailouts. The financial authorities were reluctant to send a signal that the government stood ready to help them for fear of sparking an avalanche of requests. So when one of the biggest players on Wall Street, Lehman Brothers, urgently requested help in September to avoid declaring itself insolvent, the US financial authorities looked hard at the request and refused. They made a calculated decision to stand tough and hang Lehman Brothers out to dry: '*Pour encourager les autres*', as Voltaire described the British decision to court martial and execute one of their admirals, the unfortunate Admiral Byng, for failing to prevent the French from capturing Minorca in 1756.

The decision not to deal with Lehman as the authorities had dealt with Bear Stearns turned out to be a huge misjudgement, because it sent a wave of panic through the financial markets and a stampede for the exits. If a bank as big as Lehman could collapse, then no one was safe, since almost every bank had over-borrowed in order to lend more, and so many of their loans now appeared irrecoverable. Forced to write off many loans meant that the assets on banks' balance sheets were suddenly, by a stroke of the pen, valued at only a fraction of what they had been worth only a few days before, and since banks' loans far exceeded their assets, they were very vulnerable to bankruptcy if the loans were called in. As in so many past financial crises, the solvency of the banks was seen to depend on confidence (Kindleberger 1978). There is nothing solid about monetary value. It can vanish overnight. The ability of the banks to trade and increase credit was a confidence trick in the true sense. It worked wondrously well so long as everyone suspended their disbelief and acted as though the banks really could create new wealth and were therefore content to leave their deposits with the bank and not demand their money back all at the same time. If everyone were to do so the confidence trick would fail, and once confidence was lost the high values placed on financial assets could disappear almost instantly.

This is what occurred after the failure of Lehman Brothers and the US Government's decision not to bail it out. It burst a dam, and confidence, which was already fragile after a year of the credit crunch, plummeted, putting potentially every financial institution at risk. For a few brief days at the end of September it seemed possible that there could be a complete meltdown of the financial system, with all the big banks forced to suspend trading, unable to provide any financial services, even supplying cash for ATMs, threatening a total economic and social breakdown and unimaginable disruption and disorder. This was an existential crisis of some magnitude.

The resolve of the US Government to stand firm and do nothing, 1930s style, lasted only a few hours. Then, on both sides of the Atlantic, governments swung into action to bail out and nationalize a large part of the financial system, incurring huge liabilities as they did so. Having been reluctant to bail out Lehman Brothers because the Government might be seen as a soft touch, the US administration now had to reverse itself and promise to do whatever it took to stabilize the financial system. Huge sums of taxpayers' money were committed to making the banks safe and solvent again. Giant financial institutions such as Merrell Lynch and AIG had to be rescued. In the UK one of the five biggest banks, the Royal Bank of Scotland, was nationalized outright, and another, Halifax Bank of Scotland (HBOS), was merged with another of the big banks, Lloyds, at the urging of the Prime Minister. The merger threatened to overwhelm Lloyds, which itself had to be partially nationalized, so great was the liability it had taken on. In the US, the Bush Administration proposed a $700 billion dollar fund to provide support to the banks. This was at first rejected by Congress, with fiscal conservatives in particular objecting to the open-ended nature of the bailouts. Many Senators and House Members were deaf to the pleas of their President, George Bush, who in one charged meeting told them: 'this sucker could go down'. The deadlock between executive and legislature on this occasion was quickly broken by the markets. The possibility that there might be no federal help forthcoming prompted a spectacular collapse on Wall Street.

The market rout, with its ominous echoes of 1929, concentrated enough minds to allow the Administration to get its rescue package through Congress – but the episode left scars. As critics were quick to point out, the outcome seemed to show that both in the US and in other parts of the western economy the banks had become too big to fail and would always ultimately have to be bailed out by the taxpayer if the alternative was economic collapse. If the banks were not ultimately subject to market disciplines, they could afford to take extravagant risks and act recklessly, confident that they would avoid bearing any responsibility for their mistakes if things went wrong. Over several decades the banks had acquired a structural power in the economy which was reflected not just in the huge unearned rents they were able to extract in the form of remuneration for their executives, but more significantly in the dependence of governments as well as companies and households upon them. Without credit and dynamic financial sectors modern economies could not function.

The rescue of the banks in September and October of 2008 was a political triumph. Disaster was averted. For once the politicians acted decisively and swiftly. But it was also a sign of political weakness. The politicians had no choice but to intervene as they did because the alternative of not acting was potentially so much worse. The fire-fighting was effective in stemming the slide. Stock markets continued to fall and further bail out and rescue packages had to be announced. Central banks, particularly in the US and the UK, continued to reduce their interest rates. The Federal Reserve had cut its lending rate by December 2008 to 0.25 per cent and had begun its first round of quantitative easing, flooding the market with new money to help the banks rebuild their balance sheets. By March 2009, the Fed had doubled its holdings of bank debt and mortgage backed securities, and, by June 2010, the total had reached $2.1 trillion, three times the level before the crash. The Bank of England also brought its lending rate close to zero during 2009, and commenced quantitative easing. The European Central Bank (ECB) was initially much more cautious and its rate came down only slowly, partly because at first the eurozone seemed much less affected by the crash, which was regarded in Europe as largely an affair of the bloated and reckless financial sectors of the Anglo-Saxon economies. But the ECB decision to move more slowly ultimately helped deepen the crisis when it started to grip the eurozone. Fears of inflation had vanished as everyone braced themselves for what the IMF predicted would be the worst recession for the advanced economies since 1945. Deflation was now the greater danger. By the end of 2008, no one thought any longer that the effects of the financial crash could be contained within the financial sector. It was obvious that a major recession was inevitable. The only question was how big it would be.

Although the crisis was confined mainly to the western economy, located in the world's two leading financial centres, Wall Street and London, the ripples soon spread outwards. Most national economies had become linked in varying degrees to these two financial centres, and banks around the world had taken on to their balance sheets the novel financial assets, such as collaterized debt obligations, which the leading investment banks had created. These assets were rated AAA by the rating agencies and allowed the banks which purchased them to expand their lending. When the financial crash struck, many of these assets were quickly recognized as worthless; there was nothing behind them. They moved from AAA to junk status overnight, leaving huge holes in the accounts of many banks, forcing them to seek help from their governments and contract their lending.

The financial crash also caused a radical revision of the estimates for growth, but they still struggled to keep up with what was actually happening. By November 2008, the IMF was predicting that global growth would only be 3.25 per cent in 2008 and 2 per cent in 2009, a further sharp fall since the October projections. The forecast for 2008 was close enough to what transpired, but the figure for 2009 was way out. Instead of growth there was a contraction in the international economy of –0.7, the first contraction for the international economy taken as a whole since 1945. Activity in the western economies was predicted to contract by –0.25 per cent in 2009 – the actual figure would be –4.0 per cent on average, and much higher for some economies. Although at this stage the IMF expected a contraction, it did not think it would be greater than those of 1975 and 1982. Commodity prices which only a few months before had still been booming were now falling back as global demand weakened. The IMF noted that, in the western economies, markets had entered a vicious cycle, characterized by attempts to reduce borrowings and debt and by price falls, while the rising economies, although not about to suffer recession, were coming under pressure as the effects of the turmoil in their major trading partners began to be felt. The outlook was gloomy with spreads on sovereign debt doubling as the markets probed the weak spots in the international state system, while equity markets had lost a third of their value.

The IMF concluded that the economic outlook was now exceptionally uncertain. This was something of an understatement. Although a systemic meltdown had been narrowly averted, the cost was going to be high, particularly because of the unavoidable impact of the financial crisis on economic activity and on public sector balance sheets. Some output would be permanently lost and the smooth development of the international economy would be imperilled. The IMF now acknowledged that the process of deleveraging was likely to be more intense and protracted than it had previously estimated and emphasized the risks that this would bring. Capital flows might start reversing as companies sought to minimize their losses; exchange rate depreciations might become disorderly and competitive as governments sought to protect employment levels and living standards within national economies; and a general deflation might take hold in the western economies. What might prevent recession turning into depression was the action already taken by governments to reduce interest rates to practically zero, to stand behind the financial system, and to be willing to engineer a broad-based fiscal and monetary stimulus. These were all measures which the IMF firmly endorsed.

Phase 2: the slump and the first recovery 2009–10

The recession proved far deeper than expected. By July 2009, the IMF had revised its view that this recession was comparable to the ones of 1982 and 1975, and now judged it to be unprecedented in the post-Second World War era, making the only comparable event in the previous century the Great Depression in the 1930s. However, the IMF was confident that the risk of another Great Depression had been averted, although narrowly, and the forces making for further contraction were now receding. But it warned that stabilization was uneven across national economies and regions and that the recovery was likely to be sluggish. One of the main reasons for this was that, because the crash and the recession had been unprecedented in their severity, the macroeconomic and financial support required to counter them had also had to be unprecedented, and so states were now faced with the difficult task of unwinding this support and returning to business as usual. In 2009, the western economies were not expected to show a marked pick-up in economic activity until the second half of 2010. This was a gloomy forecast, but even so it was to prove a serious underestimate of the time it would take for the western economy to recover.

The IMF painted a picture of an international economy still in shock following the financial crash. Global trade had fallen sharply and there had been a general increase in uncertainty and a collapse of confidence, especially in the western economies. The IMF voiced a number of particular fears. The housing markets had still to bottom out and the financial markets remained seriously impaired, with the banks that had survived very reluctant to start lending again. Private consumption was likely to be structurally weaker in the western economies over the next few years. There were grave doubts about the sustainability of the rising public debt incurred as a result of the huge sums put in to stabilize the banking sector as well as the sharp contraction of public revenues during the recession. Finally, there were risks to social stability from higher unemployment and popular discontent with falling living standards, which might lead political parties to propose protectionist remedies. The new IMF forecast now expected world output overall to contract by 0.8 per cent in 2009 with the main force of the contraction being felt in the western economies with their GDP declining 3.8 per cent in 2009 and only growing by 0.6 per cent in 2010. Once again it was the rising economies which were much better placed. Their growth was still continuing, helped in China by a huge fiscal stimulus. For their growth to be sustained the rising economies needed a full recovery in the western economies to provide the markets for the output of their new industries.

The special character of this crisis is reflected in the way in which the IMF responded to it, and the remedies which it prescribed. The insistence for the past 25 years that market solutions were always preferable to government solutions, and that government spending should not be allowed to crowd out private spending, had been a hallmark of orthodox IMF thinking and had conditioned the advice it gave to states, mostly developing economies seeking to integrate into the western international economy, when they encountered problems of debt and financial crisis. Yet in 2008, because the crisis affected the core states of the international economy, the advice changed and the IMF endorsed radical emergency measures to stabilize the financial system and to provide extensive and unconditional fiscal and monetary stimulus to keep the economy afloat. By the end of 2009, it was describing the recovery as 'policy driven' and 'multi-speed'. Growth in the rising economies had barely dipped, but it had plunged so much in the leading western economies that the recovery there required careful nurturing. The growth of the rising economies was proving stronger than anticipated, which allowed the IMF to raise its forecast for global output in 2010 to 4 per cent, though growth in the western economies was still expected to be sluggish, despite the sharp fall in output in 2009. In 2010, the growth rate was expected to be no more than 2 per cent, and in 2011 only 2.5 per cent. In contrast the average growth in the rising economies was expected to increase to 6 per cent in 2010, having fallen to 2 per cent in 2009, which had at least still been positive.

The IMF attributed the rebound in confidence to government action: 'extraordinary policy support' had 'forestalled another great depression' (IMF 2009); but it warned that no quick economic recovery was in prospect. Output in many western economies would remain below the pre-crisis level until at least 2011, and this would mean for many of these economies high and rising levels of unemployment and public debt, alongside still very high household, corporate and bank debt. As all these sectors continued to deleverage, the flow of credit across borders was continuing to contract. The sluggishness of the advanced economies meant that for the first time the global recovery would be led by rising economies, particularly those in Asia. The biggest threat which the IMF could see to the recovery was 'a premature and incoherent exit' from the policies of support for the banks and for national economies that would undermine global growth and the rebalancing of the international economy. The financial system remained fragile and, together with the levels of unemployment, seemed certain to hold back any quick recovery in household spending.

Despite its endorsement of the exceptional policy actions, such as quantitative easing and zero interest rates, which governments had taken to prevent something much worse happening to the international economy, the IMF still regarded what had happened as an exceptional event, like a meteorite hitting the earth. The international economy had been pushed off course, but the medium and long-term aim should be to get back to the state of affairs before the crash as quickly as possible. Nothing fundamental needed changing. The policy task as the IMF saw it in January 2010 was to 'rebalance' demand away from the public towards the private sector and away from economies with excessive external deficits towards those with excessive surpluses, while repairing the financial sectors and fostering restructuring in the industrial and service sectors.

Through 2010 the mood was fairly upbeat at the IMF. A steady recovery was in progress and confidence was gradually returning. The IMF raised its global growth forecast to 4.5 per cent for 2010 in its *July Update* and to 4.25 per cent for 2011. At the same time it noted new signs of financial turbulence, particularly in the euro area, which showed that the recovery remained fragile and could easily be pushed off course. In 2010, the focus of concern moved away from the banks to the problem of sovereign debt, and this put the spotlight firmly on the eurozone, because of the number of countries there whose sovereign debt problems in the wake of the financial crash suddenly looked unmanageable. For the next two years the main concern of the IMF was to be the euro area and in particular the debt crises in Greece, Portugal, Ireland, Spain and Italy, the first three of which required bailouts. These countries encountered great difficulty in managing their national economies and their sovereign debts within the constraints of the single currency. Since these states were unable to devalue their currency the only way they could deal with the market perception that they were a bad credit risk was to lower their costs through an internal deflation to allow their economies to compete with the more productive ones of northern Europe. The alternative would have been an orderly break-up of the eurozone and the reintroduction of national currencies which would then be allowed to devalue against other currencies – but this was ruled out by all the member states as politically unacceptable.

The IMF endorsed the decision to keep the eurozone together and significantly shifted the tenor of its advice during 2010, and helped form the new consensus in favour of fiscal consolidation and austerity. It noted that current fiscal consolidation plans for 2011 envisaged a fiscal retrenchment of around 1.25 per cent of GDP and endorsed this as broadly appropriate. It argued that in the western economies policy needed to focus on credible fiscal consolidation, by which it meant measures that could improve medium-term prospects for growth, including reforms to entitlements and tax systems, such as making people work longer before drawing their pensions and lowering tax thresholds. It did so against a background of worsening financial turbulence, which took the form of sharp movements in currency, equity and commodity markets. The problems in Greece and some of the other heavily indebted euro economies raised concerns over how they might solve their problems unaided. If they were unable to do so, the weakness of the euro area threatened to derail the global recovery and certainly raised questions about how strong and how sustainable it was. The IMF accordingly backed the new European Financial Stabilisation Mechanism agreed by the members of the eurozone in May 2010, which made provision for up to 60 billion of loan funds to provide financial assistance to member states. It recognized that the implementation of this mechanism would at first mean a reduction in growth, but it judged that this would help conditions in the financial markets to stabilize and gradually improve. The euro had begun to depreciate against other major currencies and this in part was offsetting the effects of fiscal tightening. However, the longer the deadlock in the eurozone persisted, the greater the risks of contagion of its problems both within the eurozone and outside.

The hope that 2010 would see the recovery properly established waned as the year went on. Even growth in the 'emerging economies' was marked down for 2011 as anxieties increased that the crisis in the eurozone might provide a new financial shock in the form of a cascade of sovereign defaults, leading to the disorderly breakup of the eurozone. The IMF estimated that such an outcome would create financial shocks to banks, companies and households as great as those in 2008, reducing global growth in 2011 by up to 1.5 per cent. With such uncertainties overhanging the international economy, the IMF recognized that the conditions were unfavourable for successful fiscal adjustment of the kind it was urging on the western economies, since that would be difficult unless accompanied by strong growth. Structural reform particularly in labour and product markets was needed to raise the potential growth of the western economies and improve their competitiveness, and the need for this tended to be greatest in those economies facing the greatest fiscal adjustment.

Nevertheless, despite these fears 2010 was broadly a year in which the economic recovery advanced, even though it remained very uneven. By the end of the year, the recovery was still very much a two-speed one. In the western economies economic activity had slowed rather less than expected but growth remained sluggish and unemployment still high. The Federal Reserve in the US, which had temporarily halted further quantitative easing in June 2010, had decided by December that the recovery was in danger of stalling again and launched a second round of quantitative easing, involving the purchase of $600 billion of Treasury securities. In the rising economies, activity was still buoyant, even if there were already some signs of overheating because of the massive fiscal stimulus, particularly in China. Other non-western economies were also growing strongly, particularly many states in sub-Saharan Africa, where growth was predicted to be 5.5 per cent in 2011 and 2012. Global output was now expected to grow at 4.5 per cent in 2011, a slight improvement on previous forecasts. But the biggest risk to the recovery remained the eurozone which continued to be subject to new crises as it became clear that the rescue packages and institutional reforms which had been put in place were insufficient to satisfy the markets. The scepticism of the markets continued to push up the cost of servicing the debt of the weakest eurozone economies. Progress on reducing fiscal imbalances and repairing financial systems was too slow and as a result there was renewed financial turbulence in the last quarter of 2010, in many respects repeating the May crisis, leading to an agreement in the Council of Ministers that a new permanent rescue facility needed to be established. EU leaders agreed to set up a European Stability Mechanism to come into force in 2012.

Despite the continuing risk of an implosion in the eurozone, the IMF concluded that the recovery was set to continue, provided policies to prevent contagion from the euro area were successful. It predicted that growth in the western economies would be 2.5 per cent in both 2011 and 2012, which was still quite slow, given the depth of the recession in 2009, and insufficient to make much of an impact on unemployment. The extent of the fiscal deficits in the western economies was also a cause of concern, not just in the eurozone but also in the US, where the deficit was projected to be 10.75 per cent in 2011, double that of the eurozone, with the gross government debt on course to exceed 100 per cent of GDP.

Phase 3: the impact of the eurozone crisis 2011–12

If 2010 was overall a year of gradual improvement compared to 2009, despite the deepening crisis in the eurozone, 2011 proved to be a year in which the engine stalled again. By July the IMF was reporting a mild slowdown in global growth amidst increasing risks to the recovery. The gap in performance between the western economies and the rising economies remained marked, with problems in the US and the eurozone the main risks. One-off shocks such as the Japanese tsunami also had a marked negative effect. But in the first half of the year the IMF remained confident, reminding its readers that the fundamental drivers for a sustained recovery were still in place, namely accommodative macroeconomic policies (particularly the very low interest rates throughout the advanced economies); the strong pent-up demand for consumer durables and investment; and the strong potential growth in the non-western economies. It was confident enough to proclaim in July 2011 that the global economy had turned the corner from the Great Recession (IMF 2011, p. 7), even if there was still much to do to secure the transition from recovery to sustainable long-term growth. The eurozone had to persist with its reforms and the US had to address the problem of its debt ceiling and the deadlock which had emerged between the President and Congress over the conditions under which it might be raised. The IMF urged the US to adopt a deficit reduction plan to include the reform of some entitlements and reforms to taxation to increase government revenues. Japan was also giving some cause for concern because of the problem of its national debt and the policies it had in place to deal with it and keep it contained. It had the largest national debt of the leading economies, over 200 per cent, although much of it was held internally.

By the end of the year, much of the relative optimism of July had disappeared. The IMF now conceded that the recovery had not just slowed but had stalled. The problems of the eurozone had exploded again and many fragilities in other western economies had been exposed, while the rising economies had been growing at a slower pace than expected. The global growth prediction for 2012 was revised down to 3.25 per cent and the euro economy was now expected to experience a mild recession in 2012. Restoring the health of the eurozone was reaffirmed as the top priority for getting the recovery back on track, and the IMF for the first time appeared to be having second thoughts about the wisdom of the fiscal austerity which it had pressed on all the western economies. It now advised that it was important not to overdo fiscal consolidation. Too much austerity could delay recovery rather than hasten it, and at worst might plunge economies into deflation, which as Japan had discovered in the 1990s might be very hard to escape.

The year 2012 also proved at first disappointing. The IMF noted in July that new setbacks to growth had been encountered and that further policy intervention was needed if the flagging recovery was to regain momentum. The Federal Reserve announced a third round of quantitative easing, spending $40 billion a month, later raised to $85 billion, and indicated that it wanted to keep the lending rate near zero until 2015. The eurozone was still the major area of weakness, with new anxieties in the financial markets over whether some members of the eurozone could remain within it and still pay down their debts. The prediction for global growth was slightly higher, at 3.5 per cent, and was expected to reach 3.9 per cent in 2013. The IMF praised the EU summit in June 2012 for taking steps towards banking and fiscal union which it now judged necessary in order to resolve the crisis in the eurozone, but it noted that both Greece and Spain for different reasons would have great difficulty in resolving their economic problems within its constraints. Resolving the crisis in the eurozone was still the single most important priority, but the approaching fiscal cliff in the US, a result of the breakdown of cooperation between the Democratic President and the Republican House of Representatives, was also a matter of great concern.

Phase 4: the second recovery from 2013

By the end of 2012, the mood was more optimistic again. A gradual upturn in global growth for 2013 was projected, and a further rise in 2014. The improvement in the outlook was ascribed mainly to the policy actions in both Europe and the US, which had reduced some of the more threatening risks and lessened the chances of another major financial shock which could plunge the international economy back into recession. But the IMF concluded that much more was needed to secure the fragile global recovery. The accent was still on fragile. During the first half of 2013 there were signs that growth was picking up, although global growth was expected to be no more than 3 per cent, the same as the eventual outcome for 2012. The western economies, even the eurozone, were all growing again in the second half of 2013, and the US in particular was performing more strongly, predicted to achieve 1.75 per cent growth in 2013 and 2.75 per cent in 2014. The eurozone was still expected to be in recession in 2013, but to show modest growth in 2014 of 0.9 per cent. But huge uncertainties remained. Governments faced the problem of deciding how to start withdrawing the huge stimulus provided through quantitative easing which had provided liquidity, kept interest rates low and helped keep asset prices up.

The signal by the Federal Reserve Chairman, Ben Bernanke, in June 2013 that the Fed was to begin scaling back its quantitative easing programme from $85 billion a month to $65 billion immediately triggered a sharp sell-off in equity markets, the Dow dropping 4.3 per cent. This was partly because the quantitative easing in which the Fed had engaged since 2008 was widely seen as the reason why asset prices had remained so high. In particular a bond bubble had developed, fuelled by the huge purchases of bonds made by central banks to inject more liquidity into the economy. Even more important was that the winding down of quantitative easing aroused fears that the Federal Reserve was preparing for the time when it would raise interest rates again, even though it was clear that for the moment it wished to keep rates near zero and would not consider raising them until unemployment was down to 6.7 per cent. In 2013, unemployment in the US was still well above 7 per cent. The reaction of the markets to the possibility that quantitative easing might disappear showed the extent to which the markets had come to depend on it, and why the recovery could not yet be considered very robust. The patient was still on life support. The market reaction also drew attention to another controversial aspect of the policy of quantitative easing and zero interest rates: their regressive effects on wealth distribution and on pensioners.

The task of returning the economy to a position where interest rates could rise to more realistic levels was the next key stage of the recovery, but policy-makers were conscious that if it was mishandled it could easily once more undermine the recovery. Even if these reefs could be safely navigated there was also concern that many of the deeper problems exposed by the crisis had still not been solved, including the future governing architecture of the eurozone and a credible programme to bring down US debt. By 2013, this was already the longest and slowest recovery from recession since 1945, and a strong sustainable recovery was still far from guaranteed, although the outlook was more promising than it had been for a while. The memory of what happened in 2010 was still fresh. There had been widespread hopes then that a sustained recovery was taking hold, but they had not been fulfilled. In 2013, the outlook for the western economies, particularly for the US and Japan, was more bullish than in 2010, while the outlook for the rising economies had become more clouded, with growth in China moderating and financial turbulence increasing and growth falling sharply in some other major rising economies, particularly Brazil and India. The western economies were still responsible for more than one-half of global output, so the rebalancing of the international economy towards the emerging economies had a long way to go, and any slowdown in their growth rates relative to western economies would lengthen that process.

Political resilience

The crash and its aftermath placed many western governments under huge strain. The years of prosperity had suddenly vanished and governments found themselves plunged into a situation of great uncertainty and great peril created by the financial turbulence. Unsurprisingly many governments struggled to cope, and many did not get re-elected. But the overall picture in the five years following the crash was the ability of regimes to adjust. Mainstream parties continued to rule in all major western democracies. Even in the eurozone, the area of greatest political stress, the line held.

The impact of the crash and the recession has inevitably been uneven, reflecting in part accidents in the timing of different election cycles and national circumstances. In the US, the presidency changed hands just after the crash in 2008 from Republican to Democrat, but then the House of Representatives changed hands in the mid-term elections in 2010 from Democrat to Republican. Since then, US elections have been won by the incumbents in both the presidency and Congress. Japan ousted an incumbent government twice, in 2009 and in 2012, as did the UK in 2010. The region which has experienced the greatest number of government changes since the financial crash has been the EU. Of its 28 members in 2013, 21 experienced at least one change of government between 2008 and 2013, and only 7 stayed with the same incumbent. Within the 17 states of the eurozone, 4 have had the same party in government throughout the period since the crash; 13 have experienced at least one change of government.

Several countries (Iceland, Greece, Italy and Cyprus) suffered major political crises as a result of the financial crash, accompanied in Greece by widespread social breakdown as well. But this has not been typical, and even here mainstream parties remain in government. It has been much more common for incumbent governments to lose office, sometimes accompanied by a meltdown in the ruling party's support. Local factors have been involved, and each case is different, but a general pattern has nevertheless emerged. Incumbents have tended to be blamed by voters for the financial crash and the economic stagnation which followed. Notable examples of landslides destroying the incumbent governing party include Iceland (2009), Greece (2012) and Hungary (2010). In other cases the movement of support has not been so pronounced. What is striking is that so far there has been no example of regime change in the sense of the victory of an anti-system party, whether from the Right or the Left, pledged to break with or fundamentally renegotiate existing international treaties and memberships which would isolate the country from the international economy. All the parties which have succeeded in ousting an incumbent have been parties within their particular national consensus, pledged to the same core external relationships, such as membership of the EU, the WTO, the OECD and the IMF, all of them key components of the international market order.

Radical anti-system parties from both the Right and the Left have surged in several countries, notably in Greece and Italy, and a number of other countries have seen the rapid growth of populist parties, such as the True Finns in Finland, who captured 20 per cent of the vote in 2011. But the response of the mainstream parties has often been to form grand coalitions, which kept the populist parties at a distance from any role in government, even when they have polled over 20 per cent of the vote, as Syriza did in Greece in 2011, and Beppe Grillo's Five Star Movement did in Italy in 2012. Western democracy has been placed under great strain by the policies of austerity which most of the western states have pursued in some form since the crash – but it has not yet buckled anywhere.

The most severe political crises took place in Greece and Italy. On 27 October 2011 the European Council agreed a second major bail out for Greece, following the earlier one in May 2010. The conditions were very harsh, and George Papandreou, the Greek Prime Minister, announced that he intended to hold a referendum on whether the terms were acceptable or not to the Greek people. He then came under intense pressure from other governments in the EU, and on 4 November at the Cannes G20 summit he was told that the only referendum he could hold would be on whether Greece should leave the eurozone and the

EU. The terms of the aid package were not negotiable. Papandreou cancelled the planned referendum and resigned. He was replaced by Lucas Papademos, a former governor of the Greek central bank, and a government of technocrats was assembled to deliver the package of measures which the Troika (comprising the European Commission, the ECB and the IMF) was insisting on.

At the same time, Silvio Berlusconi, having refused to implement the kind of austerity package which the Troika was recommending for Italy, lost a vote in Parliament and was forced to resign. He was swiftly replaced by Mario Monti, a former EU Commissioner, who like Papademos assembled a government of technocrats to push through austerity measures.

But although these changes were widely denounced (not least by British Eurosceptics) as the breakdown of democracy, these technocratic governments only lasted for short periods, had to command parliamentary majorities, and were quite quickly replaced by elected governments. There was no lasting suspension of democracy in Europe. This is a major difference from the 1930s. The measures adopted to prevent economic meltdown have prevented political meltdown, at least so far. But the crisis is not yet over, and the potential for breakdown in one or more countries still exists.

An important reason for the resilience of the international market order in coping with financial crashes and economic turbulence is the strength of their democracies. The limited support which anti-system parties attract means that voters can vent their frustrations at the incumbent government and remove it from office, even though the alternative they vote in often pursues similar policies and does not offer a real change. The western democracies, however, have not had an economic downturn that was so severe to manage since the crash and Great Depression 70 years ago. At that time democracy was much less securely established, and it proved unable to cope in some states. The result was regime change and dictatorship, major factors in the collapse of the international market order which had been painfully reconstructed after the First World War. Most western commentators believe that nothing like that can ever happen again, and so far nothing has. The international market order has held, but in a number of states it has been subjected to enormous strain because of the austerity policies which their government have pursued. Levels of unemployment particularly among young people have risen so high that many have begun to fear the long-term consequences, the permanent disaffection from democratic institutions of many of the next generation of citizens.

Disengagement from politics and the disillusion with politicians and the mainstream political alternatives on offer is part of the explanation for the sudden rise of populist anti-system parties like Beppe Grillo's Five Star movement in Italy, the True Finns in Finland, Golden Dawn in Greece, and Jobbik in Hungary (Goodwin 2011; Eatwell et al. 2014, ch. 9).

The assumption of political elites throughout the West is that the anti-system movements can be held at bay and will not manage a breakthrough. So far that assumption has proved correct, but legitimacy in a number of countries has worn thin, and in most democracies there is now a problem about trust in politicians and the remoteness of the political elite from popular concerns. There is also a widespread perception that the mainstream parties, despite their perpetual bickering, their extravagant rhetoric and their fierce competition to come out on top, are actually very much alike, sharing broadly the same policy assumptions and, when in office, carrying out broadly the same policies. One of these assumptions is the imperative to resume growth as quickly as possible, because of the belief that modern democracies can only be managed if there is a rising stream of public and private goods to distribute so as to placate the many and varied interests which clamour for attention. It is not only China which needs a particular level of growth to keep its domestic political problems manageable. All modern states, except the most repressive, are the same. Rule in modern societies is not easy to justify if there is permanent austerity. It is a policy governments resort to in times of crisis, but they usually regard it as a temporary palliative and look for ways to relax it as quickly as possible (Hood et al. 2014).

All the governments in western states, including Japan, that were in office in September and October 2008, the time of the financial crash, were subsequently blamed for allowing the crash to happen on their watch. This was the most important factor in the ousting of incumbents when elections were held. Only Germany and Japan held out against this tide. The crash had an immediate electoral effect in the US with the November presidential election, where the economy and its prospects became a major election issue. The crash made the crisis response of the financial authorities and the behaviour of the banks before and during the crisis a major focus of debate.

As the ripples of the crisis began to spread during 2009 the first sovereign debt crisis and default took place in Iceland, leading to a landslide against the ruling party in the elections that were forced in April. In the immediate aftermath of the crash, however, there was relatively little impact on governments, partly because few elections took place in western democracies. Their governments found themselves coping with the worst recession since 1945, although the crisis response measures they adopted prevented a slide into deflation and depression. The extent of the long-term damage, however, was only just being assessed, and as that process began so the dominant discourse began to shift from depicting the crisis as a financial one to depicting it as a debt one. Governments and households were urged to embrace austerity programmes to reduce both public spending and private spending, to bring them into line with the reduced output of the economy.

During 2010 a new phase of the political crisis began with the eruption of the sovereign debt crisis in the eurozone. The first bail out for Greece had to be agreed by the Troika amidst the realization that a much wider group of countries, including Ireland, Spain, Portugal and Italy, were all facing similar problems and were at risk of default. Sovereign and public debt were now seen as the very essence of this crisis, and the austerity discourse was increasingly dominant throughout western economies (Blyth 2013). The result of the UK general election in May produced a change of government with the new coalition keen to embrace the austerity discourse and blame the financial crisis on the lax regulation and excess spending of the previous Labour government. By this point in the unfolding crisis, incumbents in the western democracies were falling thick and fast. The future of the eurozone and its possible breakup became a key focus of the international policy debate, reflected in IMF and OECD reports. The problem spread to Ireland, with its debt crisis producing a dramatic collapse in support for the ruling Fianna Fail government in the general election in 2011, its biggest electoral setback since the founding of the Republic. Change of the ruling party also took place in Finland, Portugal, Denmark, Spain and Slovenia.

The setbacks to the recovery across the western economies led to the beginnings of a move away from the discourse of austerity during 2012 amidst new concerns about growth and living standards. The eurozone crisis was far from solved, but there was no further major deterioration, and action by the ECB in July boosted market confidence that the euro was unlikely to fall apart and that the worst might be over. Mario Draghi, the President of the ECB, boosted the markets by declaring that the Bank was ready to do whatever it took to preserve the euro, although whether he had the powers to make good that claim was doubtful (Marsh 2013).

The continuing stagnation and growing opposition to austerity in many western economies during 2012 led to the ousting of incumbents in parliamentary elections in Slovakia, Greece, Lithuania, Croatia and Japan, and to presidential elections in France, where François Hollande replaced Nicolas Sarkozy. In Greece two elections were held. The first was inconclusive with all the mainstream parties losing ground to new insurgent anti-system parties on both the Right and the Left. Pasok, the centre-left party which had been in office when the debt crisis exploded, was the big loser. Some stability was achieved through the formation of a grand coalition led by the centre-right party, New Democracy, which in the second election significantly increased its support. The atmosphere was tense because of the growing strength of the Golden Dawn party which gained representation in the parliament at the same time as it was using street violence against immigrants and its political opponents. This revival of a classic fascist movement was a warning of what the crisis could bring forth. The murder of a left-wing activist in September 2013 gave the government the opportunity it needed to label Golden Dawn a criminal organization and arrest its leaders.

Evidence that the tide for incumbents might be turning was the outcome of the US presidential election at the end of 2012. The improvement in the US economy, although still not robust, was sufficient to help Obama to re-election in November. However, the Democrats did not win back control of the House of Representatives and only narrowly held on to the Senate, and this meant that Obama still faced the prospect of deadlock in key policy areas during his second term. In Europe, however, incumbents were still struggling. Germany was the exception, Angela Merkel's re-election, although without her preferred coalition partner, in September 2013 had been widely expected. Elsewhere in Europe, however, incumbents found it hard to cling on. A new grand coalition was formed in Italy, after the election to replace the Monti government produced no overall victor; but this did not last long. Cyprus which had just elected a new president suffered a major debt crisis, a delayed reaction to the crisis in Greece, in which the Cyprus banks had been so heavily invested. One of the most remarkable turnarounds took place in Iceland, with the return to government of the Independence Party after it had been blamed for the financial collapse and had lost office in a landslide. Iceland unlike the debtor economies in the eurozone had been able to devalue and the economy had bounced back. Even in countries which were only slightly affected by the western financial crisis, incumbents were still at risk. In Australia, which had not suffered a recession after the financial crash but had continued to grow without interruption because of its ability to supply raw materials to the rising powers, particularly China, there was a decisive victory for the centre-right coalition in September 2013, but the main explanation was not the economy but other domestic issues, including the chronic divisions within the ruling Labour Party.

The rising powers maintained a high level of political stability in the first five years after the financial crash, and political instability was concentrated in the western economies. Incumbents were almost everywhere at risk, and the majority of elections resulted in a change in the ruling party. There were often important local factors, but in most cases the economic problems created by the financial crash, and the difficulties governments had in managing the expectations of their voters and keeping control of events, were significant. Despite this, it is important to recognize how resilient political systems were in this period. Even in those countries most in the eye of the storm – Greece, Portugal, Spain, Italy, Cyprus, Iceland and Ireland – and which experienced the most dramatic electoral collapses, the parties which replaced the discredited incumbents remained committed to ensuring that their countries remained full members of the international market order. Some mainstream parties, like Fianna Fail in Ireland and Pasok in Greece, did suffer spectacular collapses of support, but although there was a marked surge in support for anti-system parties the main beneficiaries were other mainstream parties. The centre held.

The political resilience of the democracies, particularly in Europe, fed into the narrative that the worst was over, although there were still anxieties over whether the centre could hold if, for example, a new crisis in the eurozone were to erupt, requiring another round of austerity. Confidence was still fragile, but the most serious threats to world peace lay not in the EU or the US but in the Middle East, East Asia and the Ukraine. In contrast to the 1930s, the economic cataclysm had not yet detonated a political cataclysm as well in the heartlands of the West.

Chapter 4

The Global Shift

The international as well as the domestic resilience of the international market order was tested by the crisis. The financial crash took place in the heartlands of the western economy, the OECD states, and at first its direct impact on other parts of the international market order was limited. Many non-western economies continued to grow at very high rates, emphasizing that they were not dependent on western markets. But this was an illusion. They could afford to be indifferent at first to what was going on in New York and London, because they were insulated from the effects. The tide of protest which swept away so many incumbent governments between 2008 and 2013 was mainly felt in western democracies. Among the eight western powers in the G20 only Canada and Germany have had the same major party continuously in office since 2008. The reverse is true among the 11 non-western members of the G20. Only Mexico has had a change of government in this time.

The rising powers viewed the spectacular implosion of Anglo-American finance in 2008 and the recession which followed as primarily a problem for the West, which did not much affect them, although their exports suffered from the contraction of demand in some of their main markets (growth rates dipped in 2009) and some countries, notably China, applied a large fiscal stimulus to offset the lost western demand and keep their growth high. There was never much risk of recession for these economies. The gloom and pessimism which pervaded much thinking about the crisis and its aftermath was strikingly absent outside the West. The mood in many of the rising powers remained generally optimistic about the economic future, because their opportunities for growth and development continued to increase. As these powers grow, they become less dependent on the western economies, trading more with one another. This experience makes the rising powers less willing to cooperate with the western powers in finding solutions to what they see as western dilemmas and leads them to question many of the assumptions on which western policy is based.

This might suggest that the 'global financial crisis', as it is sometimes called, was a regional not a global phenomenon, rather like the Asian financial crisis in 1997, and should therefore be renamed the 'North Atlantic crisis'. What makes it different from the Asian financial crisis is that it took place in the financial nerve-centre, not just of the western economies but of the whole international economy, the financial centres of Anglo-America (Gowan 2009; Green 2013; Panitch & Gindin 2013). By threatening the western democracies it threatened the stability of the international market order which the western states had dominated for so long. In this way its impact came to be felt well beyond the North Atlantic. As events since the crisis have unfolded, it has become clearer that the rising powers cannot insulate themselves from the long-term structural crisis of the neo-liberal order, which affects them just as it affects the OECD states. In trying to insulate themselves, some of them, particularly China, have created a huge credit bubble of their own, which could cause another major financial crisis in the future. In the present crisis, the rising powers are leading players, and have a major stake in the outcome and a major role in shaping it. The importance of western finance, western consumer demand and western technology in the international economy reinforces the interdependence of all states and makes autonomous and self-reliant economic development hazardous, even for the largest states, as the slowdown in growth rates and for several of the rising powers after 2012 confirmed.

By 2013, the non-western economies accounted for over 50 per cent of global output at purchasing power parity for the first time. The gap has narrowed rapidly over the last 30 years and particularly over the last ten. The West (which for these purposes includes Japan) is still dominant, but its advantage is lessening, and if current trends continue, the balance within the international economy will continue to shift against the West. Economic weight is not the same as political weight, but if the international market order which was created over six decades by the US and its western allies is to be maintained, some way of extending it by incorporating the rising powers fully within it will have to be found.

This liberal international market order appeared to be in robust health when it was extended by default after the fall of communism to embrace the whole world, as its original designers in the 1940s always intended. For two decades after the end of the Cold War it seemed that the old dream of One World, a single international market order, with a common set of rules and institutions, underpinned by a common set of values and commitments, was once again within reach. As democracy and free markets were adopted by more and more states, the number outside the international market order, either because they would not participate or could not, began to dwindle quite sharply.

The international market order survived the financial crash. It has not come tumbling down. The dollar is still the leading currency, and the international agencies such as the IMF, the World Bank and the WTO continue to function in the western interest as they were set up to do. There have been tensions, but so far protectionism and competitive devaluations have been limited. There has been nothing like the collapse of the international market order which took place in the 1930s, nothing like the protectionist moves which followed the failure of the London Economic Conference in 1933. As noted in Chapter 2 the course of events this time is so far much more similar to the 1970s. The US has suffered some setbacks, not least in its confidence in the inexorable spread of universal prosperity and democracy around the world, but it is still in a dominant position, and still capable of refashioning the international market order in order to preserve it while safeguarding its own national interests, as it eventually succeeded in doing in the 1970s. The decision after the crash to make the G20 rather than the G8 the primary forum for discussing the management of the international economy, bringing the major rising powers into dialogue with the western powers, was a major first step.

The agenda of the G20 is focused on how to preserve and if possible strengthen the international market order. This order is not about to disappear, but it is facing serious challenges. The reasons are both internal and external. Western governments remain committed in principle to the preservation of an open and liberal international economy secured through multilateral agreements and operating according to rules, as one of the essential foundations of western prosperity, but there are fears that as internal pressures on states mount, the political will and capacity to sustain existing levels of cooperation will diminish, and restrictions on the free movement of peoples, capital and goods will multiply. The internal politics of debt and austerity in both the US and the EU have undermined domestic support for the international market order.

A second reason for concern is that when the western economy was growing, particularly in the decade and a half before the financial crash, the incorporation of rising powers seemed relatively straightforward. There were advantages on both sides to be secured. The slow down in western growth and fears about a new stagflation or secular stagnation have made the international market order, as it is currently configured, much less attractive to those who were not founder members and have hitherto been excluded from its governance. Getting agreement to deepen cooperation in this climate has become harder, partly because the crisis has emboldened the rising powers to press for reforms to the institutions of the international market order. If such reforms cannot be agreed over the next decade there is likely to be an increase in bilateral rather than multilateral deals between nations, and the formation of new regional alliances and spheres of influence, even the emergence of alternative international orders.

The changing international market order

Nothing quite like this has happened in the period of the US ascendancy since 1945, and it is not surprising that there no maps, or that no one is quite sure what the future holds (Hay & Payne 2013). This has forced reflection on the importance of the international market order for western prosperity and growth, and what the consequences might be if it cannot be sustained. The crash did not create this issue, but it has helped to highlight it, partly because of the sharp contrast in economic performance between the West and the rising powers since 2008. Underlying it is one of the most important developments of the present period – the beginnings of a global shift in wealth and power, a shift from West to East and from North to South. If present trends continue – and as we shall see there is a large dispute as to whether they will – this will be the biggest transformation of the international market order since the beginning of the modern era and the rise of the West which accompanied it. The dominance achieved by the western powers in the nineteenth and twentieth centuries grew out of the overseas territorial and commercial expansion which began at the end of the fifteenth century and was consolidated by the economic and technological transformation of the world which flowed from industrialization after 1780. This dominance was maintained by the western powers even though the leadership of the West passed from Europe to the US in the course of the twentieth century.

This western dominance which has been a constant in world politics for the last three centuries is in the course of being shattered. By 2050, and certainly by 2100, the list of leading countries is likely to be very different from what it was in 2000 or 1900. Extrapolating current growth trends and using them to predict where countries will be in 50 or a hundred years is not very reliable. So many other factors can intervene to change the trends. But certain broad judgements are possible. Just as Alexis de Tocqueville was able to see in the middle of the nineteenth century that the US and Russia would be the world's two leading powers 100 years later, it is possible at the present time to see that India and China with their vast populations and huge economic potential will once again be among the world's leading powers in 2100. The industrialization and modernization which is now under way in both countries is unlikely to be smooth during the next century, and both countries are likely to encounter setbacks, possibly major setbacks, but the direction is set and the point of no return seems to have been passed. States in the twentieth century which modernized successfully and developed advanced modern economies tended to be medium-sized such as Taiwan or South Korea, or city states such as Singapore and Hong Kong. If the successful modernization and industrialization of two states whose combined populations are more than one-third of the world's total continues, it will decisively shift the balance away from the western powers in Europe and North America.

The size of the shift that is underway is even larger than this because the change is not confined to India and China, but extends to many other countries in the global South. There has been a qualitative transformation in economic prospects taking place in Brazil, in Indonesia, in Turkey, in Mexico, in Nigeria, in South Africa and in many smaller states (O'Neill 2013). The crash has highlighted the shift through the contrast since 2008 between the rising powers and the western powers, the former still forging ahead, while the latter have been plunged into recession, painful austerity and restructuring.

The very term 'rising' powers suggests others which are declining. A fierce debate on US decline flourished in the 1980s (Kennedy 1988; Strange 1988, 1996), then subsided following the collapse of the Soviet Union and the completeness of the political and ideological triumph of the US which left it without a serious rival and created a unipolar world. By the 1980s, few supposed that the stagnant and sclerotic Soviet Union was any longer a serious challenger to the US, even if few expected how quickly it would collapse. The debate on decline was focused not on the Soviet Union but on the challenge from Japan and West Germany, two countries firmly within the 'western sphere' and protected by the US security umbrella. But in the 1990s, the Japanese challenge fell away as the country became enmeshed in deflation following financial collapse, while West Germany was preoccupied with the absorption of East Germany into the Bundesrepublik and the creation of a unified German state. For a time the US position appeared unassailable and thoughts of decline a distant memory.

The debate on decline revived after 9/11 and received a further impetus after 2008. It has become increasingly focused on China (Nolan 2004; Halper 2010; Jacques 2012), partly because China appears to many a plausible candidate to be the latest in a long line of challengers to the liberal international market orders centred on Anglo-America and its two leading states, Britain and the US (Gilpin 2001; Gamble 2003; van der Pijl 2006). China is nationalist, confident and undefeated. It is building a strong economy and strong armed forces, and may be capable eventually of seeking military parity with the US, if it chooses. It resembles in that sense Germany and Japan in the first half of the twentieth century and the Soviet Union in the second half. But in other respects the comparison is inexact, since China has been expanding in the last three decades by accepting some at least of the rules of the international market order, rather than seeking to develop outside it and establish a regional hegemony, as both Germany and Japan, and later the Soviet Union, were intent on doing. China has territorial claims in Asia, particularly in the South and East China Seas, but these are minor compared to the territorial claims made by Germany and Japan to secure their homelands and provide them with the economic resources they required. In part this is because China, unlike the other two, is already a great continental economy and has the security and confidence which such an extensive territorial and demographic base provides. But it is also because China decided that the fastest way to successful modernization was to operate within the international market order, opening its economy to trade and investment with the West.

China is the rising power which has received most attention, but what makes the global shift truly global is that it is by no means the only one. India, Brazil and several other countries are also rising at the same time. The shift that is taking place is much greater than simply the re-emergence of China. It is signalling the rebalancing of the international market order in favour of some of the most populous countries in the world, the recovery of their former importance. This is potentially the first international market order of the modern era which would not be Eurocentric or western-centric. It could signal a return to a genuinely multipolar system of the kind which existed in the nineteenth century, only this time the multipolarity would not be based on the western powers and their overseas empires, but would reflect the economic, political and demographic weight of all members of the international community.

Some scepticism at this point is necessary. A new international market order is far from achieved, at best it is in its very early stages, and may never be achieved, or at least not in the form which some are predicting. The growth of the rising powers has been impressive over the last two decades, but all of these powers are still at a relatively early stage in their transition to modern, industrial societies, and vast populations remain on the land. The unevenness of development within these societies is now often as great as the traditional unevenness between rich and poor nations. The establishment of societies in which the great majority of citizens have become part of modern urban economies, and fully integrated into the international economy, is still a long way off. Some analysts doubt whether the structural advantages of the rich western powers will be overcome so easily, and predict that the rising powers may reach a glass ceiling or that their banking and financial systems may explode (Fenby 2014). They note that the countries that have developed successfully have tended to be smaller states with unique advantages and special niches in the international division of labour.

What makes the surge of development spearheaded by India and China potentially transformative is that if it is maintained it offers new development models to the rest of the world. In China in particular, a new development model is taking shape, elements of which may be attractive to other states. In its urgent need for raw materials and energy to feed its booming economy, China is engaging in bilateral trade and development links with many states in Asia, Africa and South America. It has the potential to be an alternative pole to the US. To this the sceptics counter that the number of countries which have escaped from poverty and under-development in the last century are very few, and no country as large or under-developed as China or India has done so. The possibility is real that the rising powers may advance so far but no further. They may urbanize part of their population, raise incomes and take many of their citizens out of poverty through the development of mass production industries, copying and applying technologies already available in other countries. But whether they can break through into new, innovative technologies and start to lead economic development in key sectors rather than always catching up is still unclear. The Japanese did succeed in doing this in the 1970s and 1980s when many earlier doubted that they could. The Chinese and the other rising powers are certainly intending to follow that example, and also that of South Korea, but whether they will succeed is still uncertain. The rise of Japan and Korea was sponsored and facilitated by the US, which kept its markets open for them. In the great western financial boom of the 1990s and 2000s, the US and Europe both opened their markets to China, in which western companies invested heavily. Will the US continue to do this? The rising powers have internal deadlocks and obstacles of their own to overcome, and the structural power and capacities of the western powers to block or slow their progress remains formidable.

One of the key determinants of the outcome will be what kind of international market order emerges in the altered landscape after the financial crash. Will it be a continuation of the present western dominated international market order, or will there be a transition to a new one? The crash highlighted the anomaly of an international order still so much centred on the western powers, and in particular on the US. If there is to be a smooth transition to a new international market order the interests of the rising powers have to be accommodated and ways found to enable them to participate in existing governance structures of the present order and to shape new ones. The new importance accorded to the G20 after the crash is a start, but it will need to go much further (Wade & Vestergaard 2012).

Among many other difficult issues, there is the membership of the UN Security Council (UNSC), which still reflects the circumstances of 1945 and is out of line with current political realities (Kennedy 2001). Only five states, the US, Russia, the UK, France and China, are permanent members of the UNSC and have the right of veto. They were the victors of the Second World War, although France and China had both been occupied and temporarily lost their sovereignty. China's seat was occupied by the Chiang Kai-Shek Government in Taiwan for 22 years after the 1949 Communist Revolution, because the US refused to recognize the legitimacy of the communist government in Beijing. The five permanent members continue to be the five most powerful military powers in the world, but Germany, Japan, India, Brazil, South Africa and several other countries all have pressing claims for a permanent place, in recognition of their importance, demographically and economically. The EU has no place on the UNSC, but two of its member states, Britain and France, are members in their own right. If they were to give up their places in favour of the EU gaining a single place, that would help rebalance the Council. But the idea is anathema to both Britain and France, since it would signal a further decline from their former unquestioned status as great powers, and because it would imply that the EU had become a single state, which both oppose.

Similar considerations apply to the G8, the G20, the IMF and the World Bank. The institutions for governing the international economy were established by the US and reflect the most important economies in the US sphere of influence created after the war. Membership and voting rules of many global agencies are skewed in favour of the US and its allies. Russia excluded itself after it refused Marshall Aid and did not participate in the agencies set up at Bretton Woods. The G6, when it began meeting in 1975, comprised the US, France, Germany, the UK, Italy and Japan. Canada joined in 1976, making it the G7, and Russia joined in 1997, making it the G8. China, India and Brazil, however, have not been admitted to the G8, and Russia was expelled in 2014 after it occupied Crimea. This issue has been dealt with since 2008 by sidelining the G8 and giving priority to the G20, created originally in 1999, but now recognized as the key governance forum for the international economy.

If the international market order is to change, the initiative will have to come from the US, which has occupied a unique position in international affairs in the seven decades since the Second World War. Its structural power, measured by its military, economic, ideological and cultural capacities, has given it dominance, and at times overwhelming dominance. It was the accepted leader for all the states which identified with the West against the Soviet Union, including those in western Europe and many in Asia, including Japan. Outside this sphere, it has often imposed its will on other states and obliged them to adhere to specific policies and rules, changing their internal arrangements and the nature of their regimes to conform with American wishes and the international agencies whose agendas it controlled. The US has been unlike any previous dominant power in the international market order in consciously using all aspects of its power to contain and defeat its enemies and influence and encourage its friends, setting out a universal doctrine, specifying the institutions countries should adopt to be accepted as full members of the international market order. Democracy, the rule of law and respect for property rights head the list. The US has not always lived up to these high ideals, being quite prepared to use coercion and subterfuge to impose its will on those countries and regimes it has at various times deemed threatening to its interests, and to work with many regimes which have been authoritarian and repressive, but also reliable allies, particularly in the Middle East, Asia and South America.

The international market order established by the US in the post-war world and which is still in place today was a new incarnation of the earlier liberal international market order established under British influence, though the US order has been much more encompassing than any previous one. Dominant states tend to establish orders around them, but these have often been hierarchical orders, such as the order established in its sphere of influence by the Soviet Union, or the Greater Germany project of the Nazis or the Japanese Co-Prosperity Sphere. The hierarchical and imperial aspects of US dominance have many precedents; the attempt at the same time to establish a rule based system, based on cooperation with like-minded allies, has many fewer (Ikenberry 2004). The main previous example of an international market order (although much more qualified than the American) was that organized by Britain in the course of the nineteenth century. A liberal international market order, like other forms of international order, has to be politically constructed and requires constant political effort and political will if it is to be maintained. It is not guaranteed, and it is very easy for the understandings and agreements underlying such an order to fray and for its institutions to crumble. In the modern era there has already been one major rupture when the international market order constructed during the nineteenth century unravelled in the period between 1914 and 1945. Avoiding a second rupture is a priority for western policy-makers, as is ensuring that the order does not fragment, with major states seeking to create their own orders around them. For this to happen all major states have to agree to operate within the existing order, but up to now that has meant accepting a continuing leadership role for the US. Whether or not the new rising powers will always be willing to accept that leadership, and whether the US will be willing to participate in an international market order which it does not automatically lead, are big issues which will determine the future of that order.

Geography of the international market order

The international market order may have been battered in recent years, but it has survived. Part of the reason for this resilience can be seen in how this order is spatially organized. It helps to explain why the impact of the crisis was so uneven, though it also shows the ways in which power and resources still remain highly concentrated. It is easy to be dazzled by the remarkable transformation which occurred in the last 20 years. Significant though that was, the global shift is still at an early stage, and the hold of the neo-liberal order is still strong.

The different impact of the crisis upon different parts of the international economy has already been noted. Within particular regions, such as North America or Europe, the impact of the crisis on different states has also varied considerably. This was not a single crisis with uniform effects. Rather, the effects were always mediated through particular local circumstances. The financial sector of the US was at the epicentre of the crisis, yet the financial sector of Canada, just across the border, was largely unaffected. A different regulatory system had been established for their banks which avoided US financial contagion. Similarly in Europe the crisis exposed deep spatial variations between a northern core – of hard currency, high income, high welfare, coordinated-market, creditor states – and two peripheries – a southern one of soft currency, medium income, large public sector, clientelistic debtor states, and an eastern one of low income, low welfare, liberal market development states.

A second factor which made the effects of the financial crash very uneven from the start was that the crisis was not a single event, but a series of events, some of them closely related to one another, but others only loosely. In some instances events which had nothing to do with the financial crash, such as the political unrest in the Middle East, could become a factor in the wider economic and political malaise affecting the international market order and its leading states, and in that way deepen the problems which states are attempting to resolve. Despite the promise of shale oil and gas in the US, the Middle East remains vital to the prosperity of the international economy because of the known reserves of oil which are located there. Ensuring that the interests of the international market order (which is not the same as the interests of western companies) are protected in the Middle East remains a core concern of western governments, though, partly as a result of austerity and recession, and partly as a result of weariness because of earlier interventions, domestic support for active intervention in the region and the financial capacity to fund it has weakened. The western powers have so far proved unable to impose their preferred solution on Syria as they were able to do on Iraq.

In some countries, such as Iceland, Ireland or Cyprus, the effects of the crash were all-consuming, because those countries had developed such large financial sectors relative to the rest of their economies, and their growth model and political stability were tied so closely to the continuing success and expansion of international finance. In other countries, including many European economies, the financial sector was much smaller and more tightly regulated, so the financial crash had a more muted impact. But their exposure was partly concealed, and once it came to be fully understood, the crisis which developed around sovereign debt in the eurozone had a much larger effect upon them. The epicentre of the crisis moved, as the momentum of events revealed weaknesses which had up to then either been ignored or hidden.

The dominant spatial framework used by the IMF to understand the international economy divides states into advanced economies, emerging economies and developing economies. In the first group are the OECD economies, which have three poles – North America (the US and Canada), western Europe (predominantly the 15 states which joined the EU before 2000, but also including Norway and Switzerland, which have remained outside) and an Asia–Pacific group (Japan, Korea, Singapore, Australia and New Zealand). In the second group are the emerging economies. 'Emerging' is an odd term; 'rising' is more accurate, and I will use it in this book, since many of these countries are not just emerging economies but rising powers. They include the BRICs (Brazil, Russia, India and China). The BRICs are high population, low income states whose economies sustained high continuous growth rates at some point during the 1990s. All of them have grown even faster since 2000 and, apart from Russia, which had a severe recession in 2009, they continue to expand. A new group of potential BRICs were identified by Jim O'Neill in 2012: the MINTs (Mexico, Indonesia, Nigeria and Turkey) (O'Neill 2013). To this group can be added many other states, particularly in Asia, with smaller populations but significant growth potential – including Sri Lanka, Vietnam, Thailand, Malaysia, Cambodia, Laos and the Philippines. Rising economies also include the 13 members of the EU which joined after 2004, many of them former Soviet bloc economies, together with a group of east and south-east European states, many of whom have aspirations to join the EU.

The third part of the IMF classification are the developing economies, an amorphous category which includes the sub-Saharan economies of Africa, parts of east and central Europe, parts of the Middle East, parts of Latin America and the Caribbean, and parts of south, central and east Asia. In the excitement about the BRICs this group is often in danger of being neglected. It was not thought necessary to include any representation for it in the revamped G20 after the crash. This is partly because it is the least organized and most disparate group, which is reflected in its lack of power and capacity. It remains an important part of the international economy, however, and the location of many of its persisting conflicts. Many of these economies were adversely affected by the western financial crisis (Sen 2011).

None of the IMF classifications are totally satisfactory, because there is so much variation within each group and the boundary lines are blurred. Should Korea for example be in the advanced economies group with Japan, or in the developing economies group with China? Should Greece be in the advanced economies group or placed in a category with the 13 new entrants to the EU in 2004, 2007 and 2013? There are many regional economies, such as the Middle East, which have enormous variation within them, from the oil-rich, cash rich, low population Gulf states, which have incomes per capita as high as many of the richest western powers, to resource-poor, high population, low income states like Egypt, as well as the western enclave of Israel, which is high income but resource poor.

Within the advanced economies there are marked differences in the impact of the crisis within the three main regional groupings. The difference between Canada and the US has already been noted, as well as the division between the different groupings in the EU. Among the BRICS, Russia and to some extent Brazil with their resource rich economies are pursuing a very different economic strategy from the export surplus strategy of China. India is more self-sufficient and less open than the others, and still has many internal obstacles to realizing its full potential. The distinction between emerging and developing economies is particularly fluid. Originally the emerging economies were distinguished firstly because of the size of their populations, and secondly because of the high growth they were able to sustain, particularly in the ten years before 2007, and then continuing after 2010. Since 2013, however, economic growth has begun to falter in several key emerging economies, including Brazil, India, Indonesia and Turkey; Brazil and Turkey in particular have been wracked by internal unrest.

In exploring the impact the crisis has had on different regions and different national economies within the international economy and the reasons for the resilience of the international market order in the years since the crash, a more useful spatial classification takes into account geopolitical factors and distinguishes between the western economies and western powers on one side, and the non-western world, within which the rising economies and rising powers of the BRICs and others are increasingly important, on the other. The international economy is interwoven with the international state system, and economic power cannot be understood separately from political power. The world is divided territorially into exclusive jurisdictions and sovereignties, but powerful states have always attempted to impose their own form of international or regional order. Despite the huge changes of the past 150 years, including two world wars, numerous local wars, economic slumps and depressions, social revolutions and decolonization, the hierarchy of states has been little affected.

This understanding of international political economy draws on Giovanni Arrighi's observation that the richest and most powerful states in 1900 were still the richest and most powerful in 2000, although the relative position of some of them had changed. Japan was the only challenger in 1900 which had become one of the leading powers by 2000, despite suffering a catastrophic defeat in its war with the US (Arrighi 1994). Apart from that, the landscape was eerily the same. The core fact of the history of the international system over the previous 200 years has been that the international market order first sustained by Britain and later by the US has resisted every challenge to it, incorporating many of those challengers within it, including most notably Germany and Japan. By the 1990s, this order seemed stronger than ever. The Cold War in Europe ended with the collapse of the Soviet Union and the regaining of sovereign independence by the countries of central and eastern Europe that had been absorbed within the Soviet sphere for the previous 40 years, along with self-determination for many constituent parts of the Soviet Union and the old tsarist empire from the Baltic States to the states of the Caucasus and Central Asia.

After 1991, as noted above, the US seemed for a time a superpower without precedent in the modern period. The international state system had become unipolar. The military might of the US was overwhelming, it was the richest and most productive economy in the world, and its cultural power was extensive. It was at the centre of all the security and economic governance systems of the international market order and it had a network of alliances which allowed it to project its power throughout the international system. The US and its allies were the dominant force in the international community, comprising as they did almost all the advanced economies. There were sites of resistance to this power, notably Russia itself, which while no longer an open antagonist was not successfully co-opted into the international market order, and remained outside. There were sites of resistance too in Latin America, notably Venezuela, which formed alliances with Cuba and other left-wing regimes in the region; in the Middle East, most notably Iraq, Syria and Iran; and in East Asia, where North Korea was the most vocal opponent of the western powers. The real challenge in Asia, however, came from China, still officially communist, but now embarked on its own capitalist modernization which involved a significant, although still controlled, opening to the West.

The resilience of the international market order through the crisis has owed a great deal to the way in which this order has come to be organized as a result of key events in its history and the responses to them. These have shaped the relationship of different states and regions to this order and to the US. The order can be pictured as a ring of concentric, and at times overlapping, circles. At the centre of the ring is the US. The world has long ceased to be Eurocentric, but it remains US-centric and therefore western-centric. The US and its allies are still dominant in the governance of the international political economy since they control the bulk of the world's wealth as well as the world's armaments, even if they only have a minority of its population.

The first of the three main concentric circles around the US comprise the three poles of the western economy: Anglo-America (the UK, Ireland, Canada, Australia and New Zealand); Europe (particularly the countries which are members or associates of the eurozone); and Asia–Pacific (Japan, Korea, Singapore and Taiwan). The US is the leading state of Anglo-America but has strong economic and security ties to the other two poles as well. Each of these poles is characterized by a distinct model of capitalism – Anglo-Saxon, Rhenish/Nordic and East Asian – whose fortunes have waxed and waned but which remain institutionally and to some extent culturally distinct (Coates 2000; Clift 2014). There has been only limited convergence of the three models, partly because no one model is evidently superior, although at times different elements, such as flexible labour markets or shareholder corporate governance, have been adopted by or pressed on other states. Another way of characterizing these models has been the distinction between liberal market and coordinated market economies, which allows economies to be analysed by sectors. Most economies have both liberal market and coordinated market elements within them. The notion that there are radically different models of capitalism in the western economy has to be treated with care. In the EU for example, although there is no likelihood of a convergence to a common set of institutions and practices, the power of neo-liberal ideas is very strong, and the EU has adopted a neo-liberal rhetoric, although the willingness of its members to implement neo-liberal reforms remains patchy (Haller 2008). What is noticeable within neo-liberal discourse is that there are significant differences in policy options, even within the Anglo-Saxon countries. Most actual national political economies are in any case hybrids, so that different sectors may be more strongly associated with one particular model of capitalism than others. Nevertheless the distinction between liberal market economies and coordinated market economies (Hall & Soskice 2001) remains a useful one, as does the earlier distinction between different worlds of welfare capitalism

(Esping-Andersen 1990). A further important distinction is between the role which financial and capital markets play in national economies, and with them the proneness of economies to financial bubbles and financial instabilities. The presence of different models and varieties of capitalism in different regions of the international market order shapes the impact which the financial crisis has had as well as the policy response to it. They are different dialects within a common language.

The second circle contains many of the rising economies and rising powers, some of whom have a security relationship with the US, but most do not. They are broadly cooperative with the US while retaining their own independence and distance. They are not challengers to the US, but they are not always entirely within the tent either. Countries in this group within the G20 include India, South Africa, Saudi Arabia, Turkey, Indonesia, Brazil and Argentina. The third circle contains the two rising powers, Russia and China, which are seen by the US as potential and sometimes actual rivals, limiting the scope for cooperation. For historical reasons, but appropriately given their size and importance, both are members of the UNSC. The fourth circle contains the developing countries, found particularly among the countries of sub-Saharan Africa, central and south Asia, and Latin America and the Caribbean. The fifth circle contains states which are or have been active enemies of the US, designated (by the US) as rogue states. These states – North Korea, Iran, Cuba, Syria – are important regional players, but are not able to project their power and influence globally.

The financial crash and the economic recession it triggered has had its greatest effects, as noted above, within the first circle. By plunging the western economy into recession and weakening its financial sector the financial crash highlighted the way the economies most linked to the US and its dominance of the international economy were losing ground to the rising powers of the second and third circles. Almost all of these states had developed their own model of statist capitalism and had to varying degrees accommodated to the international market order, accepting some of the rules on trade and property rights. But one of the distinctions between rising powers as opposed to developing states is that the former are much better placed to safeguard through state action the interests of their national economy, whereas states in the fourth circle are in a much more dependent relationship with international agencies and western companies.

The G20

The major initiative in reforming the international market order and recognizing the global shift under way has been the enhanced role of the G20 agreed after the financial crash in 2008. The membership of the G20 consists of eight individual western powers together with the EU and 11 non-western powers, including all the BRICs and all the MINTs (except for Nigeria). Other states have rights of attendance. The G20 is clearly a major improvement on the G8, whose meetings before the crash had often been the focus of major anti-globalization protests, but it still excludes most of the world's 195 states (Payne 2010).

The G20 in its enhanced form began holding summits every six months. This has since been reduced to an annual meeting. As in some other international bodies the chairmanship and meeting place rotates. Agendas are formulated by the country chairing each summit; the follow-through of decisions taken depends on the secretariat and the willingness of individual nations to comply. What gave coherence and purpose to the G20 in the meetings held immediately after the 2008 crash was the determination of the US and Britain, supported by other western powers, to get agreement on a new framework for the regulation of international finance. The London Conference in 2009 saw agreement to establish a new Financial Stability Board to be operated by a panel of central bankers and regulators who would promulgate a new set of rules and determine ways to enforce them (Mackintosh 2013).

The achievement of the new framework as well as the setting up of a new international regulatory body to enforce it was a significant success, even if the new rules were not as radical or comprehensive as many thought necessary. It proved much more difficult to get agreement at later meetings of the G20 on further steps, either on increased financial regulation or on many of the other issues facing the international economy. Part of the problem was that while the western powers remained reasonably cohesive and united, the rising powers found it difficult to articulate a shared agenda, and so rarely acted together. By default this still gave the leading role to the US, but after the initial burst of energy to get financial regulation sorted, the US appeared to lose interest. The difficulty of getting agreement in a body as large as the G20 became apparent now that the immediate emergency was past. The range of different interests and concerns became obvious, and the US did not have the means to impose its solutions. The G20 now had a much higher profile, but its ability to broker further agreements or help to resolve deadlocks in other areas of international negotiations appeared limited (Hale et al. 2013).

The international monetary system

A key area where international agreement was sought was over the international monetary system. Ever since the US had detached itself from the Bretton Woods fixed exchange rate system, international currencies had been floating. Financial stability was not impossible in a fixed exchange rate system, but much more difficult because it empowered markets and traders rather than national governments and central banks, and the volume of financial flows quickly became so far in excess of any national reserves to make defences against currency movements very hard to execute. Many governments during the neoliberal era had been shipwrecked as a result. The Europeans had tried to protect themselves by introducing a regional fixed exchange rate system, first the 'snake', then the exchange rate mechanism, finally the euro. The first two were considered inadequate defences, and the euro was intended as the answer. This would be a currency so big that its defences could not be overwhelmed by the financial markets, because it would be as important a currency as the dollar and to which it would come gradually to be accepted as an alternative reserve currency.

The fatal flaw in this model, as discussed in the next chapter, was that without a fiscal or a banking union, and therefore a de facto political union, the currency union on which the Europeans embarked would prove highly vulnerable to being unpicked by the financial markets. In the aftermath of the financial crash, the effects of recession in Europe exposed those countries with large banking debts and large government deficits. Countries that could allow their exchange rates to depreciate and could use their central bank to print money to support their commercial banks were judged relatively good credit risks – but eurozone countries could use neither of these instruments because they had accepted the euro. The ECB was not prepared to act in the manner of the central banks of the US or the UK because it had no political authority to do so, and all countries were stuck with the same exchange rate. This weakness of the institutions of the eurozone meant that the financial markets were able to differentiate between the creditworthiness of individual member states and demand ever higher interest rates on the loans they increasingly required to stay afloat.

The eurozone painfully hauled itself into a better place by 2013, edging tentatively towards a banking and fiscal union, without wanting to call it that. But its underlying weakness remained and, short of a full political union, threatened further crises in the future (Marsh 2013). The crisis meant, however, that the emergence of the euro as an alternative to the dollar was no longer an immediate or even a medium-term prospect. The structural weakness of the euro had been exposed by the markets, and the dollar remained as the only viable international reserve currency. Other major currencies such as the euro and the yen were fully convertible, but subordinate to the dollar. The currencies of the rising powers, such as the *renminbi*, were mostly inconvertible, and their exchange rates were protected by capital controls. Only the Americans enjoyed the 'exorbitant privilege' of running the world's reserve currency and therefore were not subject to any external discipline on how much they spent since they could always print more dollars and oblige the rest of the world to hold them (Eichengreen 2012).

The US was able to maintain this position in the aftermath of the crash, but the situation looked increasingly unsustainable. One of its manifestations was the structural imbalances which had been created during the boom and which looked increasingly hard to manage in the recession. The structural imbalances arose from the way in which the boom had created surplus and deficit economies and states. The most visible sign of the imbalances was the huge financial flows they helped to generate. The surplus countries went on amassing surpluses and the deficit countries ran up ever larger debts. There was no mechanism for correcting the imbalances except by borrowing, which merely disguised the problem. Some argued that the crash took place when the strains of providing the loans to keep this unbalanced economy afloat grew too great. The existence of the imbalances encouraged financial innovation, the development of new financial products and the brokering of ever larger deals. The availability of credit, and the ease with which the wants of borrowers everywhere could be supplied, was one of the most characteristic features of the boom, and the need for ever more creative financial innovation existed because of the growing and uncorrected imbalances in the international economy. Many economists disputed that the balances were a problem. They argued that they were caused primarily by the failure to liberalize foreign exchange, investment and trade sufficiently. Major barriers still remained to the free flow of goods, capital and people. The cause of these barriers was primarily states and the use of their sovereign powers to interfere with market exchange and market competition. The more states exercised their jurisdiction the more they distorted market signals and prevented automatic, self-regulating mechanisms to emerge to remove the imbalances.

At the heart of this was a political problem: whether the US could continue to enjoy the privileges of running the world's reserve currency. This was symbolized by the imbalance between the US and China. The US had opened part of its huge domestic market to China in the 1990s, as had the EU. China developed a growth model which depended on supplying manufactured products of every kind at very cheap prices to the rich consumer markets of the West. The huge reservoir of labour in the countryside meant that China could grow at very high rates so long as the demand for its manufactures was sustained. The low wages and high saving of Chinese workers meant that domestic demand and prices were held down and the huge profits created by the country's explosive growth were largely appropriated by the new class of owners and by the state. The model was so successful that the Chinese saw no reason to change it and resisted demands that the *renminbi* be revalued, since its low value maintained the price competitiveness of Chinese goods and allowed the growth of the industrial districts and the steady absorption of millions of new workers from the rural areas into the coastal cities to continue. The huge foreign exchange surpluses which resulted from this policy were recycled into US Treasury bonds, helping to support the domestic credit boom in the US which made the purchase of ever greater quantities of Chinese goods possible (Thompson 2010).

As the dependence of China and the US on each other deepened it became apparent that both countries were locked into a relationship which they could not afford to exit, but which seemed impossible to continue indefinitely. Opinion was divided as to who was most dependent on the other; yet the consequences of disengagement would be painful for both of them. This 'balance of financial terror' held the two countries together, because neither could afford to withdraw, yet equally neither could carry on indefinitely along this path. From the free trade perspective the way forward was for both the US and China to subject themselves to market disciplines, the Chinese accepting a substantial rise in the value of the *renminbi*, and the Americans ceasing to exploit their command of the world's reserve currency to increase continually their spending beyond their income. The financial crash came to be seen by some as a sign of the difficulty of managing the vast financial flows which China's growth had helped make possible. Inflation had been kept very low partly because of China's exports, and huge effort had gone into finding ways to maintain and extend credit to keep demand growing and protect prosperity. Without China and the other rising powers, the boom could not have continued for as long as it did.

Since the crash, the Chinese and others have criticized the existing international system and have proposed reforms. Zhou Xiaochuan, the Governor of the Chinese Central Bank, in a speech in 2009 entitled 'Reform the International Monetary System', argued for a gradual transition to a new global reserve currency based on extending the special drawing rights of the IMF, to which all the major economies would contribute. It would no longer be necessary to have a single national currency, the dollar, as the main reserve currency. Zhou linked his proposal to the idea of a new international money, bancor, which Keynes had originally put forward at the Bretton Woods conference in 1944. Zhou regretted that this proposal, which he called 'far-sighted', had not been adopted at that time (Xiaochuan 2009).

Such ideas have always been resisted by the US. Many rising powers also are not in a position to press for them because, since they are unwilling to make their own currencies convertible, they also prefer that the dollar continues to be the reserve currency. They continue to build up reserves in dollars, funding the vast and growing US deficits in the meantime. The international monetary system has been resilient up to now, but it cannot be maintained indefinitely if the gap between the US and the rising powers continues to shrink. At some point there will be a reckoning, whose most likely form will be a crisis of the dollar, bringing an end to the US-dominated international market order, just as the crisis of the gold standard marked Britain's downfall. The resilience of the dollar is vital to the resilience of the present international market order.

Little progress towards averting that future crisis was agreed in the first five years after the crash. The US did initiate a rebalancing of the voting shares of the IMF to give more weight to the rising powers and less to the Europeans, but it still clung on to its share of 15 per cent which gave it a veto over any proposals put forward by the Fund. At some point that veto will become untenable because of the shifting balance in the world economy, and the US will have to accept it can be outvoted. But the still bigger prize of a new framework for managing international currencies and surpluses and deficits remains elusive.

International trade

The Doha Round of the WTO which began in 2001 was deadlocked before the crash and it has remained deadlocked ever since. This is a forum in which the rising powers have become major players. It is the most inclusive of all the international organizations, with currently 159 member states. The WTO still divides into developed and developing states, but this is increasingly unrealistic because the rising powers in particular are now a distinct group. They have succeeded at times in forging a common position which has prevented western solutions being imposed. The WTO has continued to play an important role in resolving trade disputes between individual members, but progress towards a new multilateral agreement has been slow, and the deadlock very hard to break. One reason is the wide-ranging nature of the negotiations, covering everything from tariffs and non-tariffs to labour standards, patents, the environment, competition and agriculture.

In 2013, it appeared that the US was abandoning the effort to secure a multilateral agreement and was instead giving priority to the conclusion of two more limited agreements: a free trade agreement with the EU (the Transatlantic Trade and Investment Programme) and a free trade agreement with parts of East Asia (the Trans Pacific Partnership). What was striking was the exclusion of China, along with some other rising powers. This suggested a turning away from multilateralism, a hardening of US attitudes towards a potential rival. Underlying it was the fundamental difficulty of agreeing a new set of rules for an emerging multipolar world in a world that was still organized in a unipolar fashion. If this trend were to take hold then a new multipolar world might still emerge but without multilateral agreements which had been so important in building the degree of international cooperation that had been achieved in the last 70 years.

Conclusion

Progress towards a multipolar world based on multilateral agreement was not preceding very fast before 2008, but since the crash it has become still more difficult. The international market order is still resilient. No one has broken away from it, and its basic rules and institutions are still in place. But at a time when greater cooperation is required between all states to create the conditions for another era of general prosperity, there is no sign of the political will or the practical steps to make it happen. The world is in a much better place than it was after the London Economic Conference in 1933, but there is also a sense that the governance of the international market order is being allowed to drift. Gordon Brown writing in *The New York Times* in 2013 warned that the world is in danger of sleep-walking into the next crash. Most of the problems which caused the 2008 crisis – excessive borrowing, shadow banking and reckless lending – have not gone away: 'too-big-to-fail banks have not shrunk; they've grown bigger. Huge bonuses that encourage reckless risk-taking by bankers remain the norm. Meanwhile shadow banking ... has expanded in value to $71 trillion from $59 trillion in 2008.' Brown urged that the G20 should finish the work it started in 2008–09 and agree global standards and rules. The alternative he warned is that the very thing world leaders had sought to avoid – 'a global financial free-for-all' – will take place again: 'political expediency, a failure to think and act globally, and a lack of courage to take on vested interests are pushing us inexorably toward the next crash' (Brown 2013).

Chapter 5

The Governance Conundrum

In the aftermath of the 2008 crash, the international market order has proved resilient, but it still faces serious challenges. The financial crisis was contained, but the deeper structural crisis of the neo-liberal order remains unresolved. This structural crisis is expressed through three conundrums which face contemporary government and which, if not addressed, threaten to unravel western prosperity. These are: the governance conundrum, how order can be achieved in an increasingly interconnected and multipolar world in the face of the global shift described in Chapter 4 (Desai 2013; Germain 2013); the growth conundrum, how sustainability can be achieved in the face of the new stagflation and environmental risks; and the fiscal conundrum, how legitimation can be achieved in the face of debt, austerity and falling living standards.

These three conundrums are aspects of a broader question: what has to change before a new era of democratic capitalist prosperity in the West can be established? This is the central theme of this and the next two chapters. The conundrums express political dilemmas around which there are fierce controversies and uncertainties. Dilemmas imply that there are alternatives, that the future is not entirely predetermined, that the choices which individuals, nations and governments make still matter, however constrained they are by circumstances and by internal and external pressures. No government has a free hand, and the calculations which political leaders and citizens make are necessarily shaped by narrow and immediate concerns. Outcomes emerge chaotically from innumerable separate decisions, and are often intended by no one. This should not surprise us. Politics is not a matter of rational design, and governments rarely control events: they react to them and make the best of them that they can.

The present period has brought heightened uncertainty and anxiety. western states have become embroiled in a long and painful process of economic restructuring, with no clear end in sight. Finding long-term solutions to the three conundrums is needed if there is to be a sustained recovery. The slow and patchy recovery which has so far taken place in western economies reflects the difficulty of finding lasting remedies. There have been sudden spurts which bring hope that the worst is over, but fears remain that at best the recovery will be weak, subject to new shocks such as a further eurozone crisis or a financial meltdown in China, and that western economies could be stuck for a decade or more with slow growth, high debt, stagnant living standards and a continuing threat of deflation. Yet even though such fears are widespread, there remains an underlying optimism. It is still generally assumed that however difficult and uneven the recovery from the crash may turn out to be, sooner or later a new era of general economic advance for the western economies will resume. After all, it always has. The uncertainty is about when that will be, or how long the process of adjustment may take. As an old Washington joke puts it: 'the good news is that there is light at the end of the tunnel. The bad news is – we can't find the tunnel.'

Hegemony

For 300 years the liberal international market order has been evolving as the economic, political, ideological and cultural system of the modern world, gradually supplanting all alternatives. In this process there has been a constant tension between the gradual transformation of the world into a single, unified economy through the operation of decentralized competitive markets, capital accumulation, the emergence of a global civil society, and the continued division of this world into sovereign political jurisdictions which seek to maximize the advantages for their citizens against other states (Wallerstein 1974). The trend towards liberalization creates governance without government, the steering of the international system through markets and other decentralized networks, while the persistence of nation states encourages attempts to impose order on the international system through rules and hierarchies. The tension between these two structural principles is one of the main sources of the dynamism of capitalism as a system of political economy, but also of its conflicts. The progress of capitalism towards the creation of a single world market has not been steady, and periodically it has been interrupted. The political fragmentation of capitalism into competing nation states and competing interests constantly shapes the way it develops, and at times it has been a huge obstacle to progress. In the 1930s, it was only overcome through war.

The long period of US supremacy and leadership of the western economy after 1945 provided one of the key conditions for the rebuilding and sustaining of western prosperity. The structural crisis of the 1970s was successfully managed and US supremacy reaffirmed. The future of the US-led international market order seemed even more secure after the collapse of the Soviet Union in 1991. A new universal commercial society was born. The results seemed at first highly positive for the neo-liberal order. A new group of rising powers, particularly China, prospered, and their growth came to underpin a long period of western prosperity. But this process also began the fundamental shift in the balance of the international economy and the international state system as described in Chapter 4.

The problem facing the international market order, and its leading architect, the US, in the aftermath of the 2008 crash, is how to accommodate this shift in ways which preserve the relatively open and relatively liberal character of this order. If the rising powers cannot be incorporated successfully then there are likely to be frictions and deadlocks, a gradual retreat from multilateralism towards bilateral and regional deals, and increasing protectionism on all sides as states seek to bolster their own security. The signs of this are already evident. The dilemma for the western powers is that they can no longer rely on their economic and military strength to force other states into line, and many of the rising powers do not have the same commitment to western values and western institutions. It becomes a very hard adjustment to get right, with plenty of scope for miscalculation of motives and interests on both sides. The dilemma facing the West is that the post-war order worked because for a variety of reasons the leading western states accepted the leadership of the US and were content to grant it 'exorbitant privileges' in exchange for security and prosperity. The US too was willing at times to take a long-term view of its own national interest because of its overriding objectives to contain the Soviet Union and prevent its territorial expansion and to build a new international market order under its leadership. The US is weaker now and unable to impose its preferred order on the rising powers, and there are voices in the US urging it to give priority once again to its own national economic interests. The prospects for a return to sustained economic growth would be greatly enhanced by the deepening of multilateral agreements to liberalize the exchange of goods and services and the movement of capital and people, but the short-term domestic pressures on political leaders are to put their national economic security first.

The great global shift can be read in contrasting ways. The optimistic view is that if appropriately managed it could extend the period of incremental growth in the international economy for at least another century. However much the mature economies of the West may seem ripe for a transition to a steady-state economy, that is far from the case for the rising powers and the global South. As these economies and states continue to rise, so some of the established powers will be forced to the margins, and the international system will gradually become less Eurocentric. Its governance will be increasingly conducted from New Delhi or Beijing or Rio. The new multipolar world will sustain multilateral cooperation but it will be different from the multilateral cooperation of the past because there will no longer be one leading power, or a cohesive West.

The more pessimistic view extends the metaphor of low hanging fruit to the international sphere. The western powers have gobbled up all the low hanging fruit in 200 years of rapacious exploitation of the rest of the world, growing spectacularly rich in the process (Cowen 2011). There is much less left for the rest of the world which now seeks to catch up, and since the environmental conditions are much tougher, so the challenges of maintaining rapid economic growth and achieving stable development will be much greater than those faced by the pioneers, even with the much greater stock of knowledge which now exists. The relationships between the rising powers and the western powers will therefore be prone to conflict and mistrust.

Which of these two prospects turns out to be more accurate will depend on whether an international market order can be sustained and deepened, which will provide rules for the exchange of goods, capital, people and information, and create institutions and deliberative forums which can increase the legitimacy of international decisions and extend international cooperation. Such orders in the past have depended on the capacity and willingness of one state to provide leadership (Cox 1996). Such leadership or hegemony is necessary because an international market order is an embryonic global polity without a global sovereign. It generates the need for many of the functions which a sovereign performs, but because sovereignty is fragmented between many individual states, there is no mechanism to ensure that these functions are discharged. Where one state acts as the hegemon, its position depends in part on its power and its capacities, but also on its ability to get other states to accept its leadership. Hegemons can impose their will by force over some nations, but if they relied only on force, their rule would be imperial rather than hegemonic (Ikenberry 2004). It is because they command more by agreement than by force that they occupy their position as hegemons. Because of the circumstances in which the US became the leading world power after 1945, it was able to provide hegemonic leadership for the western states for 60 years.

The liberal international market order which the US built to consolidate its own position and to contain Soviet power proved remarkably successful and resilient, but it now faces deadlocks in international negotiations on several issues including trade, climate change and the financial and governance architecture of the international system. It is proving very difficult to strike deals on any of them, in part because the interests of the western powers and the rising powers increasingly diverge. As indicated in Chapter 4, the Doha Round of the WTO has now been deadlocked for a decade, and the prospects of achieving the kind of trade deal which could help boost growth throughout the international economy are not high. The UN Climate Change Conference meets regularly but progress is very slow given the urgency of some of the issues being discussed. At the Durban meeting in 2012 there was a consensus to extend the Kyoto agreement, which otherwise had been due to lapse, but the countries which agreed to sign up to it only accounted for 15 per cent of global emissions. Similarly there is little consensus emerging on how global governance or the international financial architecture should be reformed (Hale et al. 2013). There has been greater progress in making the G20 a more important forum for the discussion of issues to do with the international economy, but it is still a long way from being either an efficient decision-making body, issuing rulings which are binding on its members, or of making itself legitimate in the eyes of those who are not members (Wade & Vestergaard 2012).

The international market order is also weakened by national and regional deadlocks over policy within powerful states and associations of states. These include the deadlocks over fiscal policy in the US and the eurozone, but also serious problems in many of the rising powers. These political problems at both international and national levels have lowered growth prospects in many parts of the world. The political problems look so intractable that early breakthroughs are not expected. The frustration which builds with the political process at such times leads to calls to simplify decision-making, usually by opting out of this or that treaty obligation, or by separating from an existing state or regional association. Such separatist pressures tend to amplify in periods of recession and can act as a safety valve, deflecting attention from other issues. They can also lead to a spiral of declining cooperation, which in serious cases, as in the 1930s, can depress and impoverish. These effects follow the logic of 'beggar-my-neighbour', the euphemistic name for the popular card game also more accurately known as 'beat your neighbour out of doors' or 'draw the well dry'. Sometimes forms of international and national cooperation are not working and need to be dismantled, but many separatist and nationalist movements become so desperate to win their fight that they target all forms of cooperation, pursuing a beggar-your-neighbour logic.

In the international context the greatest danger is a return of rivalry between great powers, a revival of the jealousy of trade which for eighteenth-century writers plagued the relationship between states, because it led them to attempt to restrict and undermine the trade of their rivals (Hont 2010). As new powers emerge, and as the position of the US necessarily declines in relative terms from the exaggerated position of dominance it enjoyed after the end of the Cold War, so competition is likely to intensify for resources and for markets. Relationships around energy supplies are always likely to be tense, given how indispensable energy has become to modern economies. So long as there is talk of a possible energy crunch or supplies becoming limited, either by physical depletion or political constraint, states will feel obliged to take pre-emptive action. A strong international market order can create rules to minimize conflicts and ensure that countries get access to all the resources they need. Similarly it puts in place arrangements to manage capital flows and the foreign exchange markets. But this requires a financial architecture and agreements on matters such as reserve currencies, who has them and under what conditions. It is easier to come to agreements when one country is so dominant in structural terms that acquiescing in its leadership and bargaining for concessions to protect local interests is common sense for most other states. Where states are more equal in size and power, particularly when some are declining and others rising, then agreement can be harder to reach, because states will be tempted to defend their short-term interests and privileges rather than strike a grand bargain, which might provide them with long-term benefits but require short-term sacrifices.

International market orders emerged because of the frictions which developed between the international state system and global markets. It is the interaction between these two very different logics that creates so many of the tensions and dilemmas of international politics. The two spheres are sometimes separated analytically, or a false primacy given to one or the other, in contemporary theories of international politics. But it is always more fruitful to analyse their interrelationship. One way, for example, of thinking about the relationship between power and stability in the international state system is in terms of polarity. The system can have one, two or many poles, depending on how many centres of power exist. Different sources of power (territorial, military, ideological, economic, administrative) can be combined in many different ways, so the patterns of world politics are continually shifting. Poles are often treated as hubs, which attract other states, and in this way aggregate and centralize power. The dynamism of the modern commercial economy destroys the security of states by threatening the competitiveness of their industries and their military capacity through the emergence of rivals. There have been lively debates about whether a concentration or a diffusion of power is more likely to create peace and stability or lead to conflict and war. The historical evidence is ambiguous and circumstances are so different that comparisons are often difficult. Order has been achieved at various times with one, two or many centres of power. But every order eventually collapses or decays, and the world never gets to choose collectively what kind of order it might like. Orders evolve depending on circumstances and contingencies, and on political will and capacity.

In the last 200 years since the end of the Napoleonic Wars in Europe, there have been four main phases in the development of the international system: the period between 1815 and 1914, which combined the financial and commercial hegemony of Britain with a multipolar system of security, the Concert of Powers; the period of the breakdown of this system and the wars between the great powers for supremacy between 1914 and 1945; the bipolar system of the Cold War between 1945 and 1991; and the opening of a new phase in 1991, characterized at first by unipolarity, the unchallenged dominance of the US – but the future of this unipolarity has become less certain, as limits to US power have emerged and its long-term supremacy has been questioned again in the aftermath of the financial crash.

A bipolar order was not the initial preference of the US after 1945. It favoured a single inclusive order embracing all major states in the international system, but this proved impossible to achieve because of the reluctance of the Soviet Union to take part. A bipolar system gradually emerged as a result with each of the two superpowers maintaining its own sphere of influence, and a contested periphery. Proxy wars were fought in the periphery between the two superpowers, but they succeeded in avoiding a direct clash in the four decades that the Cold War lasted. The western sphere of influence was organized as a liberal international market order, and its economy thrived under US leadership, eventually outcompeting and outclassing the economy of the Soviet bloc, contributing to the collapse of the USSR in 1991. The command economy of the Soviet bloc could excel when all its resources were mobilized in pursuit of one goal, such as building a nuclear deterrent or exploring space. But it was poor at developing a diversified economy which could cater for multiple and changing wants, and it became both wasteful and inefficient, and no match for the consumer cornucopia which blossomed in the West. Always on the defensive, the USSR was forced to adopt severe protectionist measures, such as the building of the Berlin Wall to insulate the economy of its zone from the West, and keep its population from leaving. The economic success of the western economy, particularly in Europe but also in East Asia, along with the system of military alliances and forceful interventions by the US, kept the Soviet Union for the most part contained and prevented its expansion much beyond the sphere of influence which had been granted to it at Yalta in 1944. International communism proved hard to unite, and China in particular was never successfully absorbed within the Soviet Union's sphere of influence.

When the USSR eventually crumbled, it ushered in a period of unipolarity, in which the US became for a time the only superpower in the world, with no serious rivals and a military, economic and political dominance which was unprecedented. This period inspired much speculation about the return of One World, the end of history, by which was meant the final triumph of the liberal West in defining the character of the modern world. This moment of unipolarity and US primacy was real but it was also brief. There has been a pronounced shift towards multipolarity, even if there has as yet been no formal acknowledgement of this apart from the enhancement of the role of the G20. The US is still supreme militarily, with no other state even close to challenging it, but the limits of its military power were exposed by a series of intractable conflicts – on which it struggled to impose control – and more fundamentally by the global shift in wealth and power brought about by the rapid economic advance of the rising powers in the 1990s and by the proliferation of non-state forces and networks outside the control of governments (Rosenau & Czempiel 1994).

Multipolarity: governance without government

The result of this global shift in wealth and power has been the emergence of a new kind of multipolar world in which power is being steadily diffused, not only to a wide range of states, but also to a wide range of non-state actors and transnational agents, such as NGOs and companies and global civil society organizations of all kinds. The hegemonic state may struggle to control the actions of other states, but it also has to confront the explosive growth in forces outside the control of government, including transnational corporations, international finance, new forms of communication facilitated by the internet, as well as networks of arms and drugs dealers, and international terrorists. We may not live in a borderless world, but many of these networks have found ways to get round borders and to operate as though they did not exist. States are aware of how such networks shrink their power and the control they exercise. This has long been obvious in the case of the financial markets and the huge financial flows which now exist in the international economy, but it is also increasingly true of many other networks. With the development of the internet, the control of information has slipped inexorably from governments. In this world, national governments are only one of the forces, and sometimes not the most important ones, which shape the contexts and constraints within which people live (Strange 1996; Scholte 2000).

This new multipolar world of governance without government had already been growing, at least in the western economy, during the Cold War, but it accelerated after the collapse of the USSR. The distribution of power which is emerging is complex, with multiple centres and agents, and overlapping jurisdictions. It has sometimes been described as a new medievalism, which captures something of its character. Its emergence means that there is unlikely to be a return to a bipolar world order or to the continuance of a unipolar world with a single dominant power (Telo 2014). But it may also not mean a return to the multipolar world familiar from the past. Much of the language developed to understand the international market order which developed with modernity may not help us very much to understand this new turn. Ideas of empire, hegemony, even balance of power, may all belong to the past. There is no guarantee that a multipolar world will encourage multilateral negotiations to obtain cooperation between states. It could be a world in which the leading powers reduce contact and become relatively isolated from one another.

Various possibilities can be imagined. At one extreme is *anarchy*, defined literally as the absence of order, the lack of shared rules and standards, and any kind of order being short-term, pragmatic and fragile, resting on temporary truces between powers with no trust in one another. This would be a world in which order would emerge primarily from the decentralized economic and political networks which would increasingly control it. At the other extreme is a fully fledged *cosmopolitan order*, a global polity which would be governed through institutions representative of all the peoples of the world and directly accountable to them, and also by the acceptance of universal norms and standards underpinned by networks of NGOs, civil society associations and companies (Held 2010). Between these two extreme possibilities lie a number of different kinds of order, all of which still rely upon the nation state as the crucial unit in establishing and sustaining order. In a *hegemonic order* one state plays the leading role in establishing and sustaining the governance of the whole; in a *regional order*, governance is organized through regional blocs, which can be either relatively open or relatively closed; in a *national order*, governance is organized primarily through nation states. All historical orders are combinations of elements from more than one of these possibilities. The order which is slowly emerging after the 2008 crash has aspects of all five possibilities, and these shape the scenarios which are discussed in Chapter 8.

Rupture and fragmentation is certainly one possible outcome of this period of transition and reconstruction, and the one least likely to promote a general recovery. Realization that the world might slide towards anarchy, marked by declining cooperation and greater conflict over the control and distribution of resources, is one reason why such priority is given to ensuring the continuance of some kind of international market order, though there is inevitably dispute over what kind of order that can or should be, particularly between the western powers and the rising powers, but also among these powers themselves, and whether nation states have the power any longer to create such an order. The vast transnational flows of commodities, people, finance and information frequently overwhelm or frustrate whatever it is governments are trying to do. It may no longer be possible to construct the kind of international market order that has existed in the past. Failure to control the illegal drugs trade or international terror networks or illegal immigration or international financial flows or what citizens can and cannot know through the internet have all become distinctive hallmarks of the neo-liberal order. It has unleashed forces which now undermine the rule of law.

At the other extreme is a move to a true cosmopolitan order in which a global polity would be built to complement the global economy, with direct representation of all the peoples of the world in a deliberative forum and legislative assembly, rather than their indirect representation through states. Such a world government would have the legitimacy to legislate directly to set standards and rules for the global economy and for global civil society. Nation states would continue to exist but there would now be a level of authority and a governing capacity above them. The growth of many transnational institutions and networks over the last 100 years has encouraged the belief that a transition to a form of world government is possible. The normative case for cosmopolitan government is powerful: how else, its advocates ask, can many of the challenges which confront the human species be met in the twenty-first century, and how can the principles of social justice be applied to all? But sceptics are quick to point out the difficulties involved in the transition to a true cosmopolitan government. Nation states remain important centres of power and legitimacy in the international state system, and there are no signs that this is likely to change, and it is very hard to imagine the process by which existing states would be willing to cede sovereignty to supranational authority. The slow progress of European integration is a sign of how difficult a voluntary process is; so too are the deadlocked negotiations in so many multilateral bodies. So long as the international state system remains fragmented into separate states, each claiming sovereignty, it is hard to see how a cosmopolitan state which transcends the nation state will arise (Hirst & Thompson 1996).

Avoiding either a desperate lurch back to anarchy or an unlikely leap to cosmopolitan order, one of the key questions confronting the US and its allies as they seek a way out of the present impasse is whether the kind of hegemonic order established under US leadership can be continued, and if it can, whether it should continue to be hierarchical or whether ways can be found to make the exercise of hegemony more collective and inclusive. The most favoured solution of the western powers is for the international market order promoted so successfully by the US in the post-war decades to be extended to incorporate new members such as India, China and Brazil. The US would remain the leading power, while the new powers would accept the existing rules which have already been developed. For this to be acceptable to the rising powers, the US would need to agree to some changes to accommodate their interests, but essentially this would be a continuation of the liberal international market order, not a replacement of it. Its basic rules and values would be maintained and adapted, and it would offer some prospects of limiting the scope of the forces and networks outside the control of government.

The advantages of such an evolution for the US and its allies are obvious. It would cause the least disturbance to their interests, and it is the outcome most likely to boost the prospects for an early recovery of western economies. It would also give a new lease of life to the US as the pre-eminent power in the international system. However, the chances of it happening depend on the US being prepared to make the kind of concessions which might bind the rising powers into a reformed international market order and also depend on the rising powers themselves being sufficiently interested in signing up fully to an international market order which would still be western dominated. The rising powers, especially since the crash, have become conscious of their growing strength and the increasing weakness of the established powers. Their willingness to prop up a system which has been fashioned by others may be limited, especially when they see other alternatives.

A hegemonic order, in which one state or a group of states continue to offer leadership and provide governance for the whole, came to be seen as the most desirable form of order in the post-war years. The success of the new US-led international market order which unified the West, contained communism and brought unparalleled prosperity and stability to many of the states within it, was contrasted extremely favourably with the experience of the inter-war years, when, as Charles Kindleberger (1987) argued, Britain had the will to be the hegemon but no longer the capacity, while the US had the capacity but lacked the will. The new order proclaimed so fulsomely by Woodrow Wilson at the Paris Peace Conference in 1919 was fatally wounded when the US Congress rejected the Treaty of Versailles and the participation of the US in the institutions of the new order, such as the League of Nations. The attempts to establish agreement on how to maintain the peace or how to preserve prosperity both foundered, particularly after the financial crash of 1929 and the ensuing Great Depression destroyed the gold standard, depressed international trade and encouraged the formation of closed territorial protectionist blocs built around exclusive spheres of interest, high tariff walls and regional currencies.

It did not end well. Whether greater US involvement in trying to shore up the international market order in the inter-war years would have been successful is doubtful, given the difficulty of accommodating the interests of all the great powers. But what is undeniable is the influence that the international failure of the inter-war years had on a generation of western leaders. The US emerged from the Second World War in such a dominant position that it was obliged this time to take responsibility for the international system in order to safeguard its security and economic interests. Even so, the resistance to the US taking on a strategic leadership role, acting as a hegemon, and considering the long-term interests of the system rather than only the short-term interests of the US, was still formidable, and was not inevitable. The US might have retreated after 1945 once more into a state of relative isolation and disengagement from the rest of the world. What tipped it decisively was the perception of a new security threat, posed by the Soviet Union. The mobilization for the Cold War allowed the project of a new US-led international market order to be launched and consolidated. What was critical to its success was the new geopolitical thinking about the international system and the role of the US within it. The rebuilding of the shattered economies of Japan and Germany, the launch of Marshall Aid, the willingness to help all its allies get back on their feet, the conclusion of new military alliances, and the cultural and ideological offensive – the determined attempt, first broached by Woodrow Wilson, to stamp the western world, and beyond that the whole world, in the image of the US – all this became the hallmarks of the new American hegemony and formed the basis for a cross-party consensus on the new US global role which has mostly continued up to the present.

The extent and the success of the US global project since 1941 has been remarkable. The US has never liked to be thought of as an empire, because of the associations with the European colonial empires of the nineteenth century which it was always pledged to overturn. But the term 'hegemon' to describe its ascendancy did acquire some traction, at least in policy-making circles. The hegemonic stability thesis, for example, formulated in the 1970s by Kindleberger, presented the US as performing a necessary function for the international economy, providing the public goods which it needed to function smoothly. Without a hegemon it was suggested the international economy performed poorly and might even break down, as it had done in the 1930s. In shouldering this burden, the US was serving its own long-term interests, but was also acting in the interests of the whole international community, or at least the western part of it (Kindleberger 1987).

The public goods which the hegemon supplies include the formulation and enforcement of rules, a common medium of exchange, adjudication of disputes, initiatives to widen cooperation and remove barriers to trade, and the guaranteeing of peace and security. To perform such a role the hegemon has to make some sacrifices of its immediate interests, and incur some costs, but over time the benefits it receives back far outweigh them. When its currency is the international, reserve currency, for example, the hegemon is not subject to the same constraints on its economic policies as other states, unless it chooses, as Britain did in the nineteenth century and the US did between 1946 and 1971, to tie its currency to gold. But once the US had unilaterally renounced that link, it had much greater freedom to incur as much borrowing as it chose, pushing the costs on to other countries. The US took full advantage of this in the downturn after 2008, increasing its borrowing still further while other western states submitted to austerity. Shaping the rules and the standards under which the rest of the world operate gives significant advantages to US companies and helps the US retain its competitive edge. By acting as hegemon the US helped secure huge commercial opportunities for its leading companies and enabled them to establish their brands throughout the world. It is hardly surprising that US companies should therefore still dominate the list of the world's largest companies.

Hegemony is not the same as empire, however, and though it is hierarchical it only works if it is rule-based, which means that the hegemon in some areas at least has to submit to the rules which it upholds for everyone else. This is a difficult relationship, as the example of being in possession of the world's reserve currency shows. The same rules do not apply here to the US, but it is very keen to apply them to other countries through the IMF. As the world's dominant military and economic power, the US is also in a position to decline to accept the rules which other nations want. In recent years it has refused to sign up to the Kyoto protocol or to subject its citizens to the International Criminal Court. The US has claimed for itself an exceptional status, which it partly justifies because of its role as hegemon, the supplier of public goods to the world community. It claims the privileges of Leviathan, the sovereign power which is freed from the rules it imposes on everyone else. For Hobbes that was the price of security, and a price worth paying. But the US is far from being a true Leviathan in this sense, because it is not actually the global sovereign; it has not disarmed the rest of the world's nations (it has not even disarmed its own citizens), so the peace and security it offers is partial. There are also many areas in which the US does submit to the rules it has created, for example the WTO dispute mechanism. Part of the legitimacy of the US comes from its acting as though it were a Leviathan, but another part comes from submitting to a rule-governed system, and not seeking to be exempt from these rules.

If a hegemonic order is no longer possible, either because the US is not able to sustain its leadership or because a collective leadership of the leading states is impractical, then the way is open for a new kind of multipolar order, which after the 2008 crash has come to seem the most likely option. Before the crash the idea of an extended international market order had more plausibility, partly because of the strength of the US, and partly because of the strong performance of western economies, which made the incorporation of the rising powers into a successful international market order seem a natural process. The sharply differing fortunes of different parts of the international economy after the crash have changed perceptions and made the rising powers much less willing to accept the existing institutions and the rules associated with the long period of western ascendancy. Power and wealth remain very unequal in the international economy, but less so than in the recent past, and there is greater confidence that there is more than one economic and social model that countries can follow and be successful. This is the era of many capitalisms. The complications of geopolitics and international security present during the Cold War have largely disappeared, and for the moment new military competition between great powers is muted. There has been speculation about China becoming a new challenger to the US, but its territorial ambitions are limited, and although the Chinese are slowly beginning to project military power in their region, maintaining access to the markets and resources which they need for their economic development has so far been a higher priority for them. This could change if Chinese nationalism became more assertive, but so far China has been committed to a peaceful rise.

What all the rising powers need is space and time to continue their different paths of national economic development. This makes them disinclined to accept or acquiesce in western proposals on finance, the environment and trade. The deadlocks in so many international multilateral negotiations reflect the new distribution of power. The western powers are no longer in a position to impose their wishes on the rest of the world, and they are also not prepared to make the kind of concessions that might be necessary to get other countries to sign up to new deals. They still want outcomes which broadly reflect their interests and to maintain their relative wealth and structural advantages in the international economy. This is no longer acceptable to the rising powers, who are becoming more assertive about their own interests.

The outlook for greater international cooperation often looks bleak, but it is possible that out of the stand-offs and the deadlocks will eventually come a different kind of international market order. It will be less cohesive than the old US-dominated order, and more directionless. It will also be more of a patchwork. There will be agreement in some areas but not in others, and there is likely to be a proliferation of bilateral deals alongside multilateral ones. Regional agreements are likely to become more important. The international market order will be held together by inter government networks of the kind which have proliferated in recent years, and these may well be more effective than the set piece meetings and negotiations in forums such as the G20 or the UN. Groups of nations may decide to cooperate in various ways outside formal treaties and institutions. This multipolar world will have its tensions and conflicts but it may also have considerable resilience. There will be a lot of overlapping jurisdictions, transnational bodies and intergovernmental and civil society networks, which will make the international market order highly complex, but also quite effective in promoting cooperation across many different fields.

A multipolar world implies a distribution of power in which there are several centres or poles. One possibility is that this could rise to a regional order with strong regional associations developing around core states. The EU offers one such model, although its particular features make it unlikely to be replicated easily elsewhere. If there is a regional order it will probably be loose in character, and the poles are unlikely to take the form of cohesive regional blocs around a number of regional hegemons. The situation in Africa, in East Asia, in Latin America is unlikely to yield that kind of pattern. Instead there are likely to be a range of different powers, large, intermediate and small, with some large ones, particularly the US and China, continuing as now to play a role in more than one region. This international market order is more likely to be a form of 'new medievalism', although with nation states remaining as core institutions, which was never the case for the 'old medievalism'. What the idea of new medievalism does capture quite well is the fluidity of relationships in this new order and the many different kinds of agents and institutions, including global cities, which are related to one another, often in haphazard and surprising ways.

The other way a multipolar world might be organized is as a national order, using nation states once again as the primary building blocks and the main sites for the organization and legitimation of governance. In many ways this would be a retreat from the hegemonic and even cosmopolitan features of the international market order as it developed under US leadership. But it may be preferred by some of the rising powers, who distrust the role which the US has played and seeks to continue to play. This order would emphasize instead the principles of national self-determination and non-interference in the affairs of sovereign nation states which are important founding principles of the UN Charter. It would also chime with many critics of globalization, such as Dani Rodrik who has pointed to what he calls the trilemma of globalization, national determination and democracy, arguing that it is possible to have any two but not all three together. Globalization means accepting that the logic of global markets should trump democratic choices about economic arrangements: 'democracies have the right to protect their social arrangements and when this right clashes with the requirements of the global economy it is the latter that should give way' (Rodrik 2011, p. xix). In an era of austerity and economic stagnation further globalization is increasingly resisted because it transfers still more power to a global technocracy which is insulated from democratic checks and constraints (Chang 2007).

The debate on globalization and how far it is compatible with democracy and national self-determination, which Rodrik and others have led, draws attention to the political fragility of international market orders and particularly of liberal international market orders, emphasizing once again the division between the international market system and the international state system. This is an artificial division in one sense since neither could exist without the other, but it also has real effects. The international market system is driven by the requirements of trade, finance and investment, and the migration of peoples, all of which flow across borders and seek ways around the limits that politics imposes. The international state system is organized around national jurisdictions, with each state claiming sovereignty over a defined territorial space and the population and resources within it. In a world of self-sufficient subsistence economies, trade existed only at the margins, but the expansion of trade in the modern era has made an international division of labour a political and social reality and made all states to some degree interdependent in ways in which they were not before. The world is still far from being a single global economy, but it approaches economic unity more closely than it does political unity. Political authority remains fragmented into national jurisdictions and nation states are still the main focus of identity and legitimacy; but, as the economy has become steadily more integrated, so all states have become increasingly dependent on the wealth and opportunities which participation in the international economy brings.

The democratic disconnect

The degree of economic interdependence achieved in the last 60 years has led to a need for political and governance functions to be performed above the level of the nation state. If there is a global economy there needs to be a global polity too, or at least some form of transnational authority which can cut across the local concerns of national jurisdictions and find solutions which can keep trade, investment and people flowing. Such arguments support hegemonic leadership by one state or some form of global government. In both cases there is no necessary connection with democracy. What is installed is a technocracy which pursues the policies deemed necessary for the health of the global economy. Democracy is viewed as a potential obstacle to the pursuit of good government. The international order over which the US has presided since 1945 was liberal but not democratic. The institutions of global governance and the military alliances which were established were designed to make American interests and American wishes preponderant. Its allies were accommodated and concessions often made to them, but although many of these allies were themselves democracies the structure of transnational authority was not itself democratic. The same pattern is observable in the EU. Even though the European Parliament is a directly elected representative institution, its powers are limited and real authority still resides with the unelected Commission, the Council of Ministers and the ECB. It is not that 'globalization' as such places constraints on national governments. It is that national governments impose these constraints on themselves as the price for remaining in the larger entity. In this way there is a constant tension between democracy and supranational governance which is playing out both in the US-dominated international market order and in the EU.

This anti-globalization critique has become even more powerful during the period of austerity and the recession. In the boom years, the advantages of participating as full members in the international market order and in the EU were so great that domestic coalitions in favour of maintaining these memberships, despite the sacrifice of sovereignty they entailed, were dominant throughout the West. But the costs became much more apparent when the boom ended and new populist forces arose to challenge the established parties and the consensus. So far, however, as shown in Chapter 3, no country has elected a party that has sought to make a radical change to their country's involvement in the international economy. The consequences of choosing voluntarily to move outside have so far deterred any such move. Even Greece has chosen so far to remain within the EU and the eurozone, despite the rise of radical left and right-wing parties which reject both. The question is whether this can continue indefinitely if a sustained recovery does not materialize.

For the supporters of multilateralism, falling back on national sovereignty may reflect the temporary will of democracy, but they argue that the programme of the nationalists is bound to disappoint, because their policies will necessarily impoverish the people. Protectionist measures to control all movements of capital, trade and people will gradually cut the economy off from the international one. Pooling sovereignty and agreeing to constraints on domestic policy are the price that has to be paid for membership of the wider club, whose rules have been fixed by those with the greatest power and influence, and so cannot be made subject to direct national democratic control. By pooling sovereignty, states enlarge their capacities and increase the opportunities for their citizens. To the international technocracy this is simply common sense. They know it to be true. The difficulty is that it is not perceived to be true by growing numbers of citizens, and this is one of the factors leading to a steady hollowing out of western democracy, with falling participation and disengagement, and a strong sense that the established parties in every state are much the same. It makes little difference who is in power, the same policies are pursued. The populist parties all make great play of this: parties like UKIP in Britain and the Front National in France. The problem for the established parties is that they find it difficult to prove that they are in control and that they do make a difference because of their awareness that many issues now can only be settled in transnational forums through elaborate multilateral negotiations with other states.

This problem is sometimes called the 'democratic deficit'. The tide of democracy continues to spread, encouraged by the US and the EU. But many of the new democracies are finding democracy delivers much less than it promised, while the older ones have become increasingly cynical about the political process and what it can achieve. Democracy can only be practised within tight limits, and at moments of crisis, as the eurozone crisis has shown repeatedly, attempts to step outside those limits are ruthlessly punished. At such moments the limits of national sovereignty and of democracy are revealed. Yet it is not that nations no longer have a choice. They do have a choice but often the alternatives are both unpalatable. In the crisis that Cyprus faced in 2013 the choice was between on the one hand leaving the eurozone, reintroducing the Cyprus pound and dealing with banking collapse and economic restructuring as a sovereign nation state, or on the other hand accepting the terms of the Troika, the dismantling of a large part of the Cypriot financial sector and painful cuts and austerity. At least the second choice, although bitterly resented, meant staying within the club. Many of the other members of the club whom the Troika represented viewed the terms being offered as generous.

The eurozone crisis is a microcosm of the wider crisis of the international market order. Globalization has been pushed to the point that there is a serious disconnect between the peoples of the world and their governments. This growing gap between government and governed shows itself in the declining respect for domestic politics and political institutions. At the same time there is even less respect and trust in international institutions and agencies, which appear as alien powers which act against the interests of nation states. This is one of the great dilemmas of our times. We are moving towards a multipolar world in which there are many centres of power, many overlapping jurisdictions, and many different actors, both state and non-state. The complexity of the international system is a strength but also a weakness. It is a strength because it reflects the opportunity to mobilize very diverse experiences, knowledge and resources wherever they happen to be. It is a weakness because it can seem directionless, with either no one in control, or control being exercised by malign external forces. The degree of connectedness of the contemporary international economy makes all parts of the world interdependent, although to differing degrees. The more the world approaches an integrated international economy through international flows of capital, goods and labour, so the need for some kind of multilateral regulation of these flows intensifies. A global polity evolves to complement the global economy and global civil society.

The EU is not a unified centralized state in the manner of other states in the international state system; nor does it act like other states. It is a unique multilateral experiment for developing common rules and institutions to promote integration between its 28 members without usurping the role of the nation states in providing the main focus for identity and legitimacy and for decision-making. The EU budget is only 1 per cent of the total EU GDP, and even that is too much for some members who want to reduce it. The budgets of national governments in the EU is more than 40 per cent of national GDP, in some cases a lot more. In these circumstances the ability of the EU to perform the role of a strong federal centre is very limited. The budget of the US federal government is 20 per cent of GDP. The EU has offered a different social and economic model to that of the US, and also an example of how a multilateral and multipolar world might function. Its decision-making processes are slow and cumbersome, and the process by which agreements are reached is often tortuous and exhausting, but the progress in putting together a set of common rules for a diverse collection of states, which retain national sovereignty, has been impressive. The EU's ability, however, to be a positive model for the emerging world order has been recently overshadowed by the internal problems of the eurozone and the difficulty of reconciling national sovereignty and democratic legitimacy with supranational governance. This issue is not confined to the EU, but exists in relation to all the institutions of global governance.

The problem at the heart of the eurozone crisis is that the euro project is a state project which requires the full authority of a state to stand behind it, guaranteeing the currency, authorizing the central bank to act as lender of last resort, and taking responsibility for redistributing resources across the eurozone. The EU set out to run a single currency without any of those guarantees being in place. Instead the governance of the euro was to be left to agreement between the different national governments of the eurozone. The sovereign debt crisis has tested this to destruction, and despite calmer water being reached in 2012–13, the final outcome remains uncertain. Under pressure of events the eurozone has moved significantly towards creating the institutions it needs to safeguard the euro. But this inevitably means a major transfer of sovereignty to central EU bodies. The euro only ever made sense as a political project, but it was often presented simply as an economic project with no political implications. Only if the members of the eurozone are prepared to agree to a full banking union and, in time, to fiscal union, with common budgetary as well as monetary policies, is the euro likely to survive. But giving up control of national budgets and national financial systems to remote unelected unaccountable technocratic agencies like the ECB is very difficult to do. Such a union is coming about through repeated crises, with countries needing bailouts forced to accept economic conditions which plunge their economies into deep austerity and depression. This policy is inevitable so long as the eurozone is a multilateral bargain between sovereign nation states. Many citizens of the economically stronger states such as Germany, Finland and the Netherlands think it intolerable that their taxpayers' money should be used to bail out other eurozone members without any certainty that they will change their behaviour and institutions. Without it they will need a further bail out within a short time, and the process could be endless. Only if there is a central authority which could impose reforms, redistribute taxes and share risks can the eurozone be made to work. But the difficulty is whether any of the euro members are really ready for the creation of a true European federal state, endowed with significant sovereign powers. Would such a state be legitimate in the eyes of European citizens, and to whom would it be accountable? A European state is emerging but there has been no democratic agreement to set one up. This situation is causing great tensions within the EU because the actions of the Troika in forcing through changes in the eurozone are strongly resented and are leading to the growth of anti-euro and anti-EU feeling in many places (Marquand 2011; Lapavitsas 2012).

The EU is a microcosm for the wider problem because the same issues recur in the kind of packages the IMF offers developing countries. It is not an accident that the IMF is one of the three members of the Troika which is involved in the euro bailouts. This is because the same logic is being applied. The price for receiving financial aid from the richer members of the liberal international market order since the 1980s has been the acceptance of structural reforms, which is a code for privatization, deregulation, trade liberalization and the removal of barriers to inward investment. From the standpoint of the rich powers, why should they assist developing countries if those countries are not prepared to accept the rules of the game? In order to participate and reap the benefits, sovereignty has to be ceded.

The age of empires, hegemony and territorial blocs may be over, but the need for some kind of transnational governance remains, not merely to regulate and order the international economy, but also to deal with the challenges which spill across national jurisdictions, such as climate change, terrorism, nuclear proliferation and infectious diseases. In a multipolar world with many centres of power the question is how best to organize this governance. Should it be returned to the national level, or should we persevere in seeking to organize forms of transnational governance alongside them? Existing multilateral arrangements leave everyone dissatisfied, but they are not easy to reform. There are many appealing plans to improve the legitimacy and effectiveness of international institutions, but getting agreement is elusive, often for reasons of national pride and prestige, but also because the historical origins of so many of these institutions has saddled them with inappropriate memberships and voting rules and the wrong remits for present circumstances. The EU is at the forefront of this conflict, and much depends on whether it is successful in finding a way to resolve it, which might then become a model for other regions and for the international system as a whole. Despite its current problems the EU has enjoyed success, both as a league of democratic republics and as a regional economic association. It has on the whole avoided becoming an inward-looking bloc and has instead become an example of how to achieve wider multilateral bargaining and cooperation (Telo 2006). For its admirers the EU's experience in reaching consensus among the diverse interests of its 28 members offers a template for what needs to be achieved more often in international negotiations to find common solutions to the many global challenges which the world faces. But its critics wonder if the EU finds it so hard to achieve agreement when its 28 members share so much in common, then how much harder this might be for the whole world. Nation states remain an indispensable element in any possible form of international market order, but if such an order is to be achieved it cannot stop there. Multilateral institutions take time and persistence to construct, and there will often be setbacks, but it is sometimes overlooked how much has already been achieved, how many common rules and transnational networks have been established since 1945 (Slaughter 2004).

The question of US leadership

If the world needs a hegemon to stabilize it, the US remains the most plausible contender to fill the role it has been playing since the 1940s. It was the architect of both the Bretton Woods national liberal market order after 1945 and the neo-liberal order after 1971. Doubts arise, however, as to whether the US has either the capacity or the political will to continue such a role and adapt the international market order to take account of the powerful new forces, both state and non-state, which have grown up under the neo-liberal order but which the US cannot control. Questions over the US capacity to do this might seem far-fetched. The country remains overwhelmingly dominant in military terms. No other state has attempted to match it, or to form a coalition to balance against it. Despite 9/11 and 2008, the world remains unipolar as far as military power is concerned, and does not seem to be returning to multipolarity. The EU has made little progress in developing its common foreign and defence policy. The member states are divided over armed intervention in the affairs of other countries, Germany in particular, and some members like Ireland insist on their neutrality. Even the most militarily inclined European states, the UK and France, continue to reduce their military budgets. Some of the rising powers, particularly China, are increasing their military budgets, though China so far has deliberately tried not to rival the US or to give substance to US anxieties that it is seeking military parity.

In military terms therefore unipolarity has not disappeared, but what has changed is that it is no longer so clear that the US has a strong appetite to keep playing its old hegemonic role. The Bush presidency may mark an important watershed. The doctrine of US primacy, which key members of the Bush administration articulated, sought to pursue a much more aggressive policy in which the US would use its military strength to reshape the world to suit its interests, getting rid of regimes which were hostile to it, spreading democracy and eliminating threats. The policy was a reaction to the disappointments and setbacks of the 1990s, after the initial hopes of 1991 failed to bear much fruit. But US primacy and the 'war on terror' which was its most lasting monument was an even greater failure. Far from renewing American strength and reshaping the international market order in ways which benefited the US, the policy isolated the country from many of its allies and committed it to two long drawn-out wars in Afghanistan and Iraq which demonstrated the limits of its military power. The incursion in Iraq in particular changed the balance of power in the Middle East to the advantage of Iran. As some critics pointed out, for American policy to have been successful it would have needed to be much more imperial in its conception (Ferguson 2009). On this view the US should have extended its campaign to other members of the axis of evil, particularly Iran, and be prepared for long-term occupation of the countries they invaded. What quickly became clear, however, was that there was no appetite for such long-term engagement, even among many of the original advocates of the policy, and there was certainly little support from the US public. The difficulty of any western democracy pursuing wars of intervention in other parts of the world which involved significant casualties has grown markedly in recent decades, which partly explains the enthusiasm of the US military for smart weapons and unmanned drones.

The US still has some major security commitments, but these are now mainly in Asia. Under the Obama administration, the US has signalled a switch of its concern away from Europe and also the Middle East to Asia. The financial burdens of the US security presence around the world, with its 700 bases and one million military personnel (Johnson 2006), is leading to reductions in military spending and a readiness to close bases. The Cold War gave those who wanted the US to assume a hegemonic role post-Second World War the opportunity to argue for the funds to support an expansive military and economic policy (Mann 2003). The war on terror briefly supplied another pretext for military expansion which had been lacking since the end of the Cold War, but it did not outlast the Bush Administration, and this is allowing once again traditional US sentiment in favour of disengagement from the affairs of the rest of the world to become stronger. Declining capacity and declining willingness will likely reinforce one another in the years ahead. It will take a major new security challenge to change that, and the only likely one is a full-scale military competition with China.

Such a conflict is certainly possible, and some analysts have suggested it is probable, either because they think China is a plausible challenger for hegemony of the international market order in the way that the US once was, or because China is the latest in a long line of challengers to the dominance of the liberal, Anglo-American international market order – following Germany, Japan and the Soviet Union.

Since a new great power war is rendered almost unthinkable because it would so quickly become an all-out nuclear exchange, China could not be militarily defeated as were Germany and Japan, so it would have to be contained through a new cold war. But China is very unlike the USSR, since it has embraced the global market and has become a leading player within the international economy, rather than cutting itself off and organizing its own self-sufficient autarchic economy. The problem the US faces is that it might be out competed by China, economically, which means a containment strategy would not work, since the US will find it difficult to deny China access to world markets, although it may try. But it is also implausible that China is a new hegemon in the making, since its position in the international economy is nothing like that of the US in 1900 or 1920. China is still in many respects a backward and developing economy, with a large part of its population remaining on the land and very poor. It also is only one of many rising powers, and it is very unlikely that it will ever be as dominant in the international economy as the US was after 1945. The conditions for China to become a hegemon, and to be accepted as the hegemon by other states, do not currently exist, and it is hard to foresee the circumstances under which they will exist during this century (Fenby 2014). China has many serious problems to contend with, including managing the transition from its very rapid rate of growth of the last three decades to slower rates of growth, the shift in its strategy from investment to consumption, and avoiding a major financial crisis of its own. If it is to emerge as a mature economy and really catch up with the western economies as Japan and Korea have done, it needs to make that transition, but that will be very hard while it still has a need to grow at very high rates to absorb new workers from its hinterland.

Observers of China are divided on whether China can successfully make the transition without internal political upheaval. Almost all think that China's development path is unlikely to be smooth and that there are bound to be major interruptions to its growth. The history of all past successful capitalisms is that financial crashes and recessions are necessary to ensure long-term healthy growth by giving the opportunity to wipe out inefficient and under-performing companies and sectors and introduce new institutions. China may benefit from such episodes too, but they pose difficulties for a regime whose main claim to legitimacy is its ability to deliver a successful economy. Holding China together through major economic and financial cataclysms may not prove easy. But it is difficult to see that they can be avoided altogether. That is likely to make the Chinese leadership more inward-looking and less willing to take on a wider role in international affairs. It is noticeable that, since the 2008 financial crash, the Chinese Government has become more assertive in pressing the interests of itself and the other rising powers, calling for greater recognition of these states in international bodies and suggesting that alternatives to the dollar as the main international reserve currency should be sought. China's policy, however, has been mainly noteworthy for its unwillingness to take on a leadership role. The Chinese want changes in the way international governance is organized but for the moment they are content that the US continues to take the lead. They want to stay focused on their internal affairs.

This attitude of the Chinese gives some hope to those that want the liberal international market order to continue, with the US still fulfilling its role as hegemon. But for this to be possible there needs to be evidence that the Chinese and the other rising powers are willing to become full partners in the international market order. This seems unlikely until the leading western economies are no longer suffering from the effects of the crash and have regained some confidence. The rising powers appear happy to explore new forms of order, which exist alongside the international market order and are complementary to it, but are not directly part of it. The multipolar world that is emerging may contain more bilateral and regional arrangements rather than new multilateral ones. Existing multilateral institutions will not be dismantled but they may increasingly be bypassed because of the difficulty of reaching new agreements within them. Similarly the rising powers may launch new initiatives of their own, such as a new development bank, which would exist alongside the World Bank. It is yet to be seen how far such initiatives may go, but they suggest that a single universal and inclusive international market order will be hard to obtain.

The paradox facing western policy-makers is that a renewed and more inclusive international market order would be a major step towards a full economic recovery and laying the foundations for a new phase of global economic growth in which the western economies would share. But to achieve such an outcome the US would need to be prepared to accept quite radical changes in the way this order is governed and would have to agree to submit itself much more to the common rules it insists everyone else should follow. Are the Americans ready to do this? It will be difficult for US politicians to win backing in Congress when decisions are made by international bodies that go against US interests. There is a parallel here with Britain, which has never been comfortable with a role in the EU in which decisions are made which often go against British interests and are represented by Eurosceptic newspapers and politicians as a betrayal of British sovereignty. The option of painstakingly building coalitions to win arguments within Europe has gradually been eclipsed by the desire to opt out of new multilateral arrangements, and increasingly to withdraw altogether, and regain national independence. Britain's legacy of being the power which used to shape the rules and could set the terms on which it would cooperate has meant that it has always been a reluctant partner in the EU, and is now drifting towards the exit. A similar pattern could arise for the US in a new international market order in which it is still the leading power but no longer the dominant one. Whether it will be willing or able to play that role is very uncertain. There is little in the present polarized state of US domestic politics to suggest that it will, and the longer its internal deadlock lasts the more likely it becomes that older traditions of isolation and disengagement will strengthen. There is no longer the external security threat which might enable the liberal internationalists to prevail, just as in Britain the liberal internationalists of all parties who favoured the EU have steadily lost ground.

The situation is different from the 1930s. If then the problem was that the US had the capacity but not the will to take a leading role, while Britain had the will but not the capacity, the situation today is that the US still has the capacity, although it is declining; it is its will that is in question. China lacks both the capacity and the will to take over from the US, and there are no other possible contenders. US decline has been talked about before, most notably in the 1980s, when the US appeared to be losing its edge to Japan and Germany and losing its capacity to remain at the forefront of economic and technological advance. This moment was eclipsed by the extraordinary euphoria which erupted with the fall of the Soviet Union as well as by the falling away of the competition from both Japan and Germany during the 1990s: Japan plunged into its lost decade, and Germany was preoccupied with the difficult task of integrating East Germany into the West German state and economy. But in the last ten years the theme of American decline has returned, and there are once again numerous analyses detailing the multiple problems now facing the country (Luce 2012).

Might this literature on decline prove as ephemeral as the last? It is possible. US resilience and adaptability remain formidable. US dominance is still marked in many fields, not just in its still overwhelming military strength, but also in the vigour of its civil society, its universities, its culture, its big companies with their world brands. The US has cultural and social capital along with still abundant natural resources on which to draw, which means that any decline is likely to be slow and always capable of being arrested (Nye 2011). On the other side, however, there are the long-term effects of being the hegemonic power for so long. The US has become chronically indebted because of its propensity to spend more than it earns. This propensity has become hard-wired throughout American society and shows itself both in the ever increasing national debt, but more alarmingly in the levels of household debt. The cost of sustaining the US position in the world had already moved the US from being a creditor nation to being a debtor nation by the end of the 1950s. It caused the country to abandon its fixed exchange rate system in the early 1970s and open the flood gate to worldwide inflation. The US has used the reserve currency status of the dollar to exempt itself from the financial controls which the US Treasury and the IMF are keen to impose on others. The result in recent years has been that US debt has come to be held increasingly by foreign governments, particularly China, Japan and some of the Gulf states. It has often been pointed out that in the balance of financial terror between China and the US, the US has the upper hand because China cannot call in its loans without doing huge damage to its own economy and model of growth. While true, the longer these imbalances persist and continue to increase, the more the structural position of the US is undermined. When a hegemon becomes unable to bring its level of debt under control, it is a hegemon in trouble, because when circumstances change its debt can be used against it. The US could address the problem, but only by raising taxes substantially or by cutting its domestic and overseas spending radically, which would advertise the decline in its capacity to be the kind of hegemon it has been in the past. Changing the debt-driven consumer culture in the US towards long-term investment would be costly politically because it could only be achieved by a long period of austerity and reduced consumption. The US is still the technological leader in a number of major fields, but the areas in which it has ceded the advantage to others has been growing, and it is unlikely that it will get back the commanding lead it once enjoyed. Other reasons often cited for a relative decline of the US include the state of its education system below the university level, which compares unfavourably with that elsewhere, particularly in Asian countries, and the increasingly dysfunctional nature of US politics, with Washington deadlocked and partisan. The loss of pragmatism and compromise in the formulation of policy is handicapping the US response to the many problems it faces. All this sets up pressure to disengage and disconnect. The lack of support and consensus at home makes administrations wary about committing to new agreements and undertakings abroad.

The bigger picture remains the one with which this chapter started. As happened to Britain at the end of the nineteenth century, the balance of the world is shifting, and the US, although still dominant, is seeing its power and influence shrink. As far as the wealth of the country is concerned this is a relative rather than an absolute decline, but as far as its hegemony and global reach are concerned, this has the potential to be an absolute decline. The international state system remains unipolar for the moment, but hardly anyone expects it to remain so indefinitely, and in other respects the world is already multipolar. A multipolar world is arising, and the question is how the US will adjust to it. If it can relaunch its leadership and encourage the development of a reformed and extended liberal international market order, US leadership may persist long into this century. This will depend on whether and how quickly the rising powers can fulfil their potential. If the US is either unable or unwilling to adapt to the new world growing up around it, the most likely outcome is the fragmentation of the international market order, with a much more diverse multipolar system emerging. In time this could mean that there are several international orders rather than a single one, with less scope for multilateralism and international cooperation (Wade 2011).

If some kind of liberal international market order is to be preserved, then many aspects of the present neo-liberal order will have to change, in particular the balance between national governance and supranational governance, and the gross maldistribution of the world's wealth. The rules of the international market order need to recognize the needs and interests of all nation states. 'Globalization', which has so often been a discourse of the powerful and the privileged, would no longer be allowed to overrule national choices and preferences. States would no longer have the one western model of privatization, deregulation and flexible labour markets imposed on them as a price of membership of the international market order. There would still be common rules which all states could agree, and therefore still a multilateral character to the international economy, but there would also be scope for a large number of bilateral and regional arrangements. Such a system would still try to foster greater cooperation and openness as basic principles, but there would be fewer attempts to discipline and corral states. No state for example should be obliged to accept goods that did not meet its own labour or environmental standards. National governments would gain greater autonomy, but as a result they would also have greater responsibility, and they could not count on some of the safety nets that the international market order has provided. This might be a better foundation for finding ways to develop new forms of multilateral cooperation the world so desperately needs to deal with some of the big challenges it faces. If trust between nations can be increased then there is a better chance to strengthen the cosmopolitan networks in global civil society and support for international rules which can balance the drive towards nationalism and fragmentation which are so strong at the present time.

Conclusion

The governance conundrum for the neo-liberal order is that the international market order is indispensable to guarantee a broad-based and sustained recovery but it has been undermined by the forces which the neo-liberal order itself unleashed, not least the financial markets which came to escape the control of any government. The basis for the order which was established in the 1970s has been weakened, but agreement on a new order will be hard, given the multipolar character of the world that is emerging after the crash, and the divergence of interests and power within it. The US has to choose between making concessions to the rising powers, to secure agreement on rules to promote a different kind of international market order, or making the international market order which it controls much less inclusive. This is the first of the long-term structural dilemmas which the crash has highlighted. Preserving a liberal international market order has become a lot harder.

This order, which has existed in different manifestations for 150 years, with some interruptions, has depended upon the military, financial, industrial and cultural power of first Britain and then after 1945 the US. It survived successive challenges from other powers – Germany, Japan and the USSR – and established a framework of rules and institutions for the governance of the international economy. These rules reflected the interests of the leading power, but also served the interests of many other nations through public goods, such as freer and more open trade which they provided. Such an order is not an empire, although it may contain empires. It comprises many individual states, and if it is to be sustained it requires one state either directly or indirectly to be the hegemon, building alliances and consent for common rules, and taking on governance functions for the whole system, as though it were a single jurisdiction.

The US has performed the role of hegemon more fully and successfully than any previous state, but its capacity and also its willingness to continue to perform that function is now in question. The reason is not directly due to the financial crash, but arises from trends established long before it under the neo-liberal order. What the financial crash and its aftermath has highlighted, however, is how fragile in important areas US financial and industrial strength has become, and the increasing weight of the rising powers in the international political economy. There has been no sudden collapse of US power, in the manner of the Soviet Union, nor will there be. The end of US supremacy is beyond the horizon, but that there will be an end eventually looks more likely after the financial crash than it did before. The crash and its aftermath has shone a fierce light on the present state of the international political economy. In the decades ahead the US will find it increasingly difficult to maintain its position as the undisputed hegemon of the international state system, but may not be willing or able to broaden its hegemony to encompass other powers. There is a risk therefore that the international market order will gradually erode because the US proves no longer willing or able to sustain it against the many pressures that threaten it.

Chapter 6

The Growth Conundrum

In *Capitalism, Socialism and Democracy* first published in 1943, Joseph Schumpeter wrote: 'Can Capitalism survive? No I do not think it can.' Schumpeter was a political economist, influenced by the Austrian School and by Max Weber. He was briefly Austrian finance minister, and held chairs at Bonn and Harvard. He was a realist, a pessimist and conservative in his political sympathies. He cordially disliked the liberal pretensions of the British and criticized the shallowness of their economists from Smith to Keynes. His thought that the remedies which Keynes and his followers proposed for dealing with the Great Depression treated surface phenomena only and did not understand the deep forces which had shaped capitalist civilization. Few economists were more attached to capitalism than Schumpeter, but the entrepreneurial capitalism he so much admired had run its course. The great experiment of the previous 200 years was at an end. It had lifted the rate of growth of the world economy to an unprecedented level, making the growth cumulative and progressive, rather than cyclical, and ushering in the marvels and horrors of the modern age. The sources of this great burst of human energy and creativity Schumpeter believed was being snuffed out by the rise of bureaucratic organization in the form of the modern company and the modern state, which between them were in the process of establishing a controlled, administered economy. It might call itself capitalist, but in Schumpeter's view it was in fact a form of socialism (Schumpeter 1943).

Schumpeter was not alone at that time in his pessimism about the future of capitalism. The experience of the Great Depression, and of the failed attempts to rebuild the liberal international market order after 1918, led many to conclude that the era of rapid growth was indeed over and that countries would have to adjust to a slackening of investment and to sharing out existing wealth rather than creating new wealth. There were few expectations that the world's poor would ever see a major improvement in their living standards or had the means to catch up with Europe and North America. An economic boom was predicted for the period of reconstruction following the end of the war in 1945, but it was widely believed that once that phase was over there would be a renewed slump in demand and that the western economy would go back into recession and at best fitful growth. The outcome was rather different. The capitalist world was about to embark on the most rapid and most sustained period of growth in its history (Armstrong et al. 1984; Maddison 2006).

Since the crash of 2008 and the years of painful adjustment which have followed it, there has been a new outbreak of pessimism about the prospects for future growth under capitalism, with some of the arguments from the 1930s reappearing, alongside some new ones. Schumpeter asked whether capitalism could survive, but the question for many this time is not whether capitalism as such can survive. Capitalism is flourishing in many new and unexpected places in the international economy. The question is whether western liberal capitalism, the dominant form of capitalism since the 1940s, can survive in its present form. The growth conundrum which western governments are facing comes in two parts. The first is how to overcome the new form of stagflation – stagnation combined with deflation – and return to a stable and sustainable growth path; the second is how to prepare for the environmental constraints on growth which climate change is likely to impose.

New fears about the long-term potential of economic growth in western economies have taken hold against the background of the severe recession in 2009 and the slow recovery. Where is the next era of growth to come from? The modern era has been founded on the assumption of everlasting growth, and it is hard now to imagine a world without it. Keynes memorably described in 'Economic Possibilities for our Grandchildren' how the marvel of compound interest underpinned this political economy in the nineteenth century (Keynes 1972). The steady accumulation of capital and rising productivity through a constant flow of technological innovations when combined with the flow of wealth through compound interest (the reinvestment of the income from past investments) began to double the standard of living roughly every generation.

The confidence that this magic could continue to work was certainly damaged by the economic difficulties of the 1930s and by the destruction of the Second World War. But, by the end of the 1950s, optimism was in full spate again as the pace of economic growth became greater for a time than it had ever been, and living standards, at least in the countries already launched on development, once again rose steeply.

Now that optimism is in short supply. Taking a long view, this seems surprising. If the extreme circumstances of the 1920s and 1930s, which saw not only economic slump but political revolution and financial collapse, and finally world war, could be successfully overcome, and a new economic and political prosperity established, then why cannot the political will be found to overcome the much milder problems of the present?

Optimists point to the many positive features which should enable states and economies to adjust and recover (Ridley 2011; Phelps 2013). Scientific research and technological innovation have never had such a broad base, spread across so many different countries and regions. The flow of technological innovations has increased and is expected to go on increasing. The financial system, despite its recent travails, is more sophisticated and diffused than ever before, and capable of supplying investment funds throughout the international economy; the transnational companies which dominate production and trade have extraordinary reach and capacity to launch new projects and make new investments. The world is plagued by many small wars particularly in borderlands and peripheral areas, and also by international terrorism, but conflict between the great powers is currently low and much of the world inhabits a remarkable zone of peace in which exchanges of all kinds flourish. The growth potential among the new rising powers, such as India, China and Brazil, is enormous, not least because they include such a high proportion of the world's population, which means there is a lot of catching up to do and potential demand that can fuel investment for decades.

With such favourable circumstances the optimists argue that at worst we will have to endure some years of slow growth and heightened domestic conflict over distributing resources, but that in time the western economies will recover, if not by their own efforts, then pulled out of their lethargy by the dynamism of the rising powers. If this argument is broadly correct then the question is when, not whether, there will be a resumption of growth and a new upswing. It may not happen immediately, but it will happen eventually. Even many optimists are not very optimistic about the remainder of the current decade. But looking further ahead, to the 2020s and 2030s, they foresee a major upsurge in economic growth and the start of a new boom, driven by countries and regions of the world very different from the past. The basic trajectory of liberal capitalism towards broader and deeper economic integration, despite the constraints of national political jurisdictions, would be renewed.

The optimists can claim that history is on their side. There always has been recovery in the past. Growth has never stalled indefinitely, and capitalism has always advanced. Whatever the setbacks they have eventually been overcome and new peaks of output and prosperity recorded. The idea of progress is not dead. It is deeply embedded in the modern psyche that human societies in the modern era are in a state of constant improvement, with ever rising levels of material consumption and comfort. Yet despite this presumption the pessimists have been multiplying in recent years. They point to several reasons why a return to growth is proving difficult, reflecting anxieties about the obstacles that must be overcome if a new era of growth is to be realized. These obstacles include demography and human capital, debt and technology, and environmental change, in addition to the problems of governance and legitimation discussed in Chapters 5 and 7. As we have already seen with governance, these issues not only reflect anxieties: they also pose political dilemmas.

The growth conundrum in capitalist market economies can be stated quite simply. Markets need households and states to reproduce the social, political and cultural conditions which sustain them. Capitalist market economies work by privatizing gains and socializing losses, but this requires specific institutions to allow this to happen, and there is much room for mismatches and frictions as a result, particularly in distributing the burden of the costs. Under the neo-liberal order an acute form of this conflict has emerged because of the enthusiasm of neo-liberals for giving incentives to the pursuit of private gain by cutting taxes and trying to pay for it by cutting the social costs of reproduction. This is one of the basic sources of the fiscal conundrum discussed in Chapter 7.

Reproducing labour: demography and human capital

One of the most basic forms the problem of reproduction takes in all western economies in the neo-liberal era is to find both enough workers as well as workers of the right quality and skill. One of the main sources of growth has always been an abundant labour supply, and one of the prime sources of this has been high birth rates and high survival rates. Successful economies in the last 200 years have been associated with a rapidly rising population, but one which does not rise so fast that it outpaces productivity. Economies have also managed to boost their growth through immigration. The success of the US economy, for example, in the nineteenth and early twentieth centuries depended greatly on its willingness to accept millions of immigrants. Without them its economic development would have been much slower. The demographic dividend can therefore be a crucial component of successful economic growth, but it has always raised difficult political issues around the nature of borders, the territorial integrity of nation states and the welfare of different classes and groups within them. The exclusivity of nation states has fostered a nationalist politics aimed at limiting the flow of migrants and at times attempting to stop it altogether, and in extreme cases reversing it. It is often cheaper and easier to secure a demographic dividend through increasing immigration rather than increasing the national birthrate, though it is politically more difficult.

States can avoid encouraging immigration if they can ensure that their birth rate is high enough to produce an expanding work force and prevent an ageing population. Countries in which a majority of citizens are under 30 have an obvious advantage in growing rapidly, provided other conditions are met. All successful economies have enjoyed this kind of demographic dividend at some stage. But economies, as they mature, tend to reach a population plateau and an increasing number of countries have a low or even falling birth rate, and therefore an ageing population, which imposes additional costs. The demographic dividend as far as birth rates are concerned appears to be declining for the US, for most of Europe and also for China because of the one-child policy it pursued until recently. It is, however, still potent in many of the countries of the global South, if they can find ways to launch successful development. For most of the western powers, this easiest and quickest way to higher rates of growth is no longer a possibility, both because of changing cultural expectations and because women have been recruited in ever larger numbers into the work force. The expansion of jobs and opportunities for women has been one of the successes of the neoliberal era, even if many of them have been low-paid and part-time, but reducing the amount of unpaid domestic labour has had other consequences. By decreasing one of the main non-market contributions to reproducing the work force – including cooking, cleaning, child care and large families – it has loaded greater costs on the state.

A population that is stable or falling can become a major obstacle to fast economic growth. Taking workers from the non-market sectors such as subsistence agriculture or domestic labour is one solution. But eventually such reservoirs are exhausted. This is what makes immigration so attractive. Countries with low or declining birth rates can open their borders and welcome in young workers from poor countries. This restores the demographic dividend and changes the age profile of the country. It can have beneficial effects for poor countries as well, providing income flows in the form of remittances and the eventual return of many immigrants with new skills and assets. In the ideal theory of the international market order the free movement of labour is as essential as those of goods and capital. Liberals argued and still argue that encouraging such labour flows helps to equalize conditions for all people across the international economy, bringing wages down in rich countries and raising them in poor ones, just as bringing women into labour markets creates pressures to pay them the same as men.

However, the neo-liberal order has been unable to deliver this ideal. Open borders in particular have proved impossible to sustain politically. The organization of the international state system into competing, exclusive, territorial sovereignties ensured that immigration became a toxic issue in democratic politics. Conflicts of interests developed between employers of labour in securing the cheapest and best supply of labour available and the interest of workers themselves in restricting the supply of labour and preventing foreign labour undercutting their pay and conditions. Cultural issues around life-styles and ethnicity, and entitlement issues around welfare and housing, also come into play. Under these pressures, states have moved to control their borders, to define their citizenship tightly and to restrict entry. Some countries more recently have seen high levels of immigration, such as that from Mexico into the US, or the recent high levels into the UK. Both were significant factors in providing a demographic dividend and boosting economic growth in those countries. In the US much of the immigration has been illegal, but the country appears powerless to control it. In the UK the opening of borders reflected the EU policy of free movement of all EU citizens, a key pillar of the single market which was agreed in the 1980s by the Thatcher Government. The UK also gave entry to many economic immigrants from outside the EU. This was one of the factors helping the UK between 1993 and 2008 to the longest period of continuous growth in its history. The backlash against this policy since 2008 has now produced a significant tightening of immigration criteria and demands for it to go much further. Many of the anti-immigrant parties and pressure groups, such as the UK Independence Party (UKIP), want Britain to leave the EU in part because that would allow all EU as well as non-EU immigrants to be excluded. In other EU countries many far-right and populist parties, such as the Front National in France, or the True Finns in Finland, have flourished with calls for immigration to be halted, and again this has often been linked to hostility to the EU itself for permitting the free movement of all EU citizens within its borders.

A second related issue is human capital. Economies can generally expect to grow faster if their workers are healthy, well-educated, skilled, flexible and adaptable, and enjoy protection against the risks of unemployment, ill-health, injury and old age. Enhancing human capital has been a priority for western governments seeking to achieve the same starting gate for all citizens. Such egalitarian measures can be justified on the grounds of right and entitlement, but also on grounds of efficiency. Gradually, after many struggles, these measures gained broad bipartisan support, particularly in the key areas of health and education. From the efficiency standpoint it became obvious that, for a capitalist market economy to realize its full potential, all barriers discriminating between people on the grounds of gender, race, sexual orientation, age or disability needed to be swept away. This chimed with agendas seeking equal citizenship, and although much remains to be done, there has been significant progress in many countries over the last 100 years. Human capital is not fixed, so there are always further improvements that can be made in the quality of training, education and health, the aim being that everyone fulfils their potential, and that the work force as a whole is the most productive and flexible possible.

There are two problems, however. The first is the cost, and who should bear it. Social security, education and health have been one of the central battlegrounds of political and social struggles over the last 100 years. States often tried to load many of the costs – particularly for the old, the disabled and the long-term sick, but also for health and education – on to private households, and only gradually did state provision increase. As it has increased, so too has the long-term problem of affording the entitlements which citizens now take for granted. This is explored further in the next chapter.

The second problem is that as with most things the biggest gains are always the first ones. As people gain more skills, the additional benefit from further investment in them, although not negligible, is smaller and harder to quantify. This means that the more developed economies become, the more difficult it can be to improve human capital in ways which make a significant impact on growth, although for contemporary politicians it is an unavoidable commitment, and something they feel obliged to promise, whether in the form of more university places, more apprenticeships or more lifelong learning, at the same time showering benefits on the old. None of these improvements, desirable as they are, have the dramatic impact on growth that literacy programmes can have in a society where most people are still illiterate.

The problem for governments is that, so conscious are they of the need to stay competitive in 'the global race', they are forever proposing new programmes to raise the skills and flexibility of the labour force. All this is very expensive. This is one reason why governments in many countries have begun increasing the contribution which students for example make to the cost of higher education courses. To contain costs government must either reduce the service they offer, or cut the cost, either by making the user pay, as in the student case, or by forcing households to take up the burden again. The favoured neo-liberal solution is to make the user pay because this marketizes the service and provides opportunities for a further expansion of financial services, the crucial artery of the neo-liberal growth model (Hobson & Seabrooke 2007; Langley 2008).

As the gains from investing in human capital become harder to realize, it is hardly surprising that once again employers should often prefer the option of hiring young, highly motivated and highly flexible immigrant workers to meet their needs, rather than seeking to find recruits from the domestic labour force, many of whom fail to acquire the right set of skills or attitudes which employers are looking for. This again can fuel local tensions. Immigration has become a key part of the neo-liberal order, and states have had to find ways to manage and defuse the political problems surrounding it (Geddes 1999). No states involved in the international trading system close their borders entirely. Since the crash, however, opinion in most democracies has hardened against immigration. Parties which advocate open borders and free movement of labour as a way of boosting economic growth and aiding the recovery have become few and far between, even if this is one of the pillars of the neo-liberal order. No mainstream political party in Europe for instance thinks it can get elected on such a platform. For the moment, the EU policy of allowing free movement of European citizens is holding, but it is under increasing attack from populist and anti-establishment parties. Much stricter controls are being imposed on non-EU citizens, even though domestic birth rates in many countries remain depressed and there are no longer any great reservoirs of agricultural workers or women workers on which to draw.

The facts of demography in the West in general depress rather than boost future prospects for growth, and investment in human capital only partly offsets it. Reducing controls on immigration was never very popular but it has rapidly lost favour during the period of austerity following the crash. In contrast, in many other parts of the world, the demographics to underpin fast economic growth are highly favourable. The world population has reached 7 billion but is still increasing rapidly and is expected to hit 9 billion by 2050. There have been people, ever since Thomas Malthus, who are concerned that population will outpace resources, leading to terrible famines and social collapse, but although this has happened locally, often for very particular political reasons, it has not yet happened universally. There is considerable debate at the moment about the 'carrying capacity' of the earth. Pessimistic estimates put it as low as 2 billion, optimistic estimates suggest that 9 billion or even 15 billion could be accommodated if the right policies on food, energy and water are put in place. The social reproduction costs of such a large increase in population would of course be huge, and the expectation is that non-market households, either families or the state, would need to bear most of them.

If the pessimists are right there will be no future economic growth, because the population of the earth will suffer a huge contraction as environmental problems multiply: there will be fierce conflicts for food, water, energy and resources, and living standards will collapse. If the optimists are right population growth will continue to spur economic growth, except for those states which fail to obtain a demographic dividend, either through boosting their domestic birth rate or liberalizing their immigration controls. From this perspective restricting immigration is a political choice which will impoverish the countries which pursue it. It erects a significant barrier to faster economic growth. It is also the biggest single source of protectionism within the international political economy, and undermines the basic principles of free trade which the neo-liberal order proclaims.

Debt and technology

Another problem in reproducing the conditions for stable and sustainable growth which a market economy must solve concerns profitable investment. Some of these are problems of demand and some of them problems of supply. In order to get back to growth, the burden of debt must be greatly reduced. But the easiest way to reduce the burden of debt is for the economy to grow and prices to rise, by stimulating demand. Inflation reduces the real burden of debt more quickly than anything else. If the fiscal or monetary stimulus is too strong there is a risk of creating an inflation trap, which many economies fell into in the 1970s. But the opposite seems true today. Reducing the burden of debt too quickly by cutting private or public spending can push an economy into a deflation trap of low growth and rising debt.

There is no precise relationship between debt and GDP, which has to be respected if growth is not to be inhibited, although some economists have suggested otherwise (Reinhart & Rogoff 2009). An economy can have a ratio of debt to GDP of 250 per cent, as Britain did after the Napoleonic Wars, and only gradually pay it down over a long period. What is crucial is who it borrows from and the rate at which it can borrow (Krugman 2008, 2012). Japan has a very high debt in relation to its GDP, but most of it is held by Japanese citizens. Even a high and rising debt can be managed successfully if the rate of interest which has to be paid on it remains low, as has been the case with both the US and the UK since the crash. If, however, much of the debt is held externally and the interest rate demanded to service the debt keeps rising, then a point is reached at which it becomes impossible to service without a major restructuring of the public finances. The revenue is insufficient even to meet the interest on the debt, so the debt keeps rising, leading to even greater alarm among investors about the risk of default. This is what happened to several countries in the eurozone between 2010 and 2012.

If the problem of debt cannot be managed satisfactorily then it poses a major obstacle to growth and may create a deflationary spiral in which falling prices, rising unemployment and collapsing demand all feed off one another. The return to capital becomes depressed and investment sinks. Economies can get caught in a deflationary trap. The pessimistic view about many western economies in the present crisis is that the overhang of debt has become so large, and the deleveraging required so enormous, that governments lack the capacity or the will to do anything substantial about it, even if their rhetoric suggests otherwise. The position is most serious in the eurozone, but it also affects the US, as discussed in the next chapter.

The difficulty of getting rid of debt which has already accumulated, and stopping further deficits occurring which then add to the debt, plagues all governments. The policies they adopt to contain the problem tend to make the environment for long-term investment negative and weakens business confidence. A sure sign of the depressive effect of the debt overhang has been the way interest rates have been at historic lows in both the US and the EU for an unprecedented length of time. If there were significant investment opportunities they would be seized since there has never been a better time to borrow money. But in the western economies the pattern of the last few years has been that investment has been sluggish, and banks have been reluctant to lend. Western economies have had little forward momentum.

The main problem, however, in the neo-liberal order is not principally public sector debt, although this gets most of the political attention, but the debts run up by companies, by banks, and by private households. Paying down these debts is hard in such a difficult economic climate, but until they are significantly reduced – and there may be rallies and brief upturns – there is unlikely to be a major return of confidence, because further shocks and reverses will be expected. The amount of deleveraging (both reducing the level of debt and the ratio of debt) has varied in different countries. When governments pay down their debts at the same time, that can add to the debts of the private sector and households, because government purchases from the private sector are falling and taxes are increasing. Austerity programmes, despite their intentions, often worsen the situation they are designed to improve, which is why a succession of economists from Keynes to Krugman have warned against them. They are adopted because they can be presented in simplistic terms as addressing the economic problem, while at the same time they are not as risky as the full liquidationist approach of the fiscal conservatives. The liquidationist approach would get rid of debts. They would simply be written off, but at the cost of a huge swathe of bankruptcies and a collapse of employment. Very strong societies and political systems might be able to survive and adjust, but the risk of social and political breakdown would also be very high. The lessons from the 1920s and 1930s are taken seriously by many contemporary politicians and officials, and few of them are prepared to take such risks. The quick way to reboot the neo-liberal order after the crash would have been to adopt the liquidationist approach, but politically this was ruled out. Policy is stuck.

Continuing high levels of debt reinforce the effects of an ageing population and a bias in favour of saving and risk averse investments which older people tend to favour. Decisions to bail out banks rather than liquidate them appears to signal both that high levels of debt are to be considered normal and that servicing debt is a major part of what all organizations and households, as well as governments, are obliged to do. Having large debts does not necessarily make you risk averse. It may incline you to take even more extravagant risks. But in a climate of low expectations about economic recovery and economic returns large debts can reinforce prudent behaviour and minimize risk taking. It is in this way that a deflationary bias in the economy can be established, whose hold is very hard to break. Prices start falling, and once that happens it is not rational to make investments which require positive returns to make them viable. Consumption decisions are deferred in the expectation that prices will fall. So the economy stagnates. The most recent example of this phenomenon was in Japan in the 1990s, as discussed in Chapter 1, after its very high growth rates in the previous four decades (Koo 2009). Japan became locked into a cycle of low growth and deflation which proved very hard to break. It was still one of the largest and richest economies in the world. It did not suffer a major slump or social collapse; but it did not grow very much either. It is often cited as an example of what could happen to other western economies in this new period after the crash. They might suffer the same fate as Japan: a long period of slow deleveraging, weak growth and depressed demand.

On the supply side, the major issue affecting the growth conundrum concerns technology. There has never been a time when technology and technological innovation have been more pervasive and more essential for meeting the challenges modern societies face. The organization and prosperity of modern societies increasingly rest on scientific knowledge, even if the majority of citizens generally lack the most elementary understanding of science and the process of scientific reasoning. Technological innovations are ubiquitous and seem to arrive at an ever faster pace. But technological innovations, which raise the general rate of growth by increasing productivity of labour across the whole economy affecting almost every sector, have become increasingly scarce. The innovations which currently do most to boost the prospects for growth are often past innovations when they are successfully introduced into developing economies. The dilemma for western states is that they can give priority to supporting a general advance in scientific knowledge, and helping the diffusion of knowledge to fast-growing developing economies, or they can give priority to a technological policy which protects the privileged market position of their companies and workers at the top of the value chain by promoting lines of research which have immediate commercial applications. The former becomes a transfer to the rising powers paid for by western taxpayers, while the latter may boost earnings of specific national companies, but may not have a wider impact on growth. Both can be criticized as offering a return that is small relative to the cost.

Technology plays a vital role in economic growth, raising the productivity of labour and making possible a much deeper and more extended division of it, not only within factories but across national economies. The replacement of living labour by machines has been one of the chief motors of capitalist advance and, as already noted, the pace of technological innovation appears to be gathering speed rather than diminishing. The science base in all developed economies is substantial and growing, and this great engine of research funded by governments and by corporations generates constant advances in knowledge and commercial spin offs. So at first glance it is odd to think that technology might be a barrier to growth. It is more usual to think that scientific discovery and technological innovation are steadily proceeding at their own pace, occasionally interrupted by political and economic events, which can delay the applications of technology and the growth which results from them, but cannot indefinitely prevent them from happening, so long as markets are kept flexible and free (Crafts 2012; Phelps 2013). The idea of an underlying rate of growth for the economy, which over time asserts itself, is partly derived from this kind of thinking. There is a steady trend of technological progress and economic growth, from time to time disrupted by external factors. Technological optimists believe that the process of technological discovery is accelerating, not tailing off. They argue that the internet revolution is only in its infancy and that its full effects are yet to be felt. The development of new technologies like 3-D printing, nanotechnology and developments in biochemistry and neuroscience have the potential to transform our world as thoroughly as any of the great technological innovations of the past. There are risks and uncertainties associated with all these technologies (Rees 2003), but the impact on work and productivity could be profound, with the elimination of many existing jobs in professional and retail services, as the online revolution takes hold. Such technological revolutions in the past have destroyed jobs but at the same time by increasing wealth have created a whole range of new jobs. Communities and occupations have been destroyed, but societies have become wealthier and their wants ever more diversified.

The counter-argument is that technology itself has become part of the problem of growth. This has been put in popular form by Tylor Cowen in his book *The Great Stagnation*. We are doomed to stagnate, he argues, because we have exhausted the sources of growth. We have picked all the low hanging fruit in the last 200 years, and all the other fruit we might have are higher up the tree and much harder to reach. We have had an enormous binge for 200 years, using up all the resources close to hand and developing a number of technologies, such as steam power and electricity, which made possible dramatic increases in our productivity and therefore in our wealth. But now resources are much less easy to come by and there is much more competition for them, so the prices are higher, land is no longer abundant as it was for so long in the US and we have not recently discovered a technology with the potential for transforming our productivity. The frontier has finally closed, and Cowen's advice is that we have to get used to it and adjust to an indefinite era of low growth, making do with the wealth we have already created (if we are fortunate enough to live in a wealthy country and to own assets). The 200-year productivity spree is over, at least for the western capitalist economies (Cowen 2011). For rising powers things are different. They can still catch up by adopting technologies in use elsewhere and reorganizing their societies and economies to make possible modern life-styles. But eventually they too will approach the technological frontier and be forced to slow down. The era of rapid growth was a historical anomaly. We are returning to a world in which the economy is more steady-state than progressive. We need to adjust and change our behaviour, not just our economic behaviour but our political behaviour and social behaviour. Cowen thinks we are entering an era of deleveraging and austerity in which interest rates remain low and there is no rise in average wages.

This is a revival of the secular stagnation thesis which economists such as Larry Summers and economic historians such as Robert Gordon have also advanced. Gordon argues, in a manner reminiscent of Kondratieff and other long-wave theorists, that we have had three major technological revolutions in the last 300 years, each one of which permanently raised the plateau of human productivity and therefore human wealth. The first was associated with steam, spinning and the railways; the second with electricity, the internal combustion engine and running water; and the third with computing and the internet. All have been major revolutions, but Gordon argues that the third, although important, has so far been much less significant than the first two, and the transformation of productivity which it has achieved, and its future potential, is of a different order of magnitude. He does not deny that the internet revolution has produced a flow of new products and gadgets, but he thinks few of them have the potential to raise productivity across the board in the way in which either steam power or electricity did (Gordon 2012).

This thesis of secular stagnation, like the earlier version of it propounded by Alvin Hansen, suggests that modern societies have reached a plateau. Some growth will continue and there will still be many new technological innovations, but they will not have the trans-formative character on productivity which the major technologies of the last 300 years have done. More and more will continue to be invested in science and in technology but the returns, although still significant, will diminish. The neo-liberal order is caught in a bind. Governments seek to socialize as much as possible the costs of innovation for their companies to boost their profitability. But the size of investment required to make an impact on productivity, according to the proponents of secular stagnation, is becoming larger, and therefore progressively harder to afford, particularly in a time of austerity. This unleashes further distributional struggles. The changing character of innovation may also make companies and governments generally more risk averse, more content to settle for the known and the familiar. In this way modern societies will make a gradual transition to a low growth or even a steady state economy.

Gordon readily concedes that 80 per cent of the world's population is still a long way from the technological frontier. Even after substantial progress towards meeting one of the key UN Millennium Development Goals, 11 per cent of the world's population (783 million people) were still estimated in 2011 to lack access to clean water, and 2.5 billion more were without adequate sanitation (WHO 2014), while 1.4 billion people (almost a quarter of all the people on the planet) have no access to electricity. Rolling out the technological advances of the first two technological revolutions to all the people in the world will still give a huge boost to growth and productivity. The process of catch-up will provide the best opportunities for rapid economic growth, and if new rising powers with high populations are rapidly expanding, there will be an impact on growth and living standards in the rest of the international economy. But the ability of countries to catch up depends on there being a supportive international market order. Here the contradictions of the neo-liberal order show themselves, since transfers between rich and poor countries remain small, and the foreign aid budgets which do exist are everywhere under attack. It is also hampered because, as argued in Chapter 5, the obstacles in the way of establishing a new inclusive form of governance are formidable. What is required is a different kind of international market order with different priorities from those of the neo-liberal order which are still focused on the protection of the interests of the rich countries (Wade & Vestergaard 2012).

Environmental change

The third and most intractable problem of how industrial societies will continue to reproduce themselves is interaction with the natural environment and the way that changes to the environment, such as climate change brought about by human economic activity, could in the future place severe new constraints on economies and societies. This gives rise to the deepest dilemmas, because of the uncertainty surrounding the scale of the challenge and its timing. Acting now to limit the risks which the scientific consensus identifies would be prudent, but it requires actions that at the very least would prevent a resumption of the natural path of economic growth and at worst a fundamental reorientation and reconstruction of industrial societies, outside the bounds of any conceivable democratic politics. If action is not taken the result may be a catastrophe for the whole human species, because tipping points may be passed, which precludes recovery to where we were before.

Ian Gough (2011) has set out the basic dilemma. There is a strong scientific consensus that global warming is happening, that it is largely man-made and that there will have to be major changes in policy to prevent very damaging impacts on human welfare and the environment. At the same time, getting those major policy changes is very hard because a substantial minority of western citizens are sceptical, the policy process is focused on short-term considerations of what will promote growth and safeguard living standards, lobbying from interest groups and media opposed to green measures is very effective, and the interests of future generations and non-western populations are not represented. The Stern Review estimated that if equivalent carbon dioxide (CO_2e), a measure of the concentration of greenhouse gases in the atmosphere, reaches 550 parts per million then global temperatures are likely to rise between 2.4 and 5.3 per cent (Stern 2009). The current level of CO_2e is 430 ppm. This is rising by 25 ppm every decade. A temperature rise of 3 per cent would melt the Greenland ice sheet. To stabilize the level of CO_2e at 500 ppm would imply an annual global emission by 2050 of only 20 billion tonnes. That compares with 40 billion tonnes in 1990. Divided equally between the nine billion inhabitants of the world in 2050 would imply a limit of 2 tonnes per capita. The US currently emits 24 tonnes per capita and most of Europe 10 or 12 tonnes per capita. A lower emissions target of 450 ppm would keep the global temperature rise to 2 per cent, but that would imply a limit of half a tonne of carbon emission per person on the planet. These figure show the scale of the adjustment that has to be made, and the extreme political difficulty of achieving it.

The environmental critique of our present economic arrangements did not begin with the recession. It has been developing since the 1970s, as the environmental movement and green political parties became an important voice in western politics. The environmental argument is both a moral argument and an argument about efficiency. The moral argument is about fairness and intergenerational justice and urges a cultural change and a behavioural change to support a different way of living. The efficiency argument focuses on the imbalance between the industrial system and the ecosystem and the increasing costs this is likely to impose on the industrial system, slowing the rate of economic growth through the emergence of ever more serious physical constraints upon it.

In the period since the crash in the western economies, the environmental movement has struggled to gain new support or even hold the support it already had because the political focus has shifted so much towards finding ways to restore 'normal' economic growth. Environmental measures and regulations which multiplied during the boom now appear too costly and put obstacles in the path of economic recovery. Strong campaigns have been mounted to relax environmental regulations in order to boost investment in new sources of conventional energy. One example has been the strong business and media lobby in favour of mining oil and gas shale deposits through hydraulic fracturing, or fracking, the process of drilling and injecting fluid into the ground at a high pressure in order to fracture shale rocks to release the natural gas and oil inside. The environmental lobby is opposed to fracking because of the environmental damage it can cause and the uncertainty about the environmental dangers it may pose, but also because it is yet another fossil fuel solution. It is already providing cheap energy to those countries like the US which have commercially viable deposits, but at the expense of giving another big boost to carbon emissions and delaying the adoption of carbon neutral energy. It therefore helps perpetuate the long-running reliance on gas and oil, and breathes new life into the old economic model, just at a time when the elaboration of a more sustainable industrial programme based on renewable energy and the replacement of fossil fuels was gathering pace. But the political attractiveness of a cheap source of energy in a recession is too great for most governments to resist, although several European governments, including France, have so far done so, refusing to grant licences for fracking on environmental grounds. This will become increasingly hard to maintain when other countries are taking full advantage of the benefits of this new technology.

The case of fracking illustrates a more general point. The environmental critique of current industrial behaviour depends on showing that it destroys the conditions not just for long-term growth, but for the basis of prosperity itself. In the extreme case it suggests that modern societies might start to regress because the ecosystem on which all human life depends has been so damaged. The predictions that irreversible global warming may be underway, linked to the release of carbon dioxide into the atmosphere through the burning of fossil fuels, is the most well-known instance of this. But climate sceptics do not accept the science and argue instead that the environment will be much more damaged if growth is held back, because in that case human societies will be denying themselves the extra resources they could have used to deal with environmental risks and adjust to the effects of global warming if they need to (Lawson 2009).

In an era of slow growth and austerity, scepticism about climate change and green policies is always likely to prevail, since the pressures of recession increase the chances that policy-making will be dominated by short-term considerations. The moral arguments used by environmentalists also make limited headway against the hard-headed realism of the advocates of growth. The moral argument depends in particular on making an appeal to the politics of intergenerational justice, the impact on future unborn generations of decisions made by the living generations. It provides some very powerful rhetoric, and it has been an important factor influencing the growth of the green agenda and its translation into targets in many areas of public policy. It is vulnerable, however, to the demands for removing obstacles to getting the economy moving again which have become ever stronger because of the slowness of the recovery. The green agenda risks becoming a victim of the distributive struggles over declining resources.

Environmental pessimists agree that a huge diversion of resources may be needed in the future in order to cope with the adjustments to the effects of climate change which will be necessary. But they want as much as possible done now while there is still time to reduce the size of that adjustment. The environmental pessimists were making considerable progress in establishing their case until the financial crash. Since then the optimists have been gaining the upper hand, because politicians everywhere are so keen to restore growth to the economy, and strict environmental targets and the accompanying rules and regulations get in the way of that. The optimists want to get back as quickly as possible to at least 2 per cent annual growth rates, and they see one of the major obstacles in the way of that to be environmental regulations and targets. The pessimists on the other hand see the targets and regulations as essential. Large resources will need to be allocated way into the future to deal with the consequences of the uncontrolled economic growth of the last 200 years.

The environmental critique of growth shares some features in common with the technological critique, because both see the last 200 years as exceptional, a once and for all uplift in wealth and productivity which cannot and, as far as environmentalists are concerned, should not be repeated. It is a period of transition between two more or less steady-state periods. The acceleration of growth and the expectation of everlasting growth belong to that period and promoted a politics which came to assume that there would always be a growth dividend, that every generation would be richer than the previous one, and that the trend line of growth was always upward. The environmental critique, like earlier critiques of industrial society, assumes that a sustainable steady-state economy would be morally preferable to one of ever expanding wants and appetites (Daly 1997). Creating a consensus for such a society runs up against the obstacle that most people's lives are wholly bound up with the opportunities, rewards and comforts which the modern economy supplies, so politically it has been very hard for green parties to break through and build coalitions prepared to sacrifice the assumption that the past pattern of growth will continue indefinitely. Predictions of looming ecological catastrophe will not on their own change politics. The kind of shock that might would probably mean that it was already too late; that the world had passed beyond the tipping points which scientists believe are there even if they cannot say exactly when they will be reached. This paradox of green politics has been analysed by Tony Giddens. The case for action now based on what we already know is compelling for a growing number of people, but the only way of convincing a majority is when they are confronted with incontrovertible evidence about what is happening, by which time it will be by definition too late (Giddens 2009).

The point has been put another way by the environmental historian, John McNeill. He says it is as though the human species around 200 years ago collectively decided to play dice with the planet, embarking on a great experiment to see what would happen to the ecosystem of the earth if human activity changed in fundamental ways (McNeill 2001). The world was transformed by the population explosion rising from one billion people in 1800 to six billion in 2000. At the same time industrial production rose even faster, bringing with it huge increases in the consumption of energy and other raw materials. In this extraordinary historical period the world has been transformed, mostly for the better, but there has been a cost. All societies have placed themselves on a treadmill, because having once turned on the tap of progressive economic development it has become virtually impossible to switch it off. Political and economic competition between states, and the entrenchment of new ways of living, have seen to that.

In the course of this history the interdependence of all human societies on one another has been underlined, as well as the complex interdependence of the industrial system and the ecosystem. Many of these relationships, including the impact on climate, are only imperfectly understood, but the accelerating pace of global economic advance, especially with the beginning of the industrialization of the global South, gives an urgency to understanding what the effects might be, and at the same time fuels an anxiety that the process is already beyond human control, that human beings have set in motion something which they cannot stop even if they wanted to. And for the most part, as already noted, relatively few of us do want to.

Some of the anxieties about industrial society have recurred at fairly regular intervals. The Malthusian critique that population will eventually outrun resources has been perhaps the most common fear of all. It underlay the Club of Rome's warnings about the limits to growth in the 1970s, and it has revived recently with fears about the imminence of peak oil, the exhaustion of one or more key resources. It is present in the anxieties about the effects of an accelerating population and the carrying capacity of the earth. This is no longer so much about absolute numbers and the difficulty of feeding them all. There is enough food in the world for a much larger population than currently exists. The real concern arises over the implications of a population of six billion or nine billion or fifteen billion aspiring to the same level of consumption and material wealth as in the contemporary US. The political problem can appear insoluble. The countries of the global South cannot be prevented from catching up and becoming modern societies, nor is there any easy way to persuade the rich countries that they should reduce their consumption of natural resources and with it their carbon footprint to manageable levels. To keep the global temperature rise to 2 degrees by 2050 implies a carbon ceiling for emission of 2 tonnes for every person on the planet. Currently the US emissions are running at 24 tonnes per head, Europe at 10–12 tonnes and China at 6 tonnes and rising. The scale of the change in life-styles or in technologies needed to achieve a transition to a low carbon economy is daunting.

Environmental optimists dismiss Malthusianism because every time Malthusians have predicted that one resource or another is running out, whether food, coal or oil, technological innovations have occurred which have enabled new deposits to be mined and exploited commercially (Ridley 2011; Lawson 2009). Economists question whether

resources are finite at all in the sense of having fixed limits. The availability of resources depends upon the price; if the price is high enough
it becomes commercially viable to mine hitherto inaccessible reserves.
Extrapolating trends into the future generally provides very poor
predictions of what will happen. The modern economy is much too
diverse, much too complex and much too flexible to be captured in that
way. What can seem insuperable obstacles suddenly cease to be so
because of particular turns of events. The fears over oil in the 1970s
prompted by the rise of OPEC led many to think that the era of cheap
oil had gone for ever, only for prices to collapse in the 1980s. What does
seem to be true, however, is that as more and more countries industrialize the world may not run out of any particular resource, but there will
be many local pinch points, and competition among states and communities for certain resources, including energy and water, will intensify.
This will not choke off economic growth, but it will not speed it either.
Securing cheap and reliable sources of energy, food and water in particular are fundamental contributors to strong economic growth.

Other anxieties persist around pollution, particularly of the oceans
and the atmosphere, and around the unknowable effects of new technologies, such as artificial intelligence and nanotechnology. The possibility that human societies may discover technologies which radically
alter the conditions of human existence does not just belong in the
realm of science fiction. It has already happened in the case of nuclear
fission, which made possible for the first time in human history the
creation of weapons with the capacity to eradicate the human species.
The possibility that scientists may soon find ways to lengthen human
lives substantially and change their genetic make-up would have
profound implications for the social and political organization of
human societies. As with economic growth, however, no one knows
how to stop the flow of scientific knowledge and the application of it,
even if was thought desirable to do so (Williams 1993). Human societies are required to adapt their cultures, their political systems and
their civil societies much faster than ever before to keep abreast of the
accelerating pace of technological transformation.

The environmental optimists tend to shrug, arguing that human societies have no choice. They can only go forward and seek to become more
flexible, more adaptable, more knowledgeable, in order always to stay
one step ahead. On this view there can be no steady state. It is an illusion.
Anything that holds back economic growth, they argue, weakens the
capacity of human societies to adapt to the new challenges they face.
This argument comes to the fore over climate change. Some sceptics

simply do not believe the science and argue that even if there has been in the past some global warming, it has nothing to do with human activity on the planet. Others are willing to make the assumption that climate change is happening as the scientific consensus suggests and that it is man-made. But they argue that if this is so then the response should be to maximize economic growth because adaptation to rising temperatures is the only option, and technological innovation and ingenuity will be the key resource which human societies have. It will do no good to stunt the growth of the economy by clamping targets on carbon emissions or investing in more expensive forms of energy such as wind farms. This will only hinder adjustment (Prins et al. 2010). Far better to adopt a target of cheap carbon-free energy for the whole world and drive relentlessly towards it, subordinating all other considerations to seeking the technologies which will make it possible.

The neo-liberal solution to the growth conundrum posed by climate change is to wager that the market order is the best institutional means we have to price in the risks and make whatever adjustments we need to when the time comes. It is the same approach that led to the financial crash. It denies the possibility of systemic risk and disputes the evidence for it. The green growth solution recommends a low carbon industrial revolution, giving priority to energy security and prioritizing research into technologies which might enable modern industrial societies to continue growing but in a sustainable way. It would require a major shift in the goals and instruments of economic policy. This is politically thinkable, and there are some detailed ideas as to how it would work (Giddens 2009; Jacobs 2012), but it will still require the kind of transformative change that so far the crisis has not produced. Even then it might not be enough.

The third option is more radical still. It would require the decoupling of economic activity and emissions, moving to a zero growth society (Gough 2011). This would require fundamental changes in the way we think about prosperity and well-being and how we organize our societies (Skidelsky & Skidelsky 2012). But the world at present is busily rushing in the other direction.

Conclusion: the problem of democracy

The growth conundrum poses severe problems for the neo-liberal order. The basic principle of giving as much incentive and freedom to individuals as possible to maximize their private returns, leaving non-market domestic labour and public services to bear the costs of reproducing the conditions for this kind of society, has created both huge benefits and huge negatives. It leads directly to the problems of the tax state and the problems of legitimation that are at the heart of the fiscal conundrum discussed in Chapter 7. The dilemmas that are created are particularly dilemmas for democracies. They are also dilemmas for authoritarian regimes, though here they take a different form, because such regimes are more insulated from the pressures democracies face, and their legitimacy partly as a result tend to be more fragile (Runciman 2013). For example, the issue of demographics is a dilemma for democracies because its solution requires opening borders at a time when there is strong pressure to close them. The issue of debt is a dilemma because its solution requires real and permanent cuts in living standards which encounter strong resistance. The issue of technology is a dilemma because it implies that stagnant or falling living standards for the majority may not be reversible, which if true will undermine the legitimacy of the market order. What to do about the environment is a dilemma because the long-run measures needed to avert or even adjust to future environmental changes will be deeply unpopular, and there are many siren voices saying they are not necessary.

For most of the democratic era, still remarkably short, but now stretching back over a century in some countries, and since 1945 in many others, politicians have been able to rely on the existence of a growth guarantee, the political counterpart of Keynes's compound interest. In electoral politics, during upswings politicians competed to distribute the growth dividend, balancing cuts in taxes with increases in spending. The existence of a growth dividend implied that no one's existing position had to be made worse; it was a game of distributing increments to particular groups and projects judged most deserving. In recessions the growth dividend disappears and politics becomes concerned with hard choices and withdrawing resources from some groups and projects. But there is still the expectation that relatively soon growth will return and a more benign cycle of redistributive fiscal politics will begin again. The present recession raises the spectre that growth might not return, that somehow we may have unlocked a door and passing through it now find ourselves in a strange and unfamiliar landscape. We want to go back through the door into the warmer more comfortable world we left behind. But we can no longer find the door. The possibility that investment returns could be depressed in the West for 30 years, or that we could have entered a period of Japanese style deflation, is deeply unwelcome to the political class, because they have no vocabulary to address this situation and have no clue as to how it could be managed. The rage against politicians sweeps many governments away after only one term in office during such hard times. This is why politicians urgently seek ways to restore growth and return to the politics of the growth dividend. Social conflicts are much sharper and more intense when the stock of resources to redistribute is shrinking and the way is opened for much more aggressive populist and anti-establishment parties to raise their voices.

A second difficulty lies in that of bridging the national and the international in times of economic difficulty. It becomes increasingly hard to secure greater international cooperation, yet such cooperation is required more than ever to give political leaders the resources they need for gaining greater traction in handling domestic politics. Once politicians make concessions to nationalist and separatist forces they often find themselves imprisoned by them, and it is very hard to go back.

Capitalism's popular appeal has rested upon its ability to deliver growth, and the civilization associated with it has been erected on that basis. This is why no one can believe that the tap is about to be turned off, since a different civilization is so very hard to imagine. But at least in the western world, politicians and public now have to face the possibility that growth may not return in the old way, or that at best there may be a prolonged period of hardship and restructuring before economies can expand again. This is before all the anxieties about environmental risks are considered. Economic optimists draw comfort from the fact that we have been here before. Every time there have been warnings that growth could not continue, and that capitalism was entering a state of terminal decline, capitalism has managed to confound its critics and sometimes its friends, like Joseph Schumpeter, and enter upon a new burst of progress. They think it will not be different this time. But if there is a long wait, the legitimacy of many governments and regimes may be stretched to the utmost.

Writing in 1930 just after the Great Crash and with the storm clouds gathering over the western world, Keynes was remarkably relaxed about the future. In his essay 'Economic Possibilities for Our Grandchildren' he wrote:

> Technical improvement in manufacture and transport have been proceeding at a greater rate in the last ten years than ever before in history ... for the moment the very rapidity of these changes is hurting us and bringing difficult problems to solve.
>
> Those countries are suffering relatively which are not in the vanguard of progress. We are being afflicted with a new disease ...

technological unemployment ... But this is only a temporary phase of maladjustment. All this means in the long run is that mankind is solving its economic problem. I would predict that the standard of life in progressive countries one hundred years hence will be between four and eight times as high as it is today. There would be nothing surprising in this even in the light of our present knowledge. It would not be foolish to contemplate the possibility of a far greater progress still. (Keynes 1972, pp. 325–6)

This time may perhaps be no different. There are still some huge increases in general well-being that technological innovation can deliver, such as a reliable cheap source of carbon-free energy or major advances in practical applications of artificial intelligence. But there is great unease that it might be different, unless the neo-liberal order is profoundly recast, of which there is little sign. If it is not different, growth is unlikely to cease altogether, but the kind of growth which has been common for such a long time may prove harder to revive. The idea that we are in a global race and that we must redouble our efforts to stay competitive has become the mantra of the political class. But the sacrifices it seems to require, particularly in times of recession, are increasingly hard to justify to electorates in democracies who have become increasingly angry, mistrustful and occasionally obstructive. The pursuit of everlasting growth has made states and the national economies they protect ever more dependent on a system of economic relationships which they do not control. It has made national govern-ments and the cosmopolitan elites which control them careless of local solidarities and communities, who have experienced acutely the loss of autonomy and self-rule which has been required in order to receive the gains from trade. It has just been tolerable when the total wealth of society has been increasing, and when policies of redistribution have been in place so that victims of the process of change can be compen-sated, and some solidarity and social cohesion retained. If the total wealth no longer increases, or if the increase is appropriated in the rents which elites are able to extract as a result of their structural privilege and power, then democratic legitimacy will continue to evaporate and the politics of the extremes will return. A new growth model is urgently needed if these problems and the problems of climate change are to be addressed. There are ideas as to how this might be done (Stern 2009; Gough 2011; Jacobs 2012), but little sign that any government is making this a high priority.

Chapter 7

The Fiscal Conundrum

The fiscal conundrum is the third of the great structural tensions in the neo-liberal order which threatens to unravel western prosperity. Like the governance conundrum and the growth conundrum, with both of which it is intimately linked, the fiscal conundrum is not new. It has occupied political leaders in every era of the modern liberal political economy and the international market orders associated with them. It takes a particular form in the neo-liberal era, but questions of tax and spending have always been central to how the market order makes itself legitimate. The modern state is a tax state because it is mainly dependent for its revenue and therefore for the resources at its disposal on the taxes it is able to levy and collect on private households and corporate households. The state and its spending are necessary partly to reproduce the social conditions for a liberal market economy and partly to make the institutions and outcomes of that economy legitimate for its citizens. The fiscal conundrum for the neo-liberal order since the crash has been how to achieve this legitimation in the face of threats to social cohesion, such as extreme inequality, falling living standards, cuts in public services and a flat economy. In coping with the after-effects of the crash, governments have become painfully aware of the gap between what they need to spend and what they can raise in taxes or borrow. At the heart of the dilemma is whether universal welfare states are any longer affordable within the framework of a neo-liberal order. It is a dilemma because, while in many instances the international financial markets clearly indicate that they are not, these welfare states are one of the pillars on which the legitimacy of post-war western democracies has been built. It is hardly surprising that in these democracies the austerity programmes have become the main focus of political conflict.

A prolonged fiscal crisis is the form in which the redistributive consequences of major crises such as the 2008 financial crash are fought out, now that such crises are not resolved through a major slump. By suppressing or limiting the slump the crisis is transferred to the tax state itself. This is the second major fiscal crisis of the post-war era. The first emerged in the 1970s. The first general recession in the western economies since 1945 led to claims that government had become 'overloaded' and that the post-war welfare states were no longer affordable. There was a concerted attempt in several countries, but particularly in the states of Anglo-America, to rein back the scope and scale of government. This 'new right' approach, increasingly influential on both sides of the Atlantic, claimed that the extended state of social democracy had become a problem because of the ever increasing expectations about the entitlements of citizens which it encouraged, and the difficulty of managing those expectations, because of the pressures for increased spending which they led to and which far exceeded the resources which governments had available. The 1950s and 1960s had seen unparalleled growth and prosperity for the western economies, but even so expectations and demands increased even faster, forcing adjustment and retrenchment during the 1970s as growth faltered and inflation increased. Democracy came to be seen as part of the problem: the way in which democracies worked undermined sound economic management as well as making a return to economic growth more difficult because it allowed special interests to hold sway over policy.

One of the outcomes of the political conflicts and adjustments of the 1970s was that the relationship between the state and the market was reconfigured: the 'Keynesian era', whether in the form of ordoliberalism, the social market economy developed in West Germany (Turner 2011), or embedded liberalism (Ruggie 1998), the era of relatively protected national economies, was declared to be over. These had foundered in the inflation traps of the 1970s. A different set of liberal doctrines, including monetarism and Austrian economics, gained ascendancy. What was important, however, about the neo-liberal order was not so much the various intellectual strands which justified it, but the way in which it crystallized a new set of core assumptions developed in Washington about how the international economy and national economies should be run, and their translation into a set of common-sense notions about how the economy worked (Gamble 2014).

Neo-liberalism solved the immediate problem. Inflation was brought under control and welfare Keynesianism was dethroned, even if military Keynesianism and privatized Keynesianism continued to flourish. A spate of policies to privatize, marketize and deregulate the public and private sectors was introduced. The neo-liberal order was proclaimed. But the problem of the entitlement state was not solved, and the fiscal crisis has now returned, only this time in a still more intractable form. The present crisis is a crisis of the entitlement state because part of the legitimacy of the modern state rests on the belief that citizens are entitled to certain goods and that it is the responsibility of the state to supply them. It is at the same time a crisis of the tax state because the state's commitment to fund entitlements is out pacing its ability to extract taxes. In simple terms, expenditure is out pacing revenue, not just at a particular point in the normal economic cycle, but over the long term. During the earlier fiscal crisis, James O'Connor argued that the tendency to inflation had become endemic in the modern extended state, and while it could be suppressed, it could not be eliminated. Governments were engaged in a constant struggle to prevent public spending rising faster than the growth of the private sector (O'Connor 1971). In the current fiscal crisis the problem is not inflation, but deflation. The structural crisis of the neo-liberal order for the western economies is the threat of deflation, zero growth and falling living standards. States need to spend more, but they also need to cut back. This is the heart of the fiscal conundrum.

The austerity

When the financial crash occurred in 2008 it triggered a fall in output in the western capitalist economy which turned into a deep recession. The measures needed to prevent this recession from turning into a slump and a wider economic as well as financial collapse added greatly to public expenditures. At the same time, falling output and employment meant lower tax receipts and higher spending on welfare. As always happens at such times, the share of government in GDP rose sharply, plunging the public accounts into deficit and triggering calls for urgent action to reduce it by cutting spending and raising taxes. Some countries adopted measures to reduce their deficits which were judged credible by the financial markets. Those who were not judged credible saw a sharp rise in the cost of borrowing and the imposition of austerity measures to bring them into line. This was how the financial crisis became a fiscal crisis and then a sovereign debt crisis. States took the strain and shored up the private sector by taking losses onto the public accounts. But these losses were then used to frame the political debate about austerity, the need for belt-tightening and shrinking the size of the state.

The dominant narrative of the crisis restates the arguments of the 'new right' of the 1970s (Bacon & Eltis 1976), as well as older conservative verities ('you cannot get a quart into a pint pot'). The starting point is the argument that it was the desire of governments, households and companies to fund spending beyond their income which led to rapidly rising levels of debt in many different sectors of the economy. These accounts then argued that since the reason for the crash was overspending, the necessary policy response was a prolonged period of austerity to pay down debts and reduce them to manageable levels. The economy could not start growing again until the debts had been cleared and spending had been brought back into balance with income. This view seemed to accord with common sense and polling shows it is how most people came to view the crash and its aftermath. Advocates of this view never tire of the analogy with the household. Every household it is suggested must find a way to balance its income and its spending, and the same is true for the other key households in the modern economy: the public household (government) and corporate households (companies). The fallacies in this way of thinking about the economy were long ago exposed by Keynes (Skidelsky 2009; Eatwell & Milgate 2011; Blyth 2013), but that has not dented its plausibility. Like the doctrine that the sun moves around the earth, it seems to accord with daily experience. Not adding to your debt in the midst of a recession seems like common sense. But rhetoric rarely matches actions, except when policy is externally imposed: even under those governments most addicted to austerity, levels of spending and borrowing have continued to increase.

After the initial efforts to stop an uncontrollable slump in 2008 and 2009, most western governments accordingly committed themselves to addressing their deficits and pay down their debts. As was argued in Chapter 3, the impact of the recession produced falls of 3 to 9 per cent in GDP in western economies in 2009, and this combined with the costs of the bail-out packages and fiscal stimulus to produce a rapid rise in the deficits in the public household, with consequent implications for the overall debt in relation to GDP. The public accounts took the strain, which was a deliberate policy to cushion the impact of the crash on the rest of the economy. It meant, however, that public spending rose sharply as a proportion of GDP, because tax revenues were much reduced and because governments were increasing their spending. The worsening of the position of the public finances for most countries did not precede the crash but came afterwards. Those countries, however, which had been running large public sector deficits even before the crash, saw them dramatically enlarged by the response to the crash itself.

This is not how it was often represented in the policy debate. It was convenient for governments, particularly those which had not been in office in 2007–08, to present the swelling public deficits as the principal cause of the crash, and as the single most important problem to be addressed before growth could be restarted. Critics of this policy, such as Paul Krugman in the US and Martin Wolf in the UK, argued that if the public sector deficits were reduced too quickly it would impose levels of austerity on the economy which would depress spending and threaten western economies with deflation and very weak growth (Krugman 2008; Wolf 2011). The critics maintained that the policies of fiscal stimulus and quantitative easing should be kept in place and further expanded, while the other sectors of the economy remained depressed. Until private households and corporate households had dealt with their debts it would not be safe for governments to cut back their spending to any significant extent, to raise interest rates or to reduce quantitative easing. Public debt could only be safely reduced if a significant recovery was under way in the rest of the economy.

What has been common to both these positions is a belief that the economy will 'heal', that growth will resume and that the familiar pattern of market-led economic growth can be re-established. The disagreement is largely over the timing of when, not whether, the budget deficit should be reduced. The strongest advocates of austerity policies, making reduction of deficits the priority, were found in the eurozone and the UK. The strongest advocates of maintaining fiscal stimulus, in the short term at least, came from the US. The policies actually adopted in all states were compromises, which were strongly criticized both by those who wanted the opposite policy and by those who thought the policy was being applied much too timidly.

This is such a common pattern in the political economy of western capitalist states that it seems scarcely worth noting. But underlying it is one of the deep structural principles of this political economy, which is why this pattern occurs again and again, and appears so commonplace. Why is it that when a crisis hits, the default position is always to treat it as a crisis of debt, rather than as a crisis of growth? The conventional wisdom repeated endlessly at the time is that deficits must be eliminated and debt paid down to create the conditions to allow an economic recovery. Only when public sector spending and public sector jobs have been cut can the private sector expand and propel the economy into self-sustaining growth. The assumption is that the private sector is productive, while the public sector is unproductive, a drain on the wealth-creating sector which can only be afforded when the economy is doing well, but must be drastically pruned back when the economy is in recession. Public spending is discretionary spending rather than essential spending.

If this is the case, however, the puzzle is why public spending keeps growing and is so resilient. In many western economies, the size of the public sector used to be much smaller than it is today. In Britain it was below 10 per cent of the national income in the second half of the nineteenth century when British industrial, commercial and imperial power was at its zenith. In the course of the twentieth century the state has grown in every OECD country. There are different ways of accounting for the size of the state, and the proportion of state expenditure expressed as a proportion of GDP is only one of them, and in many ways a misleading one, since if the figure is 40 per cent it does not necessarily mean that 40 per cent of GDP is directly spent by the state (Peacock & Wiseman 1961). The ratio could be 150 or 200 per cent, because a large part of state expenditure involves transfer payments to individuals, such as pensions or other welfare benefits. Some economic libertarians profess to believe that if the state spends 40 per cent of the national income, its citizens are only 60 per cent free. The freedom of the individual in this reductionist view is directly proportionate to the size of the state. However, matters are more complex than this. Although the ratio should be treated with caution, and should be the starting point rather than the end point of investigation into what the state does and how it balances its activities, it does provide a rough indication of how the state has grown in importance and become so central to the way in which economies and democracies now work.

If the state is essentially a parasite on the productive economy it is hard to understand why political governments of the Right have not succeeded in shrinking the state to the bare minimum, cutting spending and cutting taxes, so that the state is once again a limited and minimal one. One of the consequences of the 1930s slump was to build support for movements and coalitions which favoured a large extension of the state to deal with the problems of capitalism, both to increase economic efficiency and to improve social justice. Three decades of Keynesianism and welfarism significantly increased the scope and the scale of modern government. The backlash against it which came to the fore in the last great economic crisis in the 1970s led to three decades in which neo-liberal and neo-conservative ideas have been in the ascendancy, and the state has reportedly been in retreat. But when the financial crash hit in 2008 the state was immediately denounced in traditional terms as bloated, parasitical and unproductive, and calls were made to reduce it drastically. Although there had been many changes, the state was still as large in absolute terms as it had been in the 1970s. Thirty years of neo-liberal rolling back of the state had not succeeded in moving it back to where it had been in the 1920s, still less to where it had been in the 1890s or 1860s.

Will the present crisis be different? The fiscal crisis of the state in the 1970s undermined the Keynesian welfare state, which had been established after the Second World War, and ushered in at the international level a new dispensation for managing the international economy. Will this fiscal crisis of the state which followed the financial crash of 2008 turn out to be the next stage in the dismantling of the post-war extended state, or will it strengthen the principles of that extended state? The politics of debt are being played out in many different national contexts, and the outcomes will vary. What this new fiscal crisis has raised, however, are fundamental questions about the scope and scale of the state and whether the crisis is an opportunity to implement a more drastic reduction of the state than would be needed simply to restore the position before the crash.

In a telling phrase Rudolf Goldscheid, almost 100 years ago, called the budget the skeleton of the state stripped of all misleading ideologies (Schumpeter 1990). In a major fiscal crisis the outline of the skeleton appears more distinct as viewpoints merge on what should be in the budget, and what are the essential and the non-essential parts of public spending. Political lines are sharply drawn as interest coalitions form to press for the cutting or the preservation of different parts of it. Since the amount available is contracting and not increasing, the determination of the budget requires the redistribution of resources and the identification of winners and losers. The outcome of these battles depends on the relative strength of the opposing political forces and on particular circumstances – and the long-term implications of many different piecemeal decisions will not always be clear. Amidst the smoke of battle, however, there will be attempts by some political groups to question fundamental principles, asking of each programme whether the state should be providing it, whether it could be better provided by an agency outside the state, or dispensed with altogether. Crises invite radical thinking, especially long drawn-out crises.

For fiscal conservatives the main reason both for the growth of the state and for the difficulties in dismantling it lie in the way in which politicians have courted electoral success by extending entitlements to more and more citizens and in doing so have bound their successors, who have not dared propose the withdrawal of entitlements. It used to be thought by conservatives that the greatest threat to the market order was the determination of governments of all political persuasions to extend government control over investment, employment and prices, including nationalizing core industries, particularly utilities, and gradually socializing key parts of the private sector. The collectivist tide, however, has receded, and, since the 1970s, governments in many countries have pursued policies of privatization, marketization and deregulation, reducing public sectors and the involvement of governments in directly managing productive assets. This part of the neo-liberal revolution has been successfully implemented almost everywhere. But neo-liberals and conservatives still fret about what they now see as the much bigger problem: the rise of the entitlement state and their inability so far to make much of a dent in it.

The problem some conservatives and neo-liberals have with entitlements is a problem they have with democracy. Democracies are too ready to extend entitlements to their citizens without considering the cost, or how these entitlements are to be paid for in the future. Entitlements are considered instead in terms of an ideal of citizenship. All citizens of the state should be provided with the goods and opportunities necessary to live well, to enjoy prosperity in its full sense. This includes provision for health, education, pensions and child care, as well as protection against sickness, unemployment and disability. This used to be called the 'welfare state', but conservatives more often these days refer to it as the 'entitlement state'. It is the conferring of entitlements on individuals which is its hallmark, rather than the payment of welfare to meet particular needs, usually of the poorest groups in society. In the past, the payment of poor relief was an expense to government, but the amount was discretionary, and could be varied up and down depending on the resources that were available and on wider considerations of policy. The point about an entitlement culture is its universalism. All citizens who qualify under the rules are entitled to the payment. Once this is embedded in the fiscal system, it means that the costs of programmes move outside the government's control, being determined in part by demographic factors such as how long citizens live. Governments can find they have to raise increasing amounts of money through taxation or borrowing in order to fund all the entitlements which their citizens claim.

The tax state

The other side of the entitlement state is the tax state. One of the distinctive features of early capitalism was the insistence on a sharp separation of the public and the private. The flourishing of a private sphere relatively free from state control and intervention was vital for the new kind of political economy which developed. One of the key principles was the subordination of the state to the economy. Property should be predominantly privately owned, and the funds available to the state should come through taxation of the citizens. In this system it was always assumed that assets and wealth properly belonged to individuals and were created by individuals and not by the state. The state was very important in guaranteeing the framework of rules and the security without which private activity and private initiative could not flourish, but its function was always supporting and enabling the market economy, rather than supplanting it.

The difference between the state and the market is captured in the different meanings of 'economy'. 'Economy' is derived from the Greek *oikonomia* or 'household'. The household is an economy because it is controlled by a single will, which allocates resources to the members of the household and balances expenditure and income. But the word 'economy' has also come to be used for the market system, which is not a household in the original sense, but composed of many households and agents who exchange with one another: a *catallaxy* or 'market order', as Hayek (1981) called it, because it has no single directing will. Instead it is made up of innumerable exchanges between individuals, no one of whom can possess any more than a fragment of the total knowledge available, so no one is in a position to plan the activity of the whole. This system of exchange is coordinated through prices and adherence to certain rules of conduct. Most systems of production in human history have been economies rather than market orders in this sense, but in the capitalist era the idea of the economy as a household has become of lesser importance than the idea of the economy as a market. The key distinction therefore is between economies as households and economies as market orders. Households, the old form of economy, are run differently from markets. They are embedded in national and international market orders, but they are not the same as them. There is a continual tension between these two different principles of organization, which is both a source of change and dynamism, but at other times is a source of deadlock.

Households, particularly corporate households with their elaborate hierarchies, still have key roles in producing and distributing resources. They are the agents whose interactions create systems of exchange, the market orders of the modern era. But there is another kind of household, the public household, which is also key for the existence of market orders (Bell 1976). The public household is the state considered in its economic aspect. It may be more or less extensive, more or less intrusive on the sphere of the market, more or less supportive of it. The revenues that flow to the state depend on it having the capacity and the authority to extract taxes from its citizens. The secret of the relationship of the modern state to the market order is that the state maximizes its revenues if it can help the market order to thrive. The state has a strong incentive in its own interest to encourage the dynamism and the profitability of private individuals and private companies. The more the market order expands, the more the household economy of the state benefits. The state becomes a tax state which is dependent upon its legitimacy being recognized by its citizens. It establishes a tax regime which provides the funds to enable it to carry out its essential tasks, but it takes care not to encroach too far on the private incomes of citizens. This is modern liberty.

The problem with the simple model of the tax state as it was developed in the liberal political economy of the nineteenth century is that the states in question were primarily accountable to a relatively limited class of property owners. It was understood that the modern state existed to protect their interests, and that included their interest in not being over-taxed and being left alone to organize production and trade and accumulate wealth. Successful modern states, whether they were authoritarian monarchies or liberal republics, were aware of how they needed to copy the example of England and foster the development of private initiative and private profit. But the very success of these states and the huge wealth generated by the new industrial capitalism brought a fresh set of problems. Urbanization, the growth of population and the concentration of that population in cities, the ideas of universal human rights and the dreams of universal human emancipation, generated new movements of public opinion and new political parties. The narrow basis on which the early modern states were constructed could not be sustained. The emergence of popular movements of resistance and opposition to the capitalist market order became associated with calls for democracy, the demand for political and legal rights for all citizens, the extension of suffrage, and the rights of free association and free speech.

The advance of democracy transformed the state and instigated a new set of dynamics for the tax state. The state as the public household became expected to intervene much more to redistribute income and wealth, to establish social justice, to achieve full employment. Joseph Chamberlain, the British industrialist, radical Liberal and social imperialist, said that property would need to pay a ransom to the people to keep itself secure. His idea, shared by many others, was that the state should recognize that every citizen was entitled to a basic minimum of security, welfare, health and education. The state should increase taxation to fund the spending that was required so as to accommodate the demands of the newly enfranchised masses, giving them a stake in the political system and finding a way to satisfy their demands and make the capitalist market order legitimate in their eyes. This was the great prize and the subject of many of the political battles of the twentieth century.

The victory was achieved. Forms of socialism which aimed at the overthrow of capitalism and the dismantling of the market order and the tax state were defeated. But the victory was not without its costs, as the defenders of classical liberalism were quick to point out. The cost was the growth of the entitlement state, the adoption of the language of fairness and social justice, a substantial growth in the scope and scale of the state, a very large increase in taxation, and the creation of an intrusive bureaucracy managing many key services. To many economic liberals the new extended state of the twentieth century appeared as a behemoth threatening to swallow up the enfeebled private sector and extinguish liberty.

For the tax state to function as it was intended, the growth of the extended state must continue to be strictly controlled and fiscal discipline must be applied whenever there is a financial crisis, along with the reining in of state spending and the creating of the conditions required for private initiative and private profit to flourish once again and restore the economy to health. This is why the state had to continue to be labelled unproductive, parasitical, wasteful and inefficient. The primacy of the private sphere over the public had to be maintained.

The difficulty as many have pointed out is that, powerful as these old ideological tropes still are, they have to be stretched more and more to accommodate the reality of modern market orders. The picture of the expansion of the state as driven by the entitlement revolution captures one of the main drivers of this expansion but ignores others, as discussed in Chapter 6, in particular military spending, spending on infrastructure, spending to boost national competitiveness and spending to improve and reproduce human capital. The state as a public household is not just an arena to accommodate the interests of different classes and maintain the legitimacy of the capitalist order. It is also in many countries the engine for development, for catch-up, for external security and for management of citizens – and this means investing to boost industrial development, human capital and military capacity. Modern states have become agents in the international market order, which emerged as the modern world system, and they discharged their role through competing economically and militarily with one another. Alongside the entitlement state, the security state is the other great driver of the expansion of the modern state. There are libertarians like Ron Paul who are consistent in wanting to dismantle both the entitlement state and the security state, but contemporary advocates of returning to a small state are mainly so only in their rhetoric. Most members of the Tea Party, for example, favour increasing spending on the US military. Big government is tolerated for some purposes but not for others.

It is hard to cut back the modern extended state because there are so many lobbies and interests associated with its programmes. Retrenchment has become increasingly difficult. Cutting spending on a major scale invites resistance, which is why governments often talk tough but fail to implement the scale of cuts they say are necessary. The gap is filled by borrowing. In the era of the extended state, governments generally find it easier to deal with deficits, either through faster economic growth or through inflation. Implementing cuts and austerity is painful and hazardous, and most politicians flinch from it if they can find an alternative. This helps to explain why the extended state is so resilient. But there are other reasons as well. Much of the ideological construction of the modern state is a fiction. The distinction between productive and unproductive activities is deeply flawed, since it suggests that all wealth originates only in private activities and that anything that is funded publicly has to be paid for from private sources. Seeing this as a deduction from private income is an ideological fiction because private wealth could not be preserved without the public framework of law and security, and also because so much public spending takes the form of purchases from private companies or raises the productivity of the economy through investment in human capital or in infrastructure or in the science base. The state and markets are so interdependent in the modern economy that the notion that two distinct spheres can be identified is fanciful. They interpenetrate one another, their boundaries have become highly porous. Far from being reversed in the neo-liberal era these trends have intensified (Crouch 2011).

In recessions, however, the old language always comes to the fore. Those who work in the public sector are said to be 'paid for' from the taxes of those who work in the private sector, and therefore to be an incubus on the back of the 'strivers' and the wealth creators. Mitt Romney's unguarded comment at a fundraising event during his campaign to become president, designating 47 per cent of US citizens as 'takers' paid for by 'makers', may have been electorally unwise, but it expressed a widely held prejudice of the Republican base. The politics of the tax state constantly divides the population into the deserving and the undeserving. The problem as many conservatives see it is that the growth of the entitlement state does indeed mean that the numbers of the undeserving and the dependent have swelled, so that now they outnumber the deserving and the independent. This is what makes democracy a dangerous system, as nineteenth-century liberals and conservatives warned. To the extent that policy in democracies is allowed to reflect the wishes of the majority it may threaten the principles of the liberal market order by allowing the infringement of property rights and the emergence of a fiscal politics which becomes unsustainable because sufficient taxes cannot be extracted to support it.

At the root of the misconception of the modern state and its relationship to the market economy is the analogy, still constantly used in political rhetoric and still vibrant in popular attitudes, between the private household and the public household. Just as each private householder expects to balance expenditure and income, cutting back on the former when the latter falls, so the state is expected to adopt similar procedures in dealing with its finances. In the nineteenth century this was formalized as the balanced budget rule. Sound finance was held to depend on the government seeking to balance its outgoings with its income. If there was a shortfall it needed to be met by reducing the outgoings, rather than by raising taxes or by borrowing. In this way, the public household set an example to all private households and corporate households as to how they should conduct their affairs. In a financial crisis the duty of the public household was to lead the way and cut its spending, restoring its solvency and credit, and not putting any additional burdens on households in the private sector, whether individual or corporate. The strongly held UK Treasury view of how the economy worked maintained that if the government financed its expenditure by borrowing it could only do so by crowding out private borrowing. There would be no net increase in investment or in economic activity, and economic activity would be damaged because a given quantity of government spending would be inherently inferior to the same quantity of private spending. The only time when government borrowing to support much greater public spending was justified was in the exceptional case of war, but in periods of peace the task of government was to keep a tight rein on its spending and only spend what it could raise in taxes, which should be kept as low as possible so as to encourage private enterprise and initiative (Skidelsky 1967).

Keynes disturbed this ordered world by pointing out that financial crises were exceptional situations like war-time and that if governments reduced their spending at the same time that private households and companies were doing the same, the result would be to turn a recession into a slump. Government policy needed to be counter-cyclical, and in particular the government should be prepared to borrow in times of recession and falling demand in order to boost its spending. During booms governments should run surpluses, but in slumps they should run deficits. All governments since the 1930s, whether guided by Keynesian precepts or not, have learnt how to do this using the great structural weight of the modern state in the economy to influence general conditions. Keynes's political point was that it made no sense to treat the public household as though it were just another private household which should be bound by the same rules. The state had a unique role to play in the management of the economy, and traditional ideas of sound finance and the operation of the tax state were holding it back from doing so (Skidelsky 2009).

Since the eighteenth century, modern states have had to manage the tension of being members of an international state system and an international market order. As they became more dependent on the latter for their economic prosperity so their freedom of action became constrained. They had constantly to balance the needs of their domestic electorate and domestic interests with the constraints of the international markets. Obliged to compete with other nations they needed always to find ways to make their national economies more productive and more competitive. This turned all states into developmental states that did not withdraw from the international market system but engaged better with it and profited from it. States must constantly balance maintaining economic credibility with the international financial markets at the same time that they maintain political credibility with their own citizens.

The fiscal crisis in the US

The fiscal conundrum is illustrated by the deadlocks which have emerged both in the US and in the EU over the fiscal issues that have occurred since the 2008 crash. They illustrate different aspects of the same problem. In the US, it is the deadlock over the future of the entitlement state and how it should be funded, which on two recent occasions, in 2011 and again in 2013, has threatened the country not only with the shutdown of the government but with a national default on its debts. In the EU, the deadlock is over how to make the monetary union work. This brings out particularly the problem of reconciling externally imposed financial discipline with democratic autonomy and legitimacy.

There have been many shutdowns of the federal government in the past because of disagreements over the budget between the president and Congress. But the divide is much harder to bridge now, and the stakes are a lot higher. A fundamental disagreement has emerged over what counts as legitimate policy. The fiscal stimulus of the Obama Administration to try and counter the effects of the financial crash on the economy was regarded by some Keynesian economists as too small to have much chance of promoting an early recovery, but it was denounced by fiscal conservatives in the Republican Tea Party movement as having the wrong priorities, because not only did it fail to tackle the ever-rising national debt, but it also accepted that it was going to rise still further.

The debt began rising right at the start of the neo-liberal era under Ronald Reagan and George H. Bush. Although Reagan was elected on a pledge to balance the budget, he tripled the national debt, and by 1992 it stood at $3 trillion, the headline figure seized on by Ross Perot in his presidential bid that year. The debt stabilized during Bill Clinton's presidency, but it rose again sharply under George W. Bush through the effect both of tax cuts and increased spending on the military and security after 9/11. It received a further large boost from the policies adopted by Bush and Hank Paulson to stave off financial collapse in 2008, including taking over $5 trillion of liabilities from Fannie Mae and Freddie Mac. This approach to the crisis was continued by Obama. By the time of the US presidential election of 2012 the national public debt had reached $16 trillion and was still climbing. The US economy had begun growing again but much too slowly to offer an early prospect of getting current deficits down, and with it the accumulated debt total.

Opinion was polarized between Democrats and Republicans over how to deal with the public finances, the continuing deficits and the increasing debt, and whether the adjustment should come through tax increases or spending cuts. The Republicans strongly opposed the first, particularly on upper income groups, on the grounds that taxing the wealth creators would harm the prospects for economic growth. They wished all the adjustment to fall on public spending, particularly on present and future welfare entitlements, but not on defence spending, which they wished to increase. One influential set of proposals was laid out in the Ryan plan, devised by the Congressman from Indiana, Paul

Ryan, who was selected as Mitt Romney's running mate in 2012. The Ryan plan only dealt with federal spending which makes up approximately 50 per cent of total US government spending. The plan proposed over time to lower the proportion of federal spending in national income to 17 from around 22 per cent, and to do this while protecting certain core spending programmes – defence and Medicare. This would require very large cuts in all other federal programmes (Ryan 2012). Indeed in some estimates all other programmes would have virtually to disappear so as to allow the plan to work (Wolf 2012; Stockman 2012). To reduce federal spending still lower, to 15 or 10 per cent, to make possible a return to the small government of the nineteenth century desired by the Tea Party, would also require big cuts in defence and Medicare. The Democrats' solution to the debt and the deficit was an increase in taxes on all those earning more than $250,000 combined with some spending cuts on welfare and on defence, but protecting key programmes for middle-income families and the poor. The failure to agree budget proposals in August 2011 led to an agreement to disagree, postponing a decision until after the presidential election. But the election settled nothing: there was further brinkmanship, and at the end of 2013 still no agreement about the future of the budget. The threat of a sovereign default in October because of a threat by the Republicans not to raise the debt ceiling was only narrowly averted.

Some of the most radical voices in the present crisis are to be found in the Tea Party movement and in some of the libertarian think tanks, such as the Cato Institute. The conservative wing of the Republican party seeks a much smaller state, and the Cato Institute has estimated just how small it should be. In the 1980s, it was argued that above a certain level (around 40 per cent) taxation on individuals was counterproductive and led to the government receiving less income, because of the disincentive effect of high tax rates on people's willingness to work, and because of tax avoidance by the rich. This relationship became formalized in the Laffer curve and led to the policy prescription that lowering high marginal tax rates would actually net more money for the government. Helping the rich would help balance the books, while squeezing the rich would take money away from government programmes and was self-defeating. The Cato Institute promotes a new curve, the Rahn curve, named after its discoverer, Richard Rahn. The curve suggests that for each country there is a relationship between the proportion of government spending in national income and the rate of economic growth. If government spending rises above a certain level the growth rate falls progressively. The optimum level is said to be between 15 and 25 per cent, a long way below the level of 37 per cent for the US and the levels of most European countries, which range from 40 to more than 50 per cent. The curve relies heavily on data points provided by 'states' such as Hong Kong which has public spending below 20 per cent. The Cato Institute suggests that a level of 15 per cent or even lower is what governments should be aiming at (Mitchell 2013).

To reduce total public spending to 15 or even 25 per cent is a strong aspiration of the conservative movement in the US, and the Ryan Plan is an example of how such aspirations might be put into effect. But they also show the difficulty of radical plans to shrink the state. It is not that they are unthinkable. It is that the political route to them looks extremely hard, because in unwinding federal and state programmes, the federal government would need to persuade or compensate all the interest groups which have a vested interest in these programmes, built up over 80 years of the entitlement state. Part of the desire of the conservatives to scupper Obamacare before it had even started, as their price for allowing an increase in the debt ceiling, was because they feared that once many people benefit from having health insurance, often for the first time, it will be hard politically to propose to take it away.

Conservatives see the entitlement state as unaffordable and doomed to collapse. The entitlements which governments have agreed to are so many time-bombs which will eventually explode. They are generating large deficits which require ever more borrowing and the accumulation of debt. The Republicans believe that the only way to tackle this deficit is to tackle spending, while the Democrats want to broaden the fiscal base and raise more in taxes as well as making some spending cuts. The Republicans do not want any increase in taxes because they think the state is already too large and needs to be reduced. These are two quite distinct fiscal visions, and it is proving very hard to achieve any kind of compromise between the two. Instead, the US is having to endure a succession of fiscal cliffs. The compromise American Tax Payer Relief Act agreed by the Senate on a bipartisan basis in January 2013, but only passed by the House of Representatives with a majority of Republicans voting against, meant a small increase in taxes from 35 to 39.6 per cent on citizens earning more than $400,000. The Congressional Budget Office's analysis of the settlement showed that, although revenues would increase over the next decade by $600 million, the extension of tax reliefs on all other income tax payers together with additional spending proposed in the bill would push the overall deficit $4 trillion higher by 2022 (CBO 2013).

For the Republicans, the problems stem from the entitlement state which has been growing ever since the New Deal, but particularly since the Great Society programmes, including Medicare, enacted in the 1960s. Obamacare is just the latest addition, but the basic structure of the entitlement state goes back much earlier to the 1960s, the 1940s and the 1930s. It is the mounting cost of health care and pensions as Americans live longer and new treatments are constantly discovered which makes these programmes look unsustainable in the long term, unless Americans are willing to pay more taxes.

The nature of this deadlock in the US over fiscal politics warrants closer examination into the arcane dispute over whether the debt ceiling should be raised or not, which first appeared in the summer of 2011 and then returned in 2013. A law dating back 70 years requires explicit Congressional approval for raising the debt ceiling. In the era of deficit finance and the reliance of the US state to fund a large part of its expenditure through borrowing, the debt ceiling has been raised as a matter of course whenever the Administration has requested it. Not to do so would push the country into default on its loans. The willingness of House Republicans in 2011 to use this obscure law as a weapon in the battle between Congress and the White House to reduce the deficit was greeted with some incredulity. Austan Goolsbee, the Chairman of the Council of Advisors, declared in January 2011: 'if we get to the point where you've damaged the full faith and credit of the US, that would be the first default in history caused purely by insanity. I don't see why anybody's talking about playing chicken with the debt ceiling' (Goolsbee 2011). But that is what the Conservative blogs were talking about endlessly, and again in 2013. Glenn Beck declared that not raising the ceiling might cause financial meltdown, but raising it would spell the end of the Republican Party. Apparently he regarded avoiding the latter as a higher priority than avoiding the former. As the August 2011 deadline for raising the debt ceiling approached it became clear that House Republicans were prepared to push their case for a major new fiscal direction right to the wire, emboldened by the mounting size of the deficit. Government expenditure was now ten times government debt obligations (*Wall Street Journal* 2011). Republicans argued that it should be a simple matter for government to trim its spending so as to avoid a default, and that the onus should therefore be on the Administration to announce major spending cuts to keep the need for borrowing below the debt ceiling.

The confrontation in 2011 was exacerbated by the faltering recovery in the US. By the third quarter of 2011 the international economy was deteriorating again. After a period in which the US together with the leading OECD economies had begun to recover from the financial crash of 2008, posting a reasonably healthy growth rate of 3 per cent in 2010, during 2011 there was a pronounced slowdown in economic output and job creation. In August of that year in the US there was no net increase in jobs at all: 14 million were registered unemployed, another 9 million part-time workers were seeking work and an estimated 6.5 million were off the register altogether. It was estimated that to reduce unemployment to 5 per cent over five years would need 17 million new jobs, or approximately 282,000 jobs a month (Samuelson 2011). Even during the boom of the 1990s only 240,000 jobs were being created, and during the post-2008 recession that dropped to 105,000. Furthermore, high unemployment has exerted downward pressure on many wages, leading to take-home pay stagnating or falling, making the prospect for recovery still worse.

The confrontation over the deficit came to a head in July and August 2011, and a default on US debt was only narrowly averted by a last minute deal. The President was seen as having conceded the most. Though achieving an increase in the debt ceiling, he had to drop his demands for higher taxes on the rich and to concede a package of spending cuts which if implemented would trim $2.4 trillion from state spending over the next decade. Even so, the compromise which ended the stand-off was judged insufficient by many traders, and Standard & Poor took the opportunity to downgrade the US credit rating from AAA to AA+. This was largely symbolic, although it helped to cause another sharp drop in the stock market because of renewed fears of slowing growth. The failure of the US economy to keep growing as fast in 2011 as it had in 2010 meant a potential loss of output of $350 billion. This complicated the task of reducing the deficit, making it more likely that it would go on rising because of lower tax revenues and more spending on benefits.

Both sides on Capitol Hill appreciated the seriousness of the economic situation, but their solutions were diametrically opposed. For the Republicans, and particularly for the many supporters of the Tea Party elected in the Congressional mid-terms, government had become too big and had to be drastically reduced in size. Until the deficit was tackled, there could be no lasting recovery. For the Democrats the deficit was a secondary issue. The key issue for them was jobs and growth. If the federal government could stimulate a recovery and avoid the economy sliding back into recession, then the deficit would be manageable and could be reduced in the longer term. The deadlock between these two positions was complicated by the fact that 2012 was an election year. The American Jobs Act which Obama unveiled on 8 September proposed both a further stimulus and a sizeable payroll tax cut. Many Republican commentators and blogs immediately branded it a continuation of the same failed approach, tinkering with the problem rather than seeking a long-term solution, and designed mainly with an eye to the forthcoming presidential election. The bill was subject to a filibuster in the Senate and eventually went down to defeat.

The hostility of the Tea Party faction is not just to fiscal stimulus but to monetary stimulus as well. They are against any kind of interventionist policy to manage the economy. Ben Bernanke at the Fed had followed Milton Friedman's advice on how to learn from the mistakes of the monetary authorities after 1929 by reducing interest rates to 0.25 per cent and pursuing quantitative easing to ensure there was sufficient liquidity in the economy to avoid bank failures. Although Bernanke's monetarist credentials were impeccable, his desire in 2011 to see a third stage of quantitative easing was widely condemned by many conservatives, and even described as treasonable by Rick Perry, briefly the front-runner among Republican presidential hopefuls in 2012. The argument between Keynesians and monetarists in the 1970s and 1980s had been focused on whether the government should give priority to jobs or to inflation in its management of the economy and on the relative efficacy of fiscal and monetary policy. But the debate was always within the framework of the extended state which had developed since the New Deal, the war-time economy and the Cold War. This extended state meant both an active interventionist policy to manage the economy, with government accepting overall responsibility for its performance, and the granting of entitlements in areas like health and pensions to all US citizens.

The Tea Party seeks to reverse this and revive arguments that pre-date the New Deal. At times it seems to echo the debate between Keynes and Hayek over the causes of the Great Crash and the Depression and what the appropriate policy response should be (Wapshott 2012). For Hayek the basic problem was the misallocation of resources which had occurred during the boom of the 1920s. The fictitious values which it had created needed to be destroyed, and as quickly as possible, through a sharp deflation to make possible a rapid and soundly based recovery. If governments intervened and tried to prevent the market destroying the inflated values which had been created in the boom, it could only do so by distorting economic activity and risking inflation, paving the way to a further and more damaging collapse in the future. Andrew Mellon had a similar approach derived from his business experience, declaring that the good thing about a recession was that assets returned to their rightful owners. His liquidationist approach was the kernel of sound finance before the Great Depression and the New Deal. It was to be held responsible subsequently not just by Keynesians but also by monetarists for turning the slump into a depression. American conservatives, however, and the Tea Party in particular, are intent on rehabilitating this approach, arguing that a supply-side approach to taxation and a balanced budget approach to fiscal policy are correct, and that it is the New Deal which is responsible for America's current difficulties by making possible the growth of big government and the culture of entitlement and dependency.

Andrew Mellon would probably not have approved of the Tea Party, however much they currently approve of him. He was an unbending fiscal conservative. He only favoured tax cuts during the upswing of the cycle. In a downturn he gave priority to tax increases to balance the budget, rather than spending cuts, because they were much quicker and more certain in their impact. Refusing to raise taxes to deal with a budget deficit would for him have been the height of irresponsibility. Mellon was, however, dealing with a much smaller state. From the Tea Party perspective, the growth of the extended state since that time has changed the context for fiscal policy. What is necessary is a radical attack on the causes of the debt and deficits which have so afflicted the US. Anything less will just perpetuate the problem. Since the New Deal era the federal government has been directly spending 18 to 22 per cent of GDP, particularly on entitlements such as social security, infrastructure and defence. In the last 30 years, however, and starting with the Reagan era, the US government has persistently wanted to spend more than it has been prepared to raise in taxes. Reagan both cut taxes and boosted spending, but supply-side policies did not generate enough extra tax dollars to pay for the big increases in military spending which he sanctioned. By 2012 the annual deficit was running at 10 per cent of GDP. While there are individuals and states willing to lend to the US, fiscal realists argue that this does not matter. So long as the dollar is the world's leading currency it will always be treated as a safe haven, whatever the credit agencies decide. But it causes anxiety nonetheless that large parts of US debt are held by the sovereign wealth funds of states which are not democracies, particularly China, Saudi Arabia and the Gulf States, and it raises the spectre that the time will come when the dollar is no longer accepted as the international currency, and at that point it would suffer a major collapse in value. This after all is what happened to the pound.

In 1933, Roosevelt was elected on a balanced budget ticket but began to experiment with many different kinds of policies to try and get the economy moving again. Obama has had to work with the extended state he inherited with all its inefficiencies and inflexibilities. His supporters urged him to be bolder. After the 2011 stand-off the satirical magazine *The Onion* declared that Obama bragged at having demanded tough concessions from Democrat and Democrat alike! But he had little room for manoeuvre. The slogan of the Tea Party was 'cut, cap and balance'. They wanted cuts in spending, a cap on the debt ceiling and a balanced budget amendment to remove discretion from the federal government to run fiscal deficits at any time, including during recessions. Even more moderate voices on the Republican side, such as *The Wall Street Journal*, argued for permanent across-the-board tax cuts, a regulation moratorium and fiscal discipline, claiming that Obama's Keynesian stimulus was supposed to have created 3.5 million jobs, but instead unemployment had risen from 8 to 9 per cent. Obama's measures were designed simply to give money to government workers and to protect them at the expense of the private sector. It calculated that the Obama stimulus since 2009 had totalled an initial $830 billion, to which it added the GM/Chrysler bailouts, Obamacare ($1 trillion health care entitlement), the Dodd–Frank financial regulation legislation, credit card price controls, Build America bonds and the extension of benefits for the jobless. This made the total stimulus almost $3 trillion (*Wall Street Journal* 2011).

Underlying this acrimonious debate were the long-term fiscal challenges which the US was facing even before the financial collapse and the recession. A couple retiring in 2011 earning $89,000 would have paid $114,000 in Medicare payroll taxes, but they could expect three times that in medical services. In social security what people pay in and what people get out is much more nearly in balance, but this is expected to change once more of the 70 million baby boomers reach retirement. The sense of entitlement to Medicare is very strong, even among members of the Tea Party, but paying for it will be a major challenge for future American governments unless they can either raise the rate of growth of the economy and thus fiscal revenues, or increase tax rates. Every year of weak growth, recession or stagnation compounds the problem. Total liabilities of all programmes are currently estimated at $61 trillion.

A long period of slow or interrupted growth in the economy will make the task of affording the entitlements that citizens have been promised that much harder. Some analysts standing back from the bitter partisan dispute in Washington have also argued that the problem may be that both the stimulus packages put forward by the Democrats and the supply-side packages put forward by the Republicans are doomed to disappoint because they will only have limited effectiveness. If the recession in 2009 was not an ordinary cyclical downturn, lasting recovery will not come about by traditional means. What is required instead are measures that would tackle the excessive household debt which doubled as a share of household income between 1982 and 2007. On this view the policy choice is either to accept stagnation while the economy slowly deleverages, or try to hasten the deleveraging by boosting demand. Pessimists think that the second choice will not work, that governments will be stuck with the first, and that the return to capital could be depressed for a long time ahead. The overhang of debt is so large, and the deleveraging required so enormous, that governments lack the capacity or the will to do anything substantial about it, even if the rhetoric often suggests otherwise. The deadlock in the US over the deficit means that there are regular confrontations and small adjustments, but the bottom line each time is that the deficit keeps rising.

The crisis in the eurozone

The eurozone crisis, which has been discussed as part of the governance conundrum in Chapter 5, also sheds important light on the fiscal conundrum. When the financial crash erupted in 2008, the eurozone at first was a haven of stability. The epicentre of the storm was in London and New York, and it seemed for a time that the European economies might be only mildly affected. This changed, however, in 2010 with the emergence of the sovereign debt crisis which was felt most acutely in the eurozone economies after it became apparent that European banks and European governments were much more exposed to the international financial markets than had at first been thought. The eurozone came to be seen as the weakest link in the international economy because, unlike the US or the UK, there was no central bank to act as lender of last resort, no political authority standing behind the single currency to take decisive action to defend it. Market traders were quick to sense that the architecture of the euro was not robust enough to withstand a crisis of such magnitude.

The different levels of productivity in the eurozone and the concealed surpluses and deficits on the balance of payments of each country within the framework of the single currency and the single interest rate meant that the only way these imbalances could be removed and debt reduced was through internal devaluations (Sinn 2011). This required very large deflations through tax increases and public spending cuts, the creation of mass unemployment and a sharp reduction in the level of wages, which if persevered with long enough might make investment profitable once more in the eurozone periphery. The problem for the eurozone after 2008 was that shrinking tax receipts and rising outlays meant that many governments had to borrow more just to stay afloat. The weaker members were made to pay penal rates on the bond markets to finance their borrowing, because those markets doubted they could make the adjustments that would allow them to grow again and pay down their debts within the eurozone. They doubted also that the rich northern members of the euro would be prepared to allow the significant transfers of wealth required to stabilize the public finances of the periphery. In this way the eurozone became the epicentre of the sovereign debt crisis. Other countries, including the US and the UK, which had as bad or worse debt ratios as some of the peripheral eurozone economies, were not targeted by the bond markets, partly because they still possessed what the peripheral eurozone countries did not have: strong central banks and national governments willing to intervene to support the currency and allow whatever external devaluations were necessary to ensure its health.

Between 2008 and 2012, the European economy, including the UK, suffered economic stagnation, high unemployment rates and very weak growth. Only in 2013 did the picture begin to change, and then not for all. The weakest economies in the eurozone, particularly Greece, have suffered very large falls in output and employment and rising social unrest. The average unemployment in the eurozone at the end of 2012 was 11 per cent, but this concealed Germany and Austria at one end with unemployment at 5 and 4 per cent respectively, while Greece and Spain both had 25 per cent. Youth unemployment in these countries was over 50 per cent. There was some evidence the policies were producing a sharp fall in costs in the southern countries, but it was still unclear whether this would be sufficient to allow a genuine recovery to begin, or whether these countries were trapped in a loop of deflation, austerity and rising debt (Lapavitsas 2012; Patomaki 2013).

Supporters of the austerity policies in Europe argue that it is the only solution to the debts which have been incurred. Until they have been paid down there is no prospect of a lasting economic recovery. The creditor economies in the eurozone cannot be expected to pick up the costs of the overspending of the deficit economies, since that would mean permanent subsidies from their taxpayers with no prospect of the situation ever improving. The lower debt ratios and lower unemployment in some of the creditor countries is taken as a sign that they spent the years of the boom increasing their productivity and maintaining fiscal discipline, instead of increasing their spending beyond their income. Within this narrative there is little scope for leniency to what is seen as the profligacy of the debtor countries (Dyson 2010). Any loans provided for them must come with strict conditions on reforming their public finances and accepting austerity. All European countries are suffering with higher than usual unemployment rates and little economic growth. The internal redistributive struggle has sharpened, and as a result it has become politically much harder for governments of the surplus countries to make concessions to the deficit countries. There is little popular support for it. The narrative is embellished with all kinds of anecdotes about the pay and benefits which those working in the public sector in some of the deficit countries have been enjoying. The inefficiencies in many programmes, and the huge losses incurred on services like the railways and infrastructure projects, are highlighted. Cultural stereotypes about attitudes to work are also widely employed. The effect has been to strengthen further resistance to bailing out the deficit countries. It has become politically toxic, and few leaders are prepared to stand up and argue for it.

The opposition to this policy has been weak. There has been some attempt to argue for policies to increase demand and increase the money supply so as to avoid deflation and help the eurozone economies to recover. The paying down of debt, particularly the national debt, is seen as a second order priority, which can wait until the recovery is firmly established. This Keynesian programme is envisaged as a Europe-wide programme, and one that is only likely to succeed if it is Europe-wide. The benefits from all countries pooling their resources and developing common policies for dealing with the crash and the recession is seen as the surest way to restart growth. The fundamental requirement for recovery is seen as the need to boost demand and inject confidence. Without demand there can be no improvement in employment and investment, and the economy will continue to stagnate – the eurozone risks slipping into a deflationary trap from which it will be hard to emerge.

This Euro-Keynesian narrative has been powerfully argued, but in Europe it has made little headway, trumped always by the austerity narrative of the ordoliberals. The appeal to national electorates to regard the national economy and the public household as a private household – and to make the policy a priority so as to bring the public finances back into balance as quickly as possible while encouraging the private and corporate households to do the same – emphasizes the importance of sound money and the need for fiscal discipline. The degree of discipline that is required, however, to rescue the eurozone may be too great to be sustained (Marsh 2013) and risks handing the initiative to parties in Europe which are not just against the euro and the eurozone but against membership of the EU itself.

In its conception the euro was a federal project, but it was established without the federal institutions needed to sustain it. In good times all was well, but in bad times the strength of the political commitment to it was always likely to be tested by the markets. As some of the architects of the euro foresaw, at some stage the members of the eurozone would be forced to choose between on the one hand a move to fiscal union and the creation of a political authority to stand behind the currency, and on the other hand an abandonment of the single currency and a return to national currencies. This political reality has been behind the impasse in the eurozone – and the apparently endless crisis summits, anguished negotiations leading to announcements of breakthroughs and the euphoria in the markets – only for the package agreed gradually to unravel. The gap between the rhetoric of the summits and what leaders are willing in practice to implement remains too great. Yet gradually over two years of negotiations between 2010 and 2012 the eurozone appeared to inch its way towards a solution. Governments have ultimately given a higher priority to getting an agreement that will stave off a eurozone collapse than in sticking to their hard line negotiating positions and seeing the euro go down. The ECB has gradually come to play an increasing role in trying to find a solution and has started doing things which were said to be impossible and unacceptable at the start of the crisis, in particular providing greater liquidity. Many observers expected the eurozone to break apart, but so far this has not happened and the currency has limped on, although with a degree of austerity and fiscal discipline which far exceeds what has been attempted elsewhere.

The reason for the deadlock in the eurozone and why it is so hard to resolve is not difficult to understand. The determination of the hard currency creditor economies grouped around Germany to impose tough conditions on the weaker members of the eurozone bloc, forcing them to adopt stringent austerity measures in return for loans to bail them out, has met a swelling tide of popular resistance to these conditions in the debtor countries. The austerity programme can only succeed if governments continue to be elected in the debtor countries that are willing to implement the programmes. The euro is caught between the willingness of the markets and governments to continue lending and the willingness of citizens to endure deepening austerity.

The euro was a bold political experiment when it was first launched, which many doubted at the time could succeed. Currency unions not backed by a single state have always tended to fail. The euro was a currency union on a scale never before attempted. A monetary union covering a continental economy without a fiscal union or political union to support it was always likely to be tested eventually, as its founders foresaw. When tested it might disintegrate or it might provide the catalyst towards fiscal and political union. A third possibility, however, not really considered at the time, was that although the eurozone might not break up, it might also fail to overcome its internal problems and remain instead permanently deadlocked.

The disintegration of the eurozone may still happen, and if it does it will most likely be triggered by major defaults in one or more of the main debtor countries: Greece, Ireland, Portugal, Spain or Italy. There was speculation for a time that some of the creditor countries might instead leave the euro and form a new hard currency union around a revived Deutsche Mark. That has receded, but the prospect of default has not gone away. It all depends on the political willingness of the creditor states to prevent it and the ability of the debtor states to continue to sell the draconian terms for staying in the euro to their people, and for there to be no further shocks. There is a great deal of international support, particularly from the US, the IMF and even the UK, for a solution to the eurozone crisis to prevent its break-up, since the consequences for the international economy would likely be grave. But the creditor countries, although much vilified for the tough conditions they have imposed on the countries seeking loans, are constrained in how far they can go by their own domestic electorates. This is how the politics of the tax state at transnational levels operates. Each national jurisdiction faces outwards and inwards at the same time. Its leadership must please its international partners and the financial markets, and at the same time keep the support of its electorate. The suggestion that Germany and the other creditor states should have to bail out the southern EU states in perpetuity, paying for the waste and inefficiencies of their public sectors, is an extreme version of the entitlement state, because those with the entitlements are not even citizens of the core national community, but only of the much looser regional association, which has forged nothing like the same bonds and solidarity on which to draw in a crisis.

If the impasse cannot be broken, the eurozone crisis risks becoming truly a crisis without end. The eurozone would manage to hang on, continuing to make small adjustments sufficient to avoid the implosion of the euro, but never enough to resolve the crisis definitively and prevent its recurrence (Münchau 2013, 2014; Marsh 2013; Stephens 2013). The eurozone economy remains stagnant, with grinding austerity, high unemployment, deflation and little prospect of growth. Somehow governments manage to contain the unhappiness of their citizens, and also to keep the markets at bay. It is a balancing act which has been performed with no little skill since 2010. But whether it can be performed indefinitely is much more doubtful.

The obvious solution which many propose is for the eurozone to complete the journey to full fiscal, banking and political union. Some steps were taken towards this during 2012, which lightened the gloom, but there is still a long way to go, and many observers see big obstacles. Further progress depends on a political judgement that the risk of a collapse outweighs the risks of reform. For it to work, the members of the eurozone will have to agree to a major pooling of their sovereignty and the creation of a federal power to govern the economy of the eurozone and stand behind the euro. The main obstacle is how to ensure the legitimacy of any such arrangements in the countries concerned, given the level of suffering and resentment in the debtor states.

The deflation that has been imposed on the eurozone in order to save the euro is the same kind of deflationary policy that was pursued in Britain in the 1920s to maintain the gold standard. It had the same polarizing effects on living standards in different parts of the country. The austerity programme of the Troika, treats the eurozone as a single country with a single currency and sets out the conditions that all parts of the eurozone must meet in order to remain part of that currency. This is a policy dictated by the interests of the strongest members and their external backers in the governing agencies of the international market order. What is lacking is an imaginative plan, a European version of Marshall Aid, to lift the European economy into growth, ease the burden of austerity and give the citizens of Europe some hope

(Tsoukalis 2013). There is little sign that the European political class is thinking of any such plan, because of the internal difficulties of winning support for such a plan from their electorates. The US administration gained support for Marshall Aid and the reconstruction of western Europe and Japan because it linked it to the security threat of the Soviet Union. No such broader purpose is available to European leaders as they seek to deal with the problems of the eurozone. They hope that growth may come from external sources, and that the eurozone will be floated off the rocks by a recovery in the US and by faster growth in Asia. In the meantime the only hope for recovery is for wages to be forced ever lower until costs in the debtor countries are compatible with those in the creditor countries. This is a policy of slow attrition which may yet cause political explosions in some of the countries worst affected and lead to the election of governments which announce defaults and even exit from the EU.

Without a fiscal and political union the eurozone is facing an impasse. The political leadership is unwilling to break from its fiscal orthodoxy and therefore a recovery of the eurozone is unlikely to come from within the zone itself. The other possibility is that the political strain will become too much and the eurozone will explode through the election of governments which repudiate existing treaties and international arrangements. This would signal a wider fragmentation of Europe and new political danger. Political deadlocks elsewhere in the international state system are also serious, but none quite match the deadlock in the eurozone for the political cataclysm it could unleash. During 2013, the dam was still holding, but there were ominous signs of mounting unrest and increasing popularity for anti-system parties of the extreme right.

Conclusion

The two major internal political deadlocks since the crash, in the US and in the eurozone, were both widely expected at various points to set off a political earthquake. But in both cases the worst was averted. Neither deadlock has gone away, however. The underlying problems remain unsolved, but the situation has eased sufficiently to allow a return to business as usual. Both still have the capacity to destroy the recovery and initiate a much more serious phase of the crisis. An American default could bring a collapse of the dollar, while the disintegration of the eurozone would derail the recovery in the western economies and trigger a retreat into protectionism in many countries.

The worst has not happened, but the potential for miscalculation is still there. The dilemmas faced by governments within the structures and assumptions of the neo-liberal order are producing some dangerous polarizations. But the future remains open. Some of the possible paths to it are explored in the final chapter.

Chapter 8

Paths to the Future

Modern capitalism has passed through many crises in the last 200 years. Some of them seemed to mark the end of the world at the time, but in retrospect even the largest of them can be seen to be no more than temporary interruptions to the advance to ever higher peaks of output and prosperity. The powers of recuperation of capitalist economies have always been formidable, and these have not suddenly disappeared. As capitalism has evolved through crises and conflicts, so all social and political institutions have gradually been reshaped to create the best possible conditions for continued economic growth. It has become the default position of our politics, and alternatives are increasingly hard to imagine. Once several generations have lived within a society shaped by capitalism, going without the many advantages and benefits which a capitalist order provides becomes hard to imagine for most people, and even dire economic circumstances do not spark the kind of revolt and regime breakdown which were once predicted as necessary consequences of the way capitalism had developed.

That view which was common in the 1930s across the political spectrum has been replaced in more recent times by the argument that the advent of capitalism has brought an end to history in the sense of debates about alternative ways of organizing society, because capitalism is inseparable from modernity itself and experience has shown there are no plausible alternatives to organizing a modern economy (Hayek 1981; Fukuyama 1989). The problem which such a perspective poses is that it makes capitalism self-contained, rather like the financial system, and gives it no way of assessing or dealing with systemic risks which may still threaten it and which arise from its own structural principles and assumptions. As the present crisis shows, capitalism still suffers from systemic risk. It is too anarchic and loosely governed to avoid it. What seems to be true is that as capitalism has developed it has become both more resilient and more vulnerable at the same time, more prone to deep crisis, but also more able to ride out short-term emergencies. At a time of major crisis, such as the period ushered in by the financial crash, there is talk of radical reform and new directions, but it proves extraordinarily hard to implement real change, because the short-term pressures to return as quickly as possible to the known and the familiar are so strong. The intractability of the issues makes these periods increasingly long and drawn-out. They become crises without end.

Change can be slow in coming, but that does not mean that crises do not have important effects. The creative destruction they unleash is not just directed at existing economic sectors and economic values, but also at political and social institutions, both domestic and international. Crises expose points of weakness and force the recognition of new realities. They signal the rise of some sectors and some states and the decline of others. In the fog of a good crisis it sometimes takes a while for the long-term effects of what is happening to be understood, but in retrospect certain turning points can be recognized. For the present crisis, its confused aftermath and the very slow recovery from it makes it hard to be sure what its long-term impact will be. In this chapter, a number of scenarios are sketched which indicate different paths which might be taken and how the significance of this crisis might in time come to be viewed. These scenarios highlight particular aspects of the present and extrapolate from them. They present one-sided, exaggerated accounts of the future. At their best they illuminate the nature of the present by pinpointing its different aspects and clarifying the nature of the political choices which have to be made and the uncertainties which surround them.

The scenarios in this chapter discuss general possibilities up to 2050. Many of these are therefore not immediate, but glimpses of how the world might develop over the next three and a half decades. The immediate prospect is the continuation of the current dispensation. The neoliberal order has proved resilient (Schmidt & Thatcher 2013), and if there is any movement in the years ahead in the direction of policy it is more likely to be towards further liberalization within national economies, as states all embrace the disciplines of 'the global race'. Liberalization in the form of new multilateral agreements, however, looks much harder to achieve.

Among the four scenarios, the first is presented as the default scenario. The other three are variations on this scenario or, in the last case, an alternative to it, looking ahead to the period 2020–50. In order for any of them to become the default scenario the interests and institutions underpinning the first scenario would first have to be displaced. There would have to be a significant shift in both economic and political power and ideological paradigms. So far this has not happened and the effects of the crisis have been contained. In this chapter, I speculate about some of the events which might change that, and drawing on the analysis elsewhere in this book I suggest that underlying unresolved problems might produce new shocks and crises, which potentially could unravel or transform the prospects for western prosperity. These scenarios are not predictions. There are too many uncertainties for that. What they offer is a way of thinking about alternative paths of development and the trade-offs which policy-makers may face. The world is likely to be a very different place in 2050. By then we will know, among many other things: whether China has continued to rise, consolidating its position as a leading power, or whether it has imploded; whether global warming is happening, and how grave a threat it poses; whether the internet has become a source of major productivity increases across the economy; whether the EU and many other lesser unions have survived; and whether the governance of the international market order is still significantly multilateral and transnational. But there will no doubt be many new uncertainties by then to cloud the future.

Each scenario is presented along two main dimensions, geopolitics and political economy. For geopolitics the key question as to how the future might evolve is whether the international state system will stay unipolar or whether it might become either bipolar or multipolar; whether the US continues to have the capacity and the will to maintain its present position of leadership; and whether the rise of India, China and other populous, low income states will eventually lead to a major shift in the balance of power, both in the international economy and in the international state system. For political economy the key question is how the obstacles to growth are dealt with: whether the political conditions can be created for a broad-based sustainable recovery in the western economies that avoids deflationary traps; and whether the very rapid growth rates of the rising powers can be sustained.

The financial crash of 2008 should not be looked at in isolation. It is tempting to see it as the North Atlantic financial crisis, regionally focused, like the Asian financial crisis before it. But although there is a sense in which that is true, it has always had a much wider significance and a much wider impact, because it arose within the heartlands of the international market order. It needs to be placed in context, in particular the context of key geopolitical events such as the collapse of the Soviet Union in 1991 and its aftermath, which saw the creation of a unipolar world and the consolidation and extension of the liberal international market order, the opening of what many expected to be a new era of peace and prosperity. This time of relative harmony was interrupted by two events. 9/11 shattered western security and launched the 'war on terror' which advertised western weakness rather than western strength, while the 2008 financial crash shattered western prosperity and highlighted the advances being made by non-western powers, giving the glimpse of a very different future for the international order. The question after 9/11 and the financial crash is whether the geopolitical and political economy foundations of the western order can be re-knit into a new synthesis which can underpin a new era of peace and progress, or whether a different kind of order will gradually emerge to take its place.

Scenario 1: US primacy

The first scenario as suggested above is the default scenario, and the one that will dominate at least the next few years, and possibly the next few decades as well. After a major shock the initial instinct is to try to restore things to where they were before. But what will actually be achieved is resilience rather than resolution, the avoidance of collapse but the acceptance of impasses, a crisis without end.

Geopolitics

In this scenario the international state system stays unipolar. US leadership and dominance is maintained, and the challenge of the rising powers is at the very least deferred, perhaps even postponed indefinitely. The US preserves its position as the only military superpower and retains its ability to use soft power to sustain a network of alliances that make it still the centre of the international community, the indispensable nation (Nye 2011). Doubts over the willingness of the US to continue to engage with the world are stilled, as both the Democrat and Republican leaderships remain in the hands of those committed to the maintenance of the global influence and global reach of the US. The domestic pressures for disengagement and a more isolationist foreign policy from domestic lobbies such as the Tea Party are successfully resisted, although the US is less willing to get involved in major military interventions overseas. As warfare becomes more automated, US power is deployed to punish and deter enemies using drones and robots without committing large numbers of US troops on the ground. The power of non-state networks outside the control of governments continues to increase, but determined efforts by the US and by international agencies limit their growth.

A unipolar world means that no fundamental shift takes place between East and West, and that within the West the pattern of relationships remains broadly the same. The EU stays as a rather loose association of states, with a weak and undeveloped federal centre, enjoying low legitimacy among the citizens of its member states. It fails to develop a coherent foreign policy, the member states continue to disagree as in the recent past on major foreign policy issues, and it continues to free-ride on the willingness and capacity of the US to provide protection and security for Europe and other regions of the world. Even those states such as the UK and France – willing under this scenario to take military action either in support of the US, as the UK did in Iraq and Afghanistan, or occasionally taking the lead, as in Libya in 2011 – will gradually take a lesser role, as their public opinion and economic and military capability make it harder for them to do so. Many of the new entrants to the EU, especially the former communist countries in the east, will become vociferous champions of western ties and committed supporters of US leadership, but they will lack a strong military capability and are unlikely to make it a priority to build one. In this scenario Europe remains a pacified and peaceful region within the US orbit, although, because it is no longer in the frontline, it increasingly drifts away from the US. The relationship between them continues to have frictions, but they remain relatively minor. Relations between Russia and the US remain strained, particularly because of attempts by Russia to rebuild its sphere of interest by exerting greater control over former states in the former Soviet Union such as Ukraine, but do not deteriorate into open conflict.

A similar pattern might be observed in Asia–Pacific, where Japan succeeds in partially escaping from its deflationary trap, building on the economic reform it began in 2013, but content to remain within the US security guarantee and not greatly enhancing its military capacity beyond the Self Defence Force or developing the political will to deploy its forces outside Japan. Korea, Singapore and Taiwan follow suit. The security focus in Asia–Pacific remains the containment of China, and with the support of its allies in the region, including Australia and New Zealand, the US is able to maintain an effective security presence.

The rising powers are the key to this scenario. Their challenge to the dominance of the US fails to materialize. This is because, although they grow richer, they find it easier to integrate with the western order and accept US leadership rather than challenge it. Their own progress turns out to be more uneven than expected, and even by 2050 they still have not emerged as fully mature industrial societies, lacking the transnational companies, global brands and skill base which would put them in the forefront of technological advance. Their state-directed strategies keep them independent of the western order, but this does not save them from asset bubbles, financial crashes and recessions of their own. The willingness of the US to promote relatively open markets for many of the most crucial commodities being traded in the international economy means that a key security interest of these states continues to be safeguarded, which lessens the need for building up military capacity to provide their own protection of supplies, although some competition for strategic position in resource-rich areas such as sub-Saharan Africa continues. In this way the international market order in its neo-liberal form gains a new lease of life by incorporating the rising powers within it, who find more advantages from accepting US primacy than in challenging it.

The big unresolved security issue in this scenario is the Middle East. This remains a major problem for the US so long as the oil reserves there are seen as a crucial resource for the international economy and for key US allies such as Japan and the European states. The evident US reluctance to get involved again militarily in the region, seen in its uncertain response to the Arab Spring in general and to Libya in 2011 and Syria in 2013 in particular, is unlikely to change, but the difficulties of maintaining a balance of power which keeps the peace remains complex, given the strategic ambitions of Iran and the involvement of Russia in the region. US allies include some Arab nations such as Saudi Arabia, the Gulf States, Jordan, Iraq and Egypt, but these states often have divergent aims and interests, and some of them are highly unstable and might move away from the US, as Egypt began to do under the Morsi presidency. None of the Arab states collaborate easily with Israel, the US's main ally in the region, which further complicates achieving a durable order. But if the US remains the undisputed world leader then it has the resources at least to continue managing the problems of the region and containing them. Reaching an understanding with Iran is one option for achieving that in this scenario.

Political economy

A revived western order and a continued unipolar security system are only viable if the US remains the leading economy. At some stage in the next 30 years, the US is likely to be overtaken by China as the largest economy. Some have even predicted this may take place as early as 2020. But absolute size of an economy is less important than productivity, and here the gap between the US and China and all the other rising powers remains very large (O'Neill 2013) and will remain so even in 2050. In this scenario that gap may gradually diminish, but not particularly rapidly, and not sufficiently for it to be closed. The US stays ahead in many new technologies, thanks to its publicly funded defence sector, and its leading universities and advanced technology companies, which provide the stream of skilled personnel and innovation breakthroughs which continue to give the country the edge. This assumes that techno-logical innovations will continue to be made which raise productivity significantly, and that these productivity gains can be widely diffused through the economy. Under these circumstances, the extraordinary flexibility and huge accumulated wealth of the US economy, together with the political and technological ability to exploit windfall gains such as shale oil and gas, and the willingness to admit immigrants and provide amnesties for illegal immigrants, make the US economy still very competitive, particularly at the high value end of products and services. The ability of the US economy to continue to generate brands which dominate international markets will be unmatched by any other economy, and while it retains that advantage, it is unlikely to lose its leading economy status.

This scenario does not mean that all the well-known problems of the US economy are suddenly dispelled, but it does suggest that the financial crash, although a big shock, does not become the major turn-ing point in US economic fortunes: the country recovers again. This recovery is not the same as the recovery from the 1930s Depression. At that time the recovery was fitful, the full productive potential of the US economy was still to be unleashed, and the conditions when it could be did not emerge until victory in the Second World War. The US will no longer be a rising power in that sense, and it will never again enjoy the kind of dominance it had in 1945, but in this scenario it still proves to be an established power that has enough strength and political will to keep ahead of its rivals and shape the world in its own image and to its own advantage. In this scenario the recovery which takes place after the crash is U-shaped, rather than V-shaped, though the economy does get back to growing at around 2 per cent per annum. Its performance may be fitful and there may be further ups and downs, so that it might not be until the 2020s that a more even keel is established. Climate change under this scenario is managed without a major alteration of policy. The US is given enough time to adjust gradually to rising temperatures. This is the wager of the climate sceptics. It needs to be right.

In this scenario the dollar remains the leading international currency, although its writ is circumscribed by the controlled currencies of some of the rising powers and by the problem of US debt. The US has to find a way to manage its debt problem more effectively, even if it cannot eliminate it. This scenario assumes that this is possible and that a combination of a reduction of spending, both domestic and external, and tax increases, together with a reduction in the need of the country to fund its borrowing needs from external sources, makes the debt problem manageable and consistent with the dollar remaining the leading currency. This continues to be tricky since the position of the US as the global leader is dependent on the US government and US companies being able to spend freely abroad. It is also tricky because it requires a resolution of the internal deadlock between Republicans and Democrats over whether spending cuts or tax rises should have priority for bringing the US long-term finances under control. That is likely to require one party gaining control of both the Presidency and Congress for an extended period.

Another assumption of this scenario is that the US succeeds in fixing its banks. Here a tighter regulatory regime would have been put in place, but nothing on the scale of the reforms of the 1930s. The Glass–Steagall Act, for example, which was first introduced in 1933 and repealed by the Clinton Administration in 1999 following intense lobbying by the financial sector, has not been re-enacted. The Dodd–Frank Act of 2010 has so far been the main legislative response to the lessons of the crash. This is part of the business-as-usual approach, but it also reflects the dependence of the modern economy on a strong and vibrant financial sector. The urge to pronounce the banking sector safe again and open for business is very strong, because all parts of the economy, from private households to companies to government, run on debt and liquidity, and need the services of financial intermediaries. Do the regulatory authorities now have enough oversight of the system to prevent another meltdown? The business-as-usual scenario assumes that they do, and that new financial bubbles do not arise, or that if they do, they are deflated before they can do any damage.

The broader consequence of renewed US ascendancy for the international political economy is that the US would once again be in the key position for shaping the rules of the post-crash era. The shifts in wealth and power, however, that have already taken place, recognized by the increased role for the G20, may mean that the US and its allies have a harder task in imposing their rules than they did either after the Second World War or after the end of the Bretton Woods international currency system in 1971. Some concessions may have to be made to the interests of the rising powers represented in the G20 if some of the deadlocks over trade and climate change are to be broken. But a different interpretation is that these deadlocks do not need to be broken to allow a return to business as usual. If other states are not powerful enough to challenge the US so as to impose their own rules, they have a strong incentive broadly to accept the rules the US promotes, negotiating for concessions which reflect their particular interests. A business-as-usual scenario assumes that the US and the international agencies have once again the appetite and the strength to negotiate an amended international market order which preserves US primacy but takes due account of the shifts that have taken place in the wealth and power of other states.

Such an outcome might well produce over time a new phase of liberalization and deeper globalization in the international economy if it succeeded in fully integrating some of the rising powers into the western order, as happened after 1945 with West Germany and Japan, and after 1991 with the states of East and Central Europe. Such integration would require full currency convertibility and domestic programmes of economic liberalization, and the dismantling or at least weakening of state subsidies and protected development. If this could be achieved the international market order would look much stronger, even if it meant a reordering of the ranking of some states. Europe might be the loser from this widening of the international market western order to embrace the rising powers since it would no longer have a privileged security or economic position in that order and would remain vulnerable, as would the US itself, to competition from the rising powers. The cost of maintaining extensive welfare states funded through taxation would be highlighted, and a drive to shrink public sectors by reducing the entitlement state to much lower levels might become part of western politics in a bid to revive the stagnant and deflation-prone economies of Europe. The first signs of this have already been seen in the recession.

US primacy is therefore the business-as-usual scenario. It sees US leadership confirmed, even though weaker than before, and the institutional framework of the post-war western order amended but still substantially in place (Anderson 2013).

Scenario 2: the G2

The second scenario assumes that China is a rising power unlike other rising powers, because it has the will and is acquiring the capacity to challenge the primacy of the US over the next 30 years. It also assumes that the US shares this assessment and comes to perceive China as a security threat. This changes the international system from a unipolar system to a bipolar one, making the question of how the US deals with China its top priority. The relationship between China and the US comes to dominate international politics and provides a lens through which everything else is refracted.

Geopolitics

If the international system becomes bipolar again, it means that the two key players come to see the other as a threat to their security. This makes the relationship between them more important than any other. This does not make conflict inevitable, although it certainly makes it possible. It can lead to a search for ways to defuse tensions both on security and economic issues precisely so as to minimize the risks of conflict and to bring some order and certainty into the relationship, even if the level of trust that can be achieved in such a relationship is always qualified.

The only previous period of sustained bipolarity in the international system was the period of the Cold War itself, where security issues predominated. China is, however, a very different power from the Soviet Union. Its challenge to the geopolitical balance has arisen not primarily from its military strength, as was the case with the Soviet Union, but from its economic strength. China was until recently a very poor and undeveloped country. Its accession of strength stems from the deliberate opening of the country to international trade and investment in the 1980s. This has transformed its economy, which in turn has begun to transform its military potential as well. The economic development of the Russian economy was on a much narrower base than China's, and much of the productive power of the Soviet economy was devoted to maintaining military parity with the US. China by contrast has integrated quite deeply into the international economy by becoming the manufacturer and assembler of so many of the consumer goods desired by the West. It has ceased to be an autarchic economy, deliberately cut off from the international economy, and has instead become a major player within it. It is this which has also shifted the geopolitical balance in Asia by making China a positive pole of attraction and gradually renewing the basis for Chinese soft power in the region, which was once so formidable. Much has been made of the growth of Chinese nationalism inside the country and the recent strengthening of its military capacities. As yet, however, China has only a fraction of US military power and shows little intent of seeking parity (Fenby 2014). That might conceivably change if China succeeds in becoming an advanced industrial economy, because since future warfare is going to depend on new kinds of weapons using the latest developments in information technology, the strength of Chinese performance in information technology means that at some point in the future China could suddenly close the gap on the US very fast. That at least is the fear of some security analysts in the US (Halper 2010).

A key question in this scenario therefore becomes China's intentions. Does China intend to challenge the West and the US, or does it seek an accommodation with them? The evidence is mixed. The mere fact of China's existence and its resurgence makes it inescapably a challenge to the US, and this would be so even if it had the most impeccable free market constitutionalist government. The antagonism between Britain and the US after all was at one stage very marked (van der Pijl 2006), and there were several occasions when they might have gone to war. What makes the challenge of China seem particularly threatening to many in the US foreign policy establishment is that it combines its economic liberalization with an authoritarian centralized one-party state under the control of the Chinese Communist Party. Understanding the intentions of rulers in a democratic state is some-times hard enough. In an authoritarian state it is still harder because so many issues are not openly discussed but determined in secret.

There are many uncertainties about the rise of China. Whether its rate of growth can be maintained and whether its political system will in time be democratized are just two of them. As Martin Jacques has argued, one of the problems in western understandings of China is that the country is a civilization rather than a nation state, and therefore has a different understanding of itself and its place in the world which does not fit into western conceptions of the international market order (Jacques 2012). The difficulty of reconciling the American view of the world and the Chinese one is considerable, and particularly difficult for the Americans who also think of themselves as a civilization and not just as a nation state. The US wants China to join its civilization by inte-grating fully into the western order. A liberal China is not an impossi-ble concept. A liberal Japan after all was achieved, but only after a war which destroyed the old Japanese state. In the G2 scenario the signifi-cance of the two leading powers treating the world as bipolar is that China refuses full integration into the western order, but reserves the right to challenge it. In doing so it becomes the latest in a long line of powers which have challenged the liberal international market order which first the British and then the Americans constructed and managed.

China is rising within a world which since 1991 has been dominated by the US and its allies. China has relatively few allies of its own, and some of them like North Korea are a liability rather than an asset. It is surrounded by allies of the US which have a huge security presence in the Asia–Pacific region. China has no global security presence, but under this scenario it gradually acquires one. The main extensions of its reach beyond its region have been into Africa and Latin America in order to secure the supplies of raw materials its industries so urgently need to keep operating. China provides aid to many countries with few of the strings which western states attach. Its purpose so far has been to construct commercial alliances rather than military alliances. Compared with the global reach of US companies that of China is in its infancy (Nolan 2004; Breslin 2009; Fenby 2014).

The main concern from a security angle with China's rise is that although the country does not have territorial ambitions and grand imperial designs in the way some other rising states have had in the past, it does have a number of territorial disputes with its neighbours over land which it claims as part of its historical territory. There are unresolved disputes with Japan, Vietnam, India, Russia and Taiwan. One of these could at some point cause a flash point and likely bring confrontation with the US, through its security alliances. Some security analysts expect this to happen. But it is not a necessary conclusion from this scenario. It seems unlikely that the kind of major security stand-off which characterized the US/USSR relationship will develop. The real sources of friction in this scenario are more likely to be economic.

Political economy

The main strain in the G2 relationship between China and the US is that both have become dependent on the other. The US needs China's cheap manufactured goods; China needs US markets to keep its factories open. The US needs China to purchase US Treasury bonds; China is obliged to purchase them because it has no other outlet for its huge export surplus. In this scenario, although China has by no means achieved overall parity with the US, in aspects of their economic relationship there is a rough parity.

Larry Summers argues that the resulting stand-off has created a balance of financial terror which neither of the two new superpowers dare upset for fear of leading to mutually assured financial destruction. The two countries are in a game of chicken and neither wants to blink first or risk bringing down the whole house of cards which sustains their political economy. There are solutions for both sides but they are very difficult. China could allow its currency to become convertible, which would see it appreciate in value. Then Chinese citizens would become much wealthier and this would greatly increase the size of the Chinese domestic market. But it would also threaten the export boom which guarantees employment to millions of Chinese workers and allows jobs to be found for the huge numbers of workers arriving from the rural areas looking for work in the cities. At some point China will need to make the transition, if it wants to become a fully mature economy, generating its growth from its domestic economy rather than being dependent on its ability to export cheaply to the West. This is a moment of opportunity for the bilateral relationship with the US but also a moment of danger. This scenario also allows the possibility of the US reducing its dependency on China by deciding to live within its means and not using its privileged position in the international economic system to compel other nations to lend their surplus dollars back to the US. This is highly unlikely since it would undermine the US role in the world and force it to submit to the same rules which are imposed on others. There is no appetite for that in the US. The advantages the US derives from its position in the international system are seen as a reward for shouldering the burden of that system. But this is what is likely to make the relationship between the US and China in a bipolar scenario difficult. Both sides are likely to claim a privileged status and not submit to the demands of the other.

In this G2 scenario other states in the international system are forced to accommodate to the interests and strategies of the two big players. As during the Cold War there are aligned and non-aligned nations, although there are few states which cannot afford to have dealings with both the US and China because of the pivotal role of both states in the international economy. As China's strength increases so it will seek, like the US, to secure its position by encouraging other states to form bilateral relationships with it. For many states like Australia, which are dependent on trade with China, this becomes a difficult choice if relations between the US and China worsen.

The more the relationship leads to conflict and a stand-off between the US and China the more the performance of the international economy is likely to suffer. There is little prospect for resolving the deadlocks on trade and climate change or extending cooperation into new areas. The recovery in western economies as a result remains fragile and W-shaped, with short, weak rallies and a tendency to stagnation. Prospects for the rising powers and for the developing economies are more favourable, not least because the stand-off between the big two intensifies competition for energy, water, resources and regional influence. This means many countries, as during the Cold War, have options as to which great power they associate with, and this gives them some bargaining power. When the world was unipolar there tended to be only one package for aid, and it came with very precise strings attached. Superpower rivalry is not necessarily a bad thing for smaller economies.

So a patchwork of trading relationships emerges, around the two principal players. US current initiatives to launch negotiations for a Transatlantic Trade and Investment Partnership (TTIP) and a Trans-Pacific Partnership (TPP) is a foretaste of things to come under this scenario. The TTIP is with the EU and the TPP is with Japan, Korea and other East Asian economies. China is excluded. These are bilateral arrangements to promote freer trade, conducted outside the framework of the WTO and its multilateral negotiations. Under the G2 scenario China starts concluding deals of its own. China and the US still need to deal with each other, but they do so bilaterally rather than through a multilateral negotiation. There is no longer a unified order, but two separate orders, with some friction between them.

The prospects for growth under this scenario are middling. The configuration of the international market order does not encourage trade, and protectionist barriers increase. Countries which have favourable demographics find national strategies to prosper. China has to solve its population problem if it is to maintain its rise and not grow old before it grows rich. Debt remains a huge issue, primarily for the western powers, and is always likely to explode again in new crises, particularly if growth proves sluggish. The difficulty of reaching agreements on how to prevent or adjust to climate change increases under this scenario, particularly as competition for energy, water and other resources is likely to intensify. Technological innovation and diffusion still takes place, but is again likely to be a source of friction, both through espionage and the adoption of rules around intellectual property rights. Conversely a bipolar world is likely to spark competition in particular technologies, and the devotion of much effort and resources by national governments, and this may speed certain technological developments, as has occurred in the past. Whether it will lead to truly breakthrough technologies which transform the prospects for the whole international economy is the big unknown. The development of such a technology might be hampered by the degree of protectionism which might by then have become established across the international economy.

Scenario 3: multilateral governance

The third scenario assumes that the shifts in power and wealth, which have been taking place in the last 20 years and were highlighted by the 2008 crash, advance to the point where a multipolar world emerges, which provides the basis for a new era of cooperation rather than conflict. The US and China are still the leading two powers but there are several others – Russia, the EU, India, Brazil, Japan and other G20 members, such as Indonesia, South Africa, Argentina, Turkey, South Korea and Mexico – who counterbalance them and allow for a dispersal of power through the system (Kupchan 2012).

Geopolitics

In this scenario the US recognizes the emerging multipolar character of the international state system and decides to share global leadership with the other members of the G20 and build a new international market order based on a set of multilateral bargains on environment, trade, nuclear proliferation and many other issues. The value of multilateral deals when they can be reached has often been demonstrated, but they are extremely difficult to achieve because of the different starting points and interests which states have (Narlikar 2010; Hale et al. 2013). Getting multilateral deals to work is rather as Weber described politics: 'slow drilling through hard boards'. Deals can take a very long time to arrange, but once they are struck they create a framework of rules which help to increase exchanges, reducing costs and increasing trust and certainty. There are still winners and losers from this process within each state, but such deals work when winners outnumber losers. The prize is considerable, but the political complexity of achieving it is high because those nations currently occupying privileged positions in global governance structures, such as seats on the UN Security Council or voting rights on the IMF, have to be prepared either to give up those privileges or at least see them substantially diluted. This scenario assumes that breakthroughs can be made in establishing new forms of international cooperation, building on the successful international regimes which have already been achieved in the post-war era.

In geopolitical terms such a multipolar system requires underpinning by a substantial rewriting of rules and the creation of new institutions to allow more states to participate actively in global governance. States still have their particular interests, and pursue them, but within commonly agreed rules. There are mechanisms to resolve disputes, drawing on the considerable experience the international community has gained from operating the dispute resolution mechanism of the WTO. This is the part of the WTO which currently works most effectively, sorting out particular trade problems between countries, and coming to decisions which both parties to the dispute normally respect. Similar arrangements are extended to other areas of policy.

In this scenario the new multipolar order is more diverse and less western-centric than the current international order. It is assumed that the process of institution building avoids some of the pitfalls encountered by the EU, the most successful example so far of multilateral regional coordination between a group of sovereign states. The process of reaching decisions in the EU has become too opaque and remote from ordinary citizens, partly because of the complexity of the institutional structure of the EU, which obliges EU national political leaders to operate at EU and national levels simultaneously. The EU struggles to maintain legitimacy as a result, and is frequently rejected as a hostile alien external power, taking away individual liberties and interfering with the lives of its citizens. In the multilateral scenario, governance of the international economy is still rooted in intergovernmental arrangements and relies on states negotiating with one another and forging agreements.

Such a multipolar order is still vulnerable to the charge that still only a handful of elite nations participate in global governance, and do so to serve their own interests. Many of the other rising powers not in the G20, and those western powers not in the EU, as well as all developing states, feel disenfranchised. This is the main challenge for this scenario, since once the governance arrangements for the new multipolar order have been established it becomes hard to change them. This reflects the experience of the current governance arrangements instituted after the Second World War, which have largely remained frozen in time, even though the balance of power in the international system has changed radically and the old rationale for membership and non-membership no longer applies. The interests of those who occupy privileged positions is to defend their continued holding of them. A genuine multipolar order creates constitutional rules which allow for change and for new institutional regimes to evolve in the future as the balance between different states and regions shifts.

Such a scenario is regarded by many as implausible, because of the nature of states and the way they define their interests, and because of the ever-growing number of non-state actors and networks – but it is not inherently impossible. There is a growing list of examples of successful cooperation by states in organizing different forms of global governance. The world has become more interdependent, more interconnected, and the need for greater cooperation and pooling of sovereignty for a variety of purposes is more widely recognized than ever before. The main obstacle to this scenario being realized is that it could only come about through a self-denying concession by the US, which even if a president were prepared to agree to it, would also require approval from Congress, which has often in the past resolutely insisted on a relatively narrow interpretation of the US national interest. The assumption has been that the US will always choose US primacy if that option is available, so this scenario is only likely to come about if the US comes to accept that the option of primacy is no longer available and that the alternatives to multilateralism and a collective hegemony are measurably worse for its interests. There are examples in international relations, as Charles Kupchan (2012) has shown, of acts of altruism by stronger powers which have turned enemies into friends by creating trust and allowing an extended negotiation to take place which has eventually resulted in agreement. This scenario assumes that under certain conditions the US is prepared to play that role in helping to construct a new multipolar order and shaping a new collective hegemony.

Political economy

The multilateral governance scenario is the one most likely to restore confidence and build the conditions for another extended period of growth. The recovery becomes V-shaped rather than U-shaped. Agreement to remove obstacles to growth and to tackle persistent collective problems facing the world creates the conditions which most easily unleash the potential for the further expansion of the rising powers and also increasingly of developing economies in other parts of the world, particularly Africa. If problems of trade, immigration, investment, poverty and finance can be sorted out then demand can be maximized and a virtuous circle of high demand, high employment and high productivity can be established. The new boom helps to deepen and widen the global economy and it is accompanied by efforts to tackle the problems of excessive population growth, environmental damage and the gap between rich and poor. Much less attention is likely to be given to these issues in the other scenarios. This is not an abstract agenda but one which is already being pushed hard by many NGOs and social movements in global civil society. There are many transnational movements and coalitions pressing for change. But the main obstacle to creating agreement to transform the present international market order from a western-centric one into something much more inclusive is the mistrust between leading powers, reflecting their different stages of development and the very different interests which they seek to pursue. This scenario seeks to build momentum for change and inclusiveness, as well as for cooperation, to meet the many challenges the international market order faces.

This scenario does not remove all the obstacles to growth, but it makes many of them more manageable. The scenario assumes that migration becomes easier between states, helping those countries with static or falling populations to benefit from an influx of young people and relieving the pressure of rapidly rising population in some developing countries. At the same time it assumes that world population growth will level off as all countries are helped to industrialize and become modern economies. At some point population growth will cease to be a major contributor to economic growth, but this is more easily handled within a stable and cooperative international market order which is seeking to address the extremes of inequality and poverty which have characterized the international market order up to now.

A new period of extended prosperity and economic growth will help advanced economies overcome their debt problems and their deflationary traps. It carries risks of its own, as all booms have in the past, and recognizing and anticipating them will be a test of the new cooperative forms of global economic management. Economic policy under this scenario could take a number of directions, but given the balance of states in the multipolar order it is unlikely to endorse the neo-liberal framework of the previous international market order, and is more likely to embrace controls on financial flows with freer trade, which was the hallmark of the Bretton Woods agreement that established the first post-war international market order.

The pace of growth under this scenario will depend partly on the continued diffusion of old technologies to all parts of the international economy, and partly to the success in developing major new technologies. There can be no certainty about the latter, but under the condition of a reformed international market order there should be scope for significant continued progress for all economies. The big question mark is climate change, which because of the lags involved could change the prospects radically for all states and force a huge diversion of resources into mitigating the effects of a substantial warming of the earth. But this scenario maximizes the chances for green growth and for the possibility that alternative energy sources will be found and deployed in time, and that other cooperative regimes will be established to reduce the environmental harm of human activity.

Scenario 4: US decline

The first three scenarios all assume that the US maintains some kind of leadership role in a changing international market order. The fourth scenario assumes that the US for a variety of reasons disengages from its former leadership role to focus instead on its internal problems and regional interests, as it did in the 1930s. This is something which its geographical position and its resource base allows it to do.

Geopolitics

In this scenario the world is once again multipolar, only this time the relationship between the poles is characterized by conflict rather than cooperation. The task of holding the world together under one order proves too great and the international economy fragments into regional groupings which seek to limit their exposure to global markets by erecting various forms of tariff and non-tariff barriers as well as capital and currency controls. The world comes to be divided into territorial blocs and spheres of influence. Conflict may flare because of competition for scarce resources, energy and water in particular. Since countries have relative advantages or disadvantages in terms of their access to these resources, there tends to be a rash of conflicts over resource and energy issues. Once a cycle of zero-sum politics has established itself it is hard to resist (Rachman 2010), and all groups find they must defend themselves or be plundered. Although large wars are still ruled out because the leading powers all possess nuclear weapons, a rash of small wars might break out, and the involvement of one or more of the great powers in them risks turning them into larger conflicts.

The pattern of the blocs follows familiar lines, reflecting the new multipolar world. Blocs form around the US, the EU (if still in existence, or Germany if not), India, China, Russia, Brazil and possibly some others. These blocs take control of their currencies and use them to gain competitive advantage over other blocs through competitive devaluations. The flow of goods, capital and people is greatly reduced, although there are bilateral relationships between many of the blocs and between individual states. Broadly, however, the blocs turn in on themselves to organize their internal markets and plan their trade and investment. Trade becomes a more marginal activity, rather than one of the main drivers of economic growth as it had been in the past.

In some ways this world still looks familiar, because many international institutions, including the UN, continue to exist, and there are still international forums for the discussion of common issues. But less and less of substance is discussed in them, and the framework of international cooperation begins to decay, since it is so difficult to get any of the big blocs involved in a multilateral negotiation. All existing negotiations remain permanently deadlocked.

The international state system in this scenario has some resemblance to the state system of the 1930s, but there are many differences, the most important of which is that the blocs do not become military blocs and do not seek to expand their territory or control of resources through armed intervention. This assumes that the minimum needs of each bloc for resources can be met from within its own single market or from trade. That implies higher levels of cooperation than were achieved in the 1930s, but given the higher levels of interdependence achieved in the last 60 years that is hardly surprising. If this assumption proved to be unrealistic, however, then a more dangerous cycle of confrontation and conflict could begin between the blocs.

Political economy

The fragmentation of existing forms of cooperation, the deepening of deadlocks and the increased competition for resources make this scenario the one least likely to support growth. Any recovery is likely to be L-shaped, with flatlining the most likely outcome, at least for western economies. The blocs formed around rising powers are likely to grow faster while the demographics favour them, and they can still adopt existing technologies to raise productivity. But the overall rate of growth is lower than in other scenarios. This is partly because states resort to protectionism of many different kinds to safeguard themselves, including currency depreciation and restrictions on imports, and the outcome is less trade, less interdependence and less growth.

Some states and economies fare better than others in this scenario, as was also the case in the 1930s. But all economies find it difficult to adjust to a much less open world and still stay highly productive. Those that succeed do so by boosting domestic demand, encouraging investment and planning for full employment. In this way there may be considerable growth in this system as there was in the 1930s within the various blocs, but the overall level remains lower than it would have been with a more open and flexible trading order.

Demographics are a continuing problem for some of the blocs, particularly the EU. Internal state politics make a more liberal policy of labour migration difficult to attract support, and the principle of free movement of labour within the single market also comes under threat as populist extremist parties press for much tighter controls on immigration and mainstream parties accede to these demands to protect their electoral base. Under this scenario the blocs are all assumed to be relatively cohesive because the desire to centralize and close ranks against rival blocs will become strong. But it is also possible that one or more blocs may lose cohesion, and even fragment. The EU is the prime candidate in this scenario, with the most likely trigger being a collapse of the eurozone and the single market, as individual member states impose new currency, capital, trade and immigration controls. A collapse of the eurozone and the EU is not ruled out in the first or second scenarios, where it would have a devastating effect on growth in the international economy. In this scenario the wider effects are more muted because of the relative insulation of the blocs from each other, which dampens the transmission effects. The effects within the EU are, however, serious.

Since overall growth is muted, the opportunities for translating scientific discoveries into improvements in productivity is more limited than it would be under the other scenarios, but the possibilities still exist. Blocs might become more protective of their technological discoveries, and even keener than they already are to engage in espionage. Jealousy of other blocs spurs competition between them in technological innovations, but direct competition between companies is much more limited because of the barriers to trade and to movements of capital and people. Progress in pushing back the technological frontier is not particularly rapid.

Fiscal consolidation and efforts to bring debt and deficits under control are under this scenario an internal matter for each bloc, although at the beginning some blocs and individual states default on some or all of their debts, which lowers trust and confidence in a way which makes cooperation on other matters more difficult. The blocs vary in how effective they are in managing internal inflationary pressures, and also in how effective they are in collecting taxes. The creation of blocs means that standards and performance diverge, because disciplines are no longer exerted either by international regulatory agencies or by market competition. But the existence of blocs does limit the unchecked growth of imbalances between surplus and deficit countries. Financial flows are also much reduced because of capital controls.

Under this scenario problems like climate change develop more slowly, because overall growth is lower, but since it does not halt or reverse it, the weakness of cooperation between the blocs makes the eventual impact potentially greater because the blocs vary considerably in their capacity and their commitment to curb carbon emissions. Some blocs do cooperate with one another, but there are no binding agreements and the sense of an international community has become too weak to exert much influence. A fragmented multipolar world at the current stage of industrial development creates major new risks and uncertainties.

Conclusion: a time of troubles, a time of progress

The future is likely to include aspects of all four scenarios. It is very unlikely to resemble just one. None of the scenarios assumes that a further meltdown and collapse is inevitable, but they cannot be ruled out. All envisage some growth, although it will be unequally distributed. The economies in those countries most seriously affected by the crash were showing signs of recovery in 2013, with several having already regained their pre-crash output peak or on course to do so. But with interest rates still close to zero, this is the longest recession these economies have suffered since 1945, and the outlook for sustained growth remains subdued. The most serious problem identified in the scenarios is that there are several critical challenges facing the West and the international market order, but only the third scenario sees an actual increase in the political resources and political capacities required to tackle them. Politics can be very destructive of human societies, but it is also indispensable for finding stable ways to provide security and prosperity.

In the twenty-first century the world faces many problems and at least two major existential threats (Cerutti 2007). The first of these arises from the dangers of the weapons which modern technologies have introduced to human warfare, most notably nuclear weapons, with their capacity potentially to wipe out the human species altogether. The politics of nuclear weapons used to focus on whether the two superpowers could make mutual deterrence credible and refrain from first strikes to gain an advantage. The contemporary concern is how to stop nuclear proliferation, the spreading of these weapons to more and more powers around the world, which increases the likelihood of them being used in a conflict at some point. The second existential threat arises from the effect of human activities on the earth's climate, which scientists warn is fast reaching the point where it will become all but irreversible (Gough 2011). To take the warnings seriously would involve changes to the organization and lifestyle of modern societies and the form which economic growth has taken for the past two centuries which are so radical that it is hard to imagine how they can be implemented through the procedures of normal politics. Two other major problems loom as well. The first is the continuing rapid growth of the world's population and the debate among demographers about the carrying capacity of the earth. Is there any limit to the number of people who can be accommodated on the planet, and what are the implications for its finite resources in providing even the present population with the standard of living and consumption which has been achieved by the rich countries? The second problem is global poverty. With three billion people still existing on less than $2 a day, what prospect is there for ending the gap between rich and poor nations which has grown so wide in the last 200 years?

There are optimists and pessimists about the capacity of human societies to deal with these threats and problems, and there is huge uncertainty about the scale of the risk which each of them poses and what, if anything, can be done about them. The recurrence of such anxieties about the future of human society in the modern era reflects an abiding sense of the gulf between our political and social capacities on the one hand, and our economic and technological capacities on the other – and the fear that the forces the latter have unleashed have passed beyond our control. This could generate a sense of fatalism leading to inaction. This is a common reaction both among many who think the threats and problems are real, but believe that taking action is too difficult and that there are other more pressing immediate concerns, and also among the many sceptics who dismiss the threats associated with nuclear weapons or climate change as exaggerated and argue against intervention to deal with the problems of population growth or global poverty. They profess a different kind of fatalism, putting their faith in the flexibility and adaptability of markets to find acceptable solutions to every problem which emerges in the course of human development (Ridley 2011).

As has been emphasized throughout this book, the pace of change in our world still appears to be accelerating. The crisis of 2008 and its aftermath forced an interruption in the growth of many western economies and raised deeper questions about its future prospects. Anxieties over western security and prosperity and the order which once so successfully promoted them have not gone away. Not many politicians or citizens in the West are ready yet to address them. This is the sense in which this crisis has become seemingly a crisis without end. The short-term emergency has been surmounted, but not the deeper problems which gave rise to it.

The deadlocks and political crises of the last few years have slowed the western economies. But the world as a whole is still accelerating. World population, world energy consumption and world living standards are all rising. The drivers which have now been operating for the last 200 years have not stopped. In important respects they are operating with even greater force than before because of the broadening of the base of the international economy with the appearance of the new rising powers. The rollercoaster of modernity is once more transforming our world, possibly in ways which those who live in the rich and secure lands of the West will experience as both loss and threat. Much will depend on whether that mood can be resisted and the basis for new partnerships and new forms of cooperation can be created. Our present unease stems from the knowledge that our political order is fragile and cannot be taken for granted. Through myopia and inertia the world could drift into fragmentation and ever deeper deadlocks. There is nothing inevitable about this, even if much conspires to make it so. The time and space to reverse these trends is not unlimited, but there is still time if we had the imagination and the will. Ideas are important, but ideas by themselves are not enough.

One of the reasons for the period of troubles which has befallen the neo-liberal order is that the springs of countervailing power and resistance to its organizing principles and assumptions have grown so weak. Alternatives require new coalitions of interests, powerful enough to reshape some of the assumptions of neo-liberal politics. With every new generation new forms of politics emerge, new kinds of organization and new expressions of hope. In this book I have examined some deep dilemmas in the political economies of the West. If western prosperity is not to unravel in the decades ahead, but is to spread much more equitably to all peoples in the world, then ways have to be found to bring all states into a new inclusive international market order to create the governance structures which can elicit the cooperation we shall need to tackle the mounting challenges we face. We need a new model of growth, whose first priority should be to find the technologies which can begin to reverse the environmental damage we have already caused. And we need to find a new solidarity to generate the public resources we need to reverse the trends to ever greater inequality and ever more inadequate social provision (Cramme & Diamond 2009, 2012; Crouch 2013; Cramme et al. 2013). We have a long way to go, and the task may seem like the labours of Sisyphus. But it is better to think of it like Pascal's wager on the existence of God. If we wager that a better and more secure future is attainable, we gain greatly if it turns out to be true. And we are hardly any worse off if it turns out to be false. But if believing it to be true changes the way we behave, speak and act, that can help to set us free and resolve the crisis which enfolds us.

Guide to Further Reading

The literature on the crisis and its aftermath grows apace. I do not offer a comprehensive guide here, merely some pointers to sources which have been important in shaping my thinking and which may be of use to readers who want to explore further some of the themes of this book. References have also been added in the text to indicate sources on which the argument draws.

Key texts which have influenced me on the nature of our contemporary political economy and the nature of crisis include Arrighi (1994); Bell (1976); Cerutti (2007); Fraser (2013); Glyn (2006); Habermas (1976); Harvey (2011); Hont (2010); McNeill (2001); Schumpeter (1943, 1990); Strange (1988); Wallerstein (1974); and Hayek (1981).

There are three broad literatures about the causes of the financial crash. The first explores the nature of the financial markets and how financial crashes happen. For the history of financial crashes, see Kindleberger (1978) and Reinhart & Rogoff (2009). For the 2008 crash, see Gowan (2009) and Peston (2008, 2012). For the failures of economics, see Krugman (2008) and Mirowski (2013).

A second literature focuses on the structures of the international market order, particularly the growth of imbalances and the impact of globalization and liberalization on the financial markets. For this, see Desai (2013); Frieden (2006); Gilpin (2001); Green (2013); Helleiner (2010); and Thompson (2010).

A third literature focuses on the political origins of the crisis. For the failures of regulation and the pursuit of particular programmes such as the encouragement of sub-prime mortgages in the US, see Schwartz (2009) and Thompson (2009). For the role of ideas, see Blyth (2013); Hay (2011, 2013); Posner & Friedman (2011); and Schwartz (1994). On the detail of financial regulation, see Baker (2010, 2013); Engelen et al. (2011); Haldane (2012); and Hindmoor & McConnell (2013).

On the response to the crisis, and how the crisis was defined, see Blyth (2013); Grant & Wilson (2014); Hay (2011); Hay and Payne (2013); and Schmidt & Thatcher (2013).

For the governance conundrum, see Eichengreen (2012); Hale et al. (2013); Ikenberry (2004); and Narlikar (2010). For the role of the US, see Anderson (2013); Frieden (2006); and Helleiner (1996).

For the growth conundrum, the arguments about a new secular stagnation are put by Cowen (2011); Gordon (2012); Koo (2009); and Skidelsky & Skidelsky (2012). The optimists are less numerous, but see Crafts (2012); Kaletsky (2010); Phelps (2013); and Ridley (2011). On climate change, see the Stern Review (2009) and the arresting analysis of the politics provided by Giddens (2009); Gough (2011); and Jacobs (2012). Gwyn Prins and his colleagues (2010) mount a strong critique of current policy on climate change. The climate sceptic case is put by Lawson (2009) and Ridley (2011).

For the fiscal conundrum, classic accounts are to be found in O'Connor's (1971) analysis of fiscal crises and Schumpeter's (1990) analysis of the tax state. Those with strong constitutions should read the Ryan Plan (2012) and, as an antidote, Krugman (2008), along with his blog (www.pkarchive.org & economistsview.typepad.com) to learn about the fiscal issues in the US. The eurozone crisis is analysed from different perspectives by Dyson (2010); Lapavitsas (2012); Marquand (2011); Marsh (2013); and Sinn (2011). For the problems of democracy, see Rachman (2010); Runciman (2013); and Schäfer & Streeck (2013). One of the most interesting and detailed attempts to think about future scenarios is the report of the AUGUR team (Eatwell et al. 2014). The reform of global governance is considered by Hale et al. (2013); Payne (2010); and Wade & Vestergaard (2012). Critics of the existing international market order also include Chang (2007) and Rodrik (2011). For an assessment of the potential of the rising powers, see O'Neill (2013). The role of the US is considered from different perspectives by Anderson (2013); Kupchan (2013); Luce (2012); and Nye (2011). The future of China is debated by Fenby (2014); Halper (2010); Jacques (2012); and Nolan (2004). The future of progressive politics is discussed by Crouch (2011, 2013); Cramme & Diamond (2012); and Cramme et al. (2013).

There are many excellent blogs, including the SPERI blog www.dept.shef.ac.uk/comment. Commentators I always find worth reading on different aspects of the crisis include Wolfgang Münchau, Philip Stephens and Martin Wolf in *The Financial Times* (www.ft.com), Larry Elliott, Aditya Chrakrabortty, Polly Toynbee, Will Hutton in *The Guardian* (www.theguardian.com); Ambrose Evans-Pritchard and Andrew Lilico in *The Daily Telegraph* (www.blogs.telegraph.co.uk/finance). In the US the website *Real Clear*

Politics (realclearpolitics.com) is invaluable. See also *American Prospect* (www.prospect.com); *The Wall Street Journal* (www.wsj.com); and *The New York Times* (www.nytimes.com). For China see the Institute of World Economics and Politics (en.iwep.org.cn) and for India, the Indian Council for Research on International Economic Relations (www.icrier.org) and the Indian Council on Global Relations (www.gatewayhouse.in).

Bibliography

Allison, Graham (1971) *Essence of decision: explaining the Cuban missile crisis* (Boston: Little, Brown).

Anderson, Perry (2013) 'American foreign policy and its thinkers' *New Left Review* 83 (Sept–Oct), 5–167.

Armstrong, Philip, Andrew Glyn & Bob Sutcliffe (1984) *Capitalism since World War II: the making and breakup of the great boom* (London: Fontana).

Arrighi, Giovanni (1994) *The long twentieth century: money, power and the origins of our times* (London: Verso).

Bacon, Roger & Walter Eltis (1976) *Britain's economic problem: too few producers* (London: Macmillan).

Baker, Andrew (2010) 'Restraining regulatory capture? Anglo-America, crisis politics and trajectories of change in global financial governance' *International Affairs* 86:3, 647–63.

Baker, Andrew (2013) 'The new political economy of the macroprudential ideational shift' *New Political Economy* 18:1, 112–39.

Baran, Paul & Paul Sweezy (1966) *Monopoly capital: an essay on the American economic and social order* (New York: Monthly Review Press).

Barraclough, Geoffrey (1974) 'The coming depression' *New York Review of Books*, 27 June.

Bell, Daniel (1976) *The cultural contradictions of capitalism* (London: Heinemann).

Bell, Stephen and Andrew Hindmoor (2014) *Masters of the universe but slaves of the market: the great financial meltdown and how some bankers avoided the carnage* (Cambridge: Harvard University Press).

Bernstein, Peter (1996) *Against the gods: the remarkable story of risk* (New York: Wiley).

Blyth, Mark (2013) *Austerity: the history of a dangerous idea* (London: Oxford University Press).

Breslin, Shaun (2009) *China and the global political economy* (London: Palgrave Macmillan).

Brown, Gordon (2009) *Beyond the crash* (New York: Simon & Schuster).

Brown, Gordon (2013) 'Stumbling toward the next crash', www.nytimes.com/2013/12/19.

Caplan, Bryan (2009) *The myth of the rational voter: why voters choose bad policies* (Princeton: Princeton University Press).

Cassidy, John (2014) 'Is Larry Summers right about "secular stagnation"?' *The New Yorker*, 8 January, www.newyorker.com.

213

CBO (Congressional Budget Office) (2013) *The fiscal cliff deal*, www.cbo.gov/publication/43835.

Cerutti, Furio (2007) *Global challenges for Leviathan: a political philosophy of nuclear weapons and global warming* (Lanham, MD: Lexington Books).

Chang, Ha-Joon (2007) *Bad Samaritans: rich nations, poor policies and the threat to the developing world* (London: Random House).

Clarke, Peter (2009) *Keynes: the rise, fall and return of the 20th century's most influential economist* (New York: Bloomsbury Press).

Clift, Ben (2014) *Comparative Political Economy: States, Markets & Global Capitalism* (Basingstoke: Palgrave Macmillan).

Coates, David (2000) *Models of capitalism* (Cambridge: Polity).

Coggan, Philip (2013) *The last vote* (London: Allen Lane).

Council of Economic Advisors (1965) *Economic Report of the President* (Washington: US Government).

Cowen, Tylor (2011) *The great stagnation* (New York: Dutton).

Cox, Robert (1996) *Approaches to world order* (Cambridge: Cambridge University Press).

Crafts, Nicholas (2012) *Returning to growth: lessons from history* (London: Royal Economic Society).

Cramme, Olaf & Patrick Diamond (eds) (2009) *Social justice in the global age* (Cambridge: Polity).

Cramme, Olaf & Patrick Diamond (eds) (2012) *After the Third Way: the future of social democracy in Europe* (London: I.B.Tauris).

Cramme, Olaf, Patrick Diamond & Michael McTernan (eds) (2013) *Progressive politics after the crash* (London: I.B.Tauris).

Crouch, Colin (2011) *The strange non-death of neo-liberalism* (Cambridge: Polity).

Crouch, Colin (2013) *Making capitalism fit for society* (Cambridge: Polity).

Daly, Herman (1997) *Beyond growth: economics of sustainable development* (New York: Beacon Press).

Darling, Alastair (2011) *Back from the brink* (London: Atlantic).

Davies, Howard (2010) *The financial crisis: who is to blame?* (Cambridge: Polity).

Desai, Radhika (2013) *Geopolitical economy: after US hegemony, globalisation and empire* (London: Pluto).

Dunn, John (1979) *Western political theory in the face of the future* (Cambridge: Cambridge University Press).

Dyson, Kenneth (2010) 'Norman's lament: the Greek and euro area crisis in historical perspective', *New Political Economy* 15:4, 597–608.

Eatwell, John & Murray Milgate (2011) *The fall and rise of Keynesian economics* (London: Oxford University Press).

Eatwell, John, Terry McInley & Pascal Petit (eds) (2014) *Challenges for Europe in the world, 2030*, The AUGUR project (London: Ashgate).

Eichengreen, Barry (2012) *Exorbitant privilege* (Oxford: Oxford University Press).

Engelen, Ewald, Ismail Ertürk, Julie Froud, Sukhdev Johal, Adam Leaver, Mick Moran, Adriana Nilsson & Karel Williams (2011) *The great complacence* (Oxford: Oxford University Press).

Esping-Andersen, Gosta (1990) *The three worlds of welfare capitalism* (Cambridge: Polity).

Fenby, Jonathan (2014) *Why China will not dominate the twenty-first century* (Cambridge: Polity).

Ferguson, Niall (2009) *Colossus: the rise and fall of the American empire* (London: Penguin).

Financial Crisis Inquiry Commission (2011) *Financial crisis inquiry report* (Washington: Public Affairs).

Flamant, Maurice & Jeanne Singer-Kérel (1968) *Modern economic crises* (London: Barrie & Jenkins).

Flinders, Matthew (2012) *Defending politics: why democracy matters in the twenty first century* (Oxford: Oxford University Press).

Fraser, Nancy (2013) 'A triple movement', *New Left Review* 81, May/June, 119–32.

Freeden, Michael, Lyman Sargent & Marc Stears (eds) (2013) *The Oxford handbook of political ideologies* (Oxford: Oxford University Press).

Freedman, Lawrence (1990) *Signals of war: the Anglo-Argentine conflict of 1982* (London: Faber).

Frieden, Jeffry A. (2006) *The fall and rise of global capitalism* (New York: Norton).

Fukuyama, Francis (1989) 'The end of history' *The National Interest* 16, 3–18.

Galbraith, John Kenneth (1971) *The new industrial state* (Boston: Houghton-Mifflin).

Gamble, Andrew (1994) *The free economy and the strong state* (London: Macmillan).

Gamble, Andrew (2003) *Between Europe and America: the future of British politics* (Basingstoke: Palgrave Macmillan).

Gamble, Andrew (2014) 'Ideologies of global governance' in A. Payne & N. Phillips (eds) *Handbook of the international political economy of governance* (Cheltenham: Edward Elgar).

Geddes, Andrew (1999) *Immigration and European integration: towards fortress Europe* (Manchester: Manchester University Press).

Germain, Randall (2009) 'Financial order and world politics: crisis, change and continuity' *International Affairs* 85:4, 669–87.

Germain, Randall (2013) *Globalisation and its critics* (Basingstoke: Palgrave Macmillan).

Giddens, Tony (2009) *The politics of climate change* (Cambridge: Polity).

Gilpin, Robert (2001) *Global political economy: understanding the international economic order* (Princeton: Princeton University Press).

Glyn, Andrew (2006) *Capitalism unleashed* (Oxford: Oxford University Press).

Goodwin, Matthew (2011) *Right response: understanding and countering populist extremism in Europe* (London: Chatham House).

Goolsbee, Austan (2011) 'Goolsbee to Tea Party: playing chicken with debt ceiling is insanity', http://abcnews.go.com/Politics/goolsbee-tea-party-playing-chicken-debt-ceiling-vote/story?id=12522970.

Gordon, Robert (2012) *Is US economic growth over? Faltering innovation confronts the six headwinds*, www.nber.org.

Gough, Ian (2011) *Climate change and public policy futures* (London: British Academy).

Gowan, Peter (2009) 'Crisis in the heartland', *New Left Review* 55, 5–30.

Grant, Wyn & Graham Wilson (2014) (eds) *The consequences of the global financial crisis* (Oxford: Oxford University Press).

Green, Jeremy (2013) 'The political economy of the special relationship: British development and American power', unpublished PhD thesis, York University, Toronto.

Greenspan, Alan (2007) *The age of turbulence* (London: Penguin).

Greenspan, Alan (2008) 'Testimony to the Committee of Government Oversight and Reform', 23 October.

Habermas, Jurgen (1976) *Legitimation crisis* (London: Heinemann).

Haggard, Stephen (2000) (ed.) *The political economy of the Asian financial crisis* (Washington: Institute for International Economics).

Haldane, Andrew (2012) 'The Bank and the Banks', Speech at Queen's University Belfast, 18 October.

Hale, Thomas, David Held & Kevin Young (2013) *Gridlock: why global cooperation is failing when we need it most* (Cambridge: Polity).

Hall, Peter (1993) 'Policy paradigms, social learning, and the state: the case of economic policy-making in Britain', *Comparative Politics* 25:3, 275–296.

Hall, Peter & David Soskice (2001) (eds) *Varieties of capitalism: the institutional foundations of comparative advantage* (Oxford: Oxford University Press).

Haller, Max (2008) *European integration as an elite process: the failure of a dream?* (London: Routledge).

Halper, Stefan (2010) *The Beijing consensus* (New York: Basic Books).

Harvey, David (2011) *The enigma of capital* (London: Profile Books).

Hay, Colin (2007) *Why we hate politics* (Cambridge: Polity).

Hay, Colin (2011) 'Pathology without crisis? The strange demise of the Anglo-liberal growth model' *Government and Opposition* 46:1, 1–31.

Hay, Colin (2013) *The failure of Anglo-liberal capitalism* (Basingstoke: Palgrave Macmillan).

Hay, Colin & Tony Payne (2013) *The Great Uncertainty: thinking through financial crisis*, www.speri.comment.

Hayek, F.A. (1981) *Law, Legislation and Liberty* (London: Routledge).

Heffernan, Richard (1999) *New Labour and Thatcherism: political change in Britain* (London: Macmillan).

Held, David (2010) *Cosmopolitanism* (Cambridge: Polity).

Helleiner, Eric (1996) *States and the re-emergence of global finance: from Bretton Woods to the 1990s* (Ithaca, NY: Cornell University Press).

Helleiner, Eric (2010) 'A Bretton Woods moment? The 2007–2008 crisis and the future of global finance' *International Affairs* 86:3, 619–636.

Hindmoor, Andrew & Allan McConnell (2013) 'Why didn't they see it coming? Warning signs, acceptable risks, and the global financial crisis', *Political Studies* 61:3, 543–60.

Hirst, Paul & Grahame Thompson (1996) *Globalisation in question* (Cambridge: Polity).

Hobson, John & Len Seabrooke (eds) (2007) *Everyday Politics of the World Economy* (Cambridge: Cambridge University Press).

Hont, Istvan (2010) *Jealousy of Trade: international competition and the nation state in comparative perspective* (Cambridge: Harvard University Press).

Hood, Christopher (2001) *The government of risk: understanding risk regulation regimes* (Oxford: Oxford University Press).

Hood, Christopher, David Heald & Rozana Himaz (eds) (2014) *When the party's over: the politics of fiscal squeeze in perspective* (London: British Academy).

Hoover, Herbert (1952) *Memoirs: The Great Depression*, vol. 3 (New York: Macmillan).

Hutton, Will (2011) *Them and Us: changing Britain – why we need a fair society* (London: Abacus).

Hutton, Will (2013) 'The lessons I learned from my week with Japan's power-brokers', 9 February www.theguardian.com.

Ikenberry, John (2004) 'Liberalism and empire: logics of order in the American unipolar age' *Review of International Studies* 30, 609–30.

IMF (2008) *World Economic Outlook* (October) (Washington: IMF).

IMF (2009) *World Economic Outlook* (October) (Washington: IMF).

IMF (2011) *World Economic Outlook* (July) (Washington: IMF).

IMF (2012) *World Economic Outlook* (October) (Washington: IMF).

Jacobs, Michael (2012) 'Green growth: economic theory and political discourse' Working paper 92, London: Grantham Research Institute on Climate Change and the Environment.

Jacques, Martin (2012) *When China rules the world* (London: Penguin).

Jay, Peter (1976) *Employment, inflation and politics* (London: IEA).

Johnson, Chalmers (2006) *The sorrows of empire: militarism, secrecy and the end of the republic* (London: Verso).

Kaletsky, Anatole (2010) *Capitalism 4.0* (London: Bloomsbury).

Kennedy, Paul (1988) *The rise and fall of the great powers: economic change and military conflict from 1500 to 2000* (London: Unwin Hyman).

Kennedy, Paul (2001) *The parliament of man: the United Nations and the quest for world government* (London: Allen Lane).

Keynes, John Maynard (1972) 'Economic possibilities for our grandchildren', *Collected Writings IX Essays in Persuasion* (London: Macmillan).

Kindleberger, Charles (1978) *Manias, panics and crashes* (London: Macmillan).

Kindleberger, Charles (1987) *The world in depression* (London: Penguin).

Knight, Frank (1964) *Risk, uncertainty and profit* (New York: Century Press).

Koo, Richard (2009) *The Holy Grail of macroeconomics* (London: Wiley).

Kosellek (2002) 'Some questions concerning the conceptual history of "crisis"', in N. Witoszek & L. Tragärdh (eds) *Culture and Crisis* (New York: Berghahn), 12–22.

Krugman, Paul (2008) *The return of depression economics and the crisis of 2008* (London: Allen Lane).

Krugman, Paul (2012) 'Nobody understands debt', *The New York Times* 1 January, www.nytimes.com.

Kupchan, Charles (2012) *How enemies become friends: the sources of stable peace* (Princeton: Princeton University Press).

Kupchan, Charles (2013) *No-one's world* (Oxford: Oxford University Press).

Lampedusa, Guiseppe di (1974) *The Leopard* (London: Fontana).

Langley, Paul (2008) *The everyday life of global finance* (Oxford: Oxford University Press).

Lapavitsas, Costas (2012) *Crisis in the eurozone* (London: Verso).

Lawson, Nigel (2009) *An appeal to reason: a cool look at global warming* (London: Duckworth).

Lindblom, Charles (1977) *Politics and markets: the world's political and economic systems* (New York: Basic Books).

Luce, Edward (2012) *Time to start thinking: America and the spectre of decline* (New York: Little, Brown).

Mackintosh, Stuart (2013) 'The redesign of the global financial architecture: forums, institutions and state power', unpublished PhD thesis, University of Newcastle.

Maddison, Angus (2006) *The World Economy* (Paris: OECD).

Mann, Michael (2003) *Incoherent empire* (London: Verso).

Marquand, David (2011) *The end of the West: the once and future Europe* (Princeton: Princeton University Press).

Marsh, David (2013) *Europe's deadlock: how the euro crisis could be solved and why it won't happen* (New Haven: Yale University Press).

Mazzucato, Mariana(2013) *The entrepreneurial state: debunking public versus private sector myths* (London: Anthem Press).

McNeill, John (2001) *Something new under the sun: an environmental history of the twentieth century world* (London: Penguin).

Mirowski, Philip (2013) *Never let a serious crisis go to waste: how neo-liberalism survived the financial meltdown* (London: Verso).

Mitchell, Dan (2013) 'Question of the week: what's the right point on the Laffer curve' www.cato.org/blog/question-week-whats-right-point-laffer-curve.

Mount, Ferdinand (2013) *The New Few, or a very British oligarchy* (London: Simon & Schuster).

Münchau, Wolfgang (2013) 'A disunited Europe will struggle even to disintegrate' *Financial Times*, 24 November, www.ft.com.

Münchau, Wolfgang (2014) 'What euro crisis watchers should look for in 2014' *Financial Times*, 5 January, www.ft.com.

Narlikar, Amrita (2010) (ed.) *Deadlocks in multilateral negotiations: causes and solutions* (Cambridge: Cambridge University Press).

Nolan, Peter (2004) *China at the crossroads* (Cambridge: Polity).

Nye, Joseph (2011) *The future of power* (New York: Public Affairs).

O'Connor, James (1971) *The fiscal crisis of the state* (New York: St Martin's Press).

O'Neill, Jim (2001) *Building better global economic BRICs*, www.gs.com.

O'Neill, Jim (2013) *The growth map* (London: Penguin).

Panitch, Leo & Sam Gindin (2013) *The making of global capitalism: the political economy of American empire* (London: Verso).

Parker, Sophia (2013) *Squeezed middle* (London: Policy Press).

Patomaki, Heikki (2013) *The great eurozone disaster* (London: Zed).

Paulson, Hank (2010) *On the brink: inside the race to stop the collapse of the global financial system* (New York: Business Plus).

Payne, Anthony (2010) 'How many Gs are there in "global governance" after the crisis? The perspectives of the "marginal majority" of the world's states', *International Affairs* 86:3, 729–40.

Payne, Tony & Nicola Phillips (2014)*The handbook of the international political economy of governance* (London: Edward Elgar).

Peacock, Alan & Jack Wiseman (1961) *The growth of public expenditure in the United Kingdom* (Oxford: Oxford University Press).

Peston, Robert (2008) *Who governs Britain?* (London: Hodder & Stoughton).

Peston, Robert (2012) *How do we fix this mess?* (London: Hodder & Stoughton).

Phelps, Edmund (2013) *Mass Flourishing: how grassroots innovation created jobs, challenge and change* (Princeton: Princeton University Press).

Pijl, Kees van der (2006) *Global rivalries from the cold war to Iraq* (London: Pluto).

Posner, Richard (2010) *The crisis of capitalist democracy* (Harvard: Harvard University Press).

Posner, Richard & Jeffrey Friedman (2011) *What caused the financial crisis* (Philadelphia: University of Pennsylvania Press).

Prins, Gwyn et al. (2010) (eds) *The Hartwell Paper: a new direction for climate policy after the crash of 2009*, http://eprints.lse.ac.uk.

Rachman, Gideon (2010) *Zero-sum world: politics, power and prosperity after the crash* (London: Atlantic Books)

Reich, Robert (2011) *Aftershock* (New York: Vintage).

Reinhart, Carmen & Kenneth Rogoff (2009) *This time is different: eight centuries of financial folly* (Princeton: Princeton University Press).

Rees, Martin (2003) *Our final century?* (London: Heinemann).

Ridley, Matt (2011) *The rational optimist* (London: Fourth Estate).

Rodrik, Dani (2011) *The globalisation paradox* (Oxford: Oxford University Press).

Rosenau, James & Ernst-Otto Czempiel (1994) *Governance without government: order and change in world politics* (Cambridge: Cambridge University Press).

Rostow, Walt Whitman (1978) *The world economy* (London: Macmillan).

Ruggie, John (1998) *Constructing the world polity: essays on international institutionalisation* (London: Routledge).

Runciman, David (2013) *The confidence trap* (Princeton: Princeton University Press).

Ryan, Paul (2012) *The Path to Prosperity: a blueprint for American renewal,* www.prosperity.budget.house.gov.

Samuelson, Robert (2011) 'Labour Day Blues' *Nation*, 5 September.

Schäfer, Armin & Wolfgang Streeck (2013) (eds) *Politics in the age of austerity* (Cambridge: Polity).

Schmidt, Vivien & Mark Thatcher (2013) (eds) *Resilient liberalism in Europe's political economy* (Cambridge: Cambridge University Press).

Scholte, Jan-Aart (2000) *Globalisation* (Basingstoke: Palgrave Macmillan).

Schumpeter, Joseph (1943) *Capitalism, socialism and democracy* (London: Allen & Unwin).

Schumpeter, Joseph (1990) 'The crisis of the tax state' in R. Swedberg (ed.) *The Economics and Sociology of Capitalism* (Princeton: Princeton University Press).

Schwartz, Herman (1994) *States versus markets* (New York: St Martin's Press).

Schwartz, Herman (2009) *Sub-prime nation: American power, global capital and the housing bubble* (Ithaca: Cornell University Press).

Sen, Kunal (2011) 'A hard rain's a-gonna fall: the global financial crisis and developing countries', *New Political Economy* 16:3, 399–413.

Shiller, Robert (2008) *The subprime solution: how today's global financial crisis happened, and what to do about it* (Princeton: Princeton University Press).

Shonfield, Andrew (1966) *Modern capitalism* (New York: Oxford University Press).

Sinclair, Tim (2010) 'Round up the usual suspects: blame and the subprime crisis' *New Political Economy* 15: 1, 91–107.

Sinn, Hans Werner (2011) 'Target loans, current account balances and capital flows: the ECB's rescue facility' NBER Working Paper 17626, www.nber.org.

Skidelsky, Robert (1967) *Politicians and the slump: the Labour Government of 1929–1931* (London: Macmillan).

Skidelsky, Robert (2009) *Keynes: the return of the master* (London: Allen Lane).

Skidelsky, Robert & Edward Skidelsky (2012) *How much is enough?* (London: Allen Lane).

Slaughter, Anne-Marie (2004) *A new world order* (Princeton: Princeton University Press).

Spencer, Herbert (1994) *Political Writings*, ed. by J. Offer (Cambridge: Cambridge University Press).

Stephens, Philip (2013) 'Europe faces a bigger threat than German caution', *Financial Times* 12 December, www.ft.com.

Stern, Nicholas (2009) *A blueprint for a safer planet* (London: Bodley Head).

Stiglitz, Joseph (2010) *Freefall: free markets and the sinking of the global economy* (London: Penguin).

Stockman, David (2012) 'Paul Ryan's fairy-tale budget plan', *New York Times* 13 August, www.nytimes.com.

Stoker, Gerry (2006) *Why politics matters: making democracy work* (Basingstoke: Palgrave Macmillan).

Strange, Susan (1988) *States and markets* (London: Pinter).

Strange, Susan (1996) *The retreat of the state: the diffusion of power in the world economy* (Cambridge: Cambridge University Press).

Summers, Larry (2004) 'The United States and the global adjustment process', www.iie.com.

Summers, Larry (2014) 'Washington must not settle for secular stagnation' *Financial Times*, 5 January, www.ft.com.

Telo, Mario (2006) *Europe a civilian power? European Union, global governance, world order* (Basingstoke: Palgrave Macmillan).

Telo, Mario (2014) (ed.) *Globalisation, multilateralism, Europe* (London: Ashgate).

Thompson, Helen (2008) *Might, right, prosperity and consent: representative democracy and the international economy 1919–2001* (Manchester: Manchester University Press).

Thompson, Helen (2009) 'The political origins of the financial crisis: The domestic and international politics of Fannie Mae and Freddie Mac', *The Political Quarterly*, 80:1, 17–24.

Thompson, Helen (2010) *China and the mortgaging of America* (Basingstoke: Palgrave Macmillan).

Triffin, Robert (1964) *The evolution of the international monetary system: historical reappraisal and future perspectives* (Princeton: Princeton University Press).

Tsoukalis, Loukas (2013) 'The fall-out from the eurozone crisis', in O.Cramme et al., *Progressive politics after the crash* (London: I.B.Tauris), 53–62.

Turner, Rachel (2011) *Neo-liberal ideology: history, concepts and policies* (Edinburgh: Edinburgh University Press).

Voltaire (2007) *Candide* (Paris: Larousse).

Wade, Robert (2011) 'Emerging world order?: from multipolarity to multilateralism in the G20, the World Bank, and the IMF' *Politics and Society*, 39:3, 347–78.

Wade, Robert and Jakob Vestergaard (2012) 'The G20 has served its purpose and should be replaced with a Global Economic Council on a firmer constitutional foundation' *British Politics and Policy at LSE* (19 September), Blog Entry.

Wallerstein, Immanuel (1974) *The modern world system* (New York: Academic Press).

Wall Street Journal 'How to freeze the debt ceiling without risking default' (2011) 19 January.

Wapshott, Nicholas (2012) *Keynes Hayek: the clash that defined modern economics* (New York: W.W.Norton).

WHO (World Health Organization) (2014) 'Data' http://www.who.int/gho/mdg/environmental_sustainability/en/.

Williams, Roger (1993) 'Technical change: political options and imperatives', *Government and Opposition* 28:2, 152–73.

Wolf, Martin (2011) 'Struggling with a great contraction', 30 August, www.ft.com.

Wolf, Martin (2012) 'Paul Ryan's plan for America is not credible', 17 August, www.ft.com.

Wolf, Martin (2013) 'A perilous journey to full recovery', 29 January, www.ft.com.

Xiaochuan, Zhou (2009) 'Reform the international monetary system', Bank for International Settlements, www.bis.org.

Index